Copyright © 2024 Md. Sifat Hossain

The Statisticians and Their Statistics

Md. Sifat Hossain

Preface

Statistics, often described as the science of learning from data, is a field that has profoundly shaped the modern world. From the early days of probability theory to the contemporary advances in machine learning (ML), statisticians have played a pivotal role in developing tools and methodologies that underpin vast areas of science, industry, and society. This book, *The Statisticians and Their Statistics*, is a tribute to the remarkable individuals who have made these contributions, shaping not only the discipline of statistics but also the broader landscape of knowledge and discovery.

As a student of statistics and a passionate follower of its history, I have always been fascinated by the stories behind the theorems, the equations, and the concepts that form the bedrock of statistical science. In writing this book, my aim has been to bring these stories to life, exploring the lives, works, and legacies of the statisticians who have laid the foundations and driven the evolution of this vital field.

The Statisticians and Their Statistics is organized into different sections, each dedicated to a key figure in the history of statistics. Beginning with Karl Pearson, who established the foundations of modern statistics, and moving through the works of giants like R.A. Fisher, Jerzy Neyman, and William Gosset, the book covers the development of hypothesis testing, regression analysis, exploratory data analysis (EDA), and more. It also delves into the contributions of statisticians like John Tukey, who revolutionized the way we explore data, and Bradley Efron, whose work on resampling methods opened new avenues in statistical inference.

In addition to these well-known figures, I have included sections on individuals whose contributions, though perhaps less celebrated, have had a profound impact on the field. Figures like Gerard Salton, who advanced information retrieval, and Grace Wahba, whose work on splines has influenced numerous applications in science and engineering, are given the recognition they deserve.

This book also explores the broader applications and interdisciplinary impacts of statistics, examining how statisticians like W. Edward Deming and Myron Tribus applied statistical thinking to management and decision science, shaping practices that continue to influence business and industry today.

As we look to the future of statistics, the final sections of this book reflect on the ongoing evolution of the field. With the advent of big data, artificial intelligence (AI), and computational statistics, the role of the statistician has never been more critical. I hope that this book serves as both an educational resource and an inspiration to those who are passionate about statistics, whether they are students, professionals, or simply curious minds.

I would like to express my deepest gratitude to the many mentors, colleagues, and friends who have supported me throughout the process of writing this book. Their insights and encouragement have been invaluable. I also extend my thanks to the statisticians whose work forms the backbone of this book; their dedication and brilliance continue to inspire me.

Finally, to the readers: I hope you find this book as enriching and engaging to read as it was to write. May it deepen your appreciation for the rich history of statistics and the remarkable individuals who have made it what it is today.

The Author
August 2024

Dedicated to

All the statisticians

The Author

Md. Sifat Hossain
MPhil Research Fellow
Department of Statistics
University of Rajshahi
Rajshahi-6205

Contacts

+8801863504629 (WhatsApp, Telegram, Viber)
sifat.stat@gmail.com
https://www.facebook.com/msh.stat
https://www.linkedin.com/in/sifatstat
https://orcid.org/0009-0000-7265-5143
https://www.researchgate.net/profile/Md-Hossain-1441

Table of Contents

Introduction

Statistics is the science of collecting, analyzing, and interpreting data. While its application touches nearly every field, the foundations and continued advancement of statistics is due to the contributions of many brilliant thinkers over the centuries. This book profiles 25 of the most influential statisticians in history and their impact on both the theory and practice of statistical methodology.

We begin in antiquity with foundational works in probability by mathematician Carl Friedrich Gauss and philosopher-mathematician Leonhard Euler. Their early concepts would eventually blossom into the modern fields of probability and stochastic modeling. Transitioning into the modern era, agricultural scientist Ronald Fisher revolutionized experimental design while laying the groundwork for statistical inference. Concurrently, mathematicians like Karl Pearson and Jerzy Neyman cemented statistics' identity as a distinct quantitative science through their seminal works.

Major innovations accelerated following the mid-20th century. Scientists such as John Tukey, Abraham Wald, Jimmie Savage, C.R. Rao, and John von Neumann pioneered techniques like EDA, decision theory, Bayesian analysis, non-parametrics, and computational approaches. Their diverse work demonstrated statistics' widespread utility across domains. Even more recent statisticians like Bradley Efron, Grace Wahba, David Cox, and George Box have revolutionized areas including resampling methods, splines, generalized linear model (GLM), and time series.

Through these 25 biographical profiles, this book aims to chronicle statistics' evolution from philosophical curiosity to indispensable scientific tool. By showcasing statisticians both renowned and lesser known, from varied cultures and disciplines, the profound and ongoing impact of their collective works will hopefully inspire future statisticians and all those who apply this science. Whether exploring the past or looking ahead, the story of statistics is truly one of intellectual endeavor achieving practical success through continuous innovation.

Leonhard Euler and Foundations of Probability

Early Life and Education in Switzerland

Leonhard Euler, one of the most prolific mathematicians in history, began his journey in the small city of Basel, Switzerland. Born on April 15, 1707, Euler was the son of Paul Euler, a pastor and a keen amateur mathematician, and Marguerite Brucker, who came from a family deeply involved in intellectual pursuits. From a young age, Euler was exposed to an environment that valued education and scholarly discussion, laying the groundwork for his future achievements.

Euler's formal education commenced at the University of Basel, where he initially studied theology. However, his interest in mathematics soon took precedence. Under the guidance of Johann Bernoulli, a leading mathematician of the time, Euler's mathematical abilities flourished. Bernoulli recognized Euler's potential and encouraged him to pursue mathematics more seriously. Euler's exceptional talent became evident during his studies, and he graduated with a degree in philosophy and mathematics in 1726.

Following his graduation, Euler continued his studies at Basel while engaging in advanced mathematical research. His work caught the attention of the academic community, leading to his move to St. Petersburg in 1727. At the young age of 20, Euler was invited to join the St. Petersburg Academy of Sciences, marking the beginning of a highly influential career. His move to Russia not only marked a new chapter in his life but also set the stage for his groundbreaking contributions to various fields of mathematics, including the foundations of probability.

Foundations of Graph Theory

Leonhard Euler's contributions to graph theory, which he laid out in his 1736 paper "Solutio Problematis ad Geometrum Situs," fundamentally changed how we understand and approach network structures. This seminal work, often considered the first paper in the field of graph theory, began with a seemingly simple but profound problem: the Seven Bridges of Königsberg.

The city of Königsberg, in what is now Kaliningrad, Russia, was divided by the Pregel River into four landmasses connected by seven bridges. The challenge was to find a route that would allow one to cross each bridge exactly once and return to the starting point. Euler approached this problem not by finding a solution but by analyzing the problem's structure through a novel mathematical lens. He abstracted the city's layout into a graph, where the landmasses were vertices and the bridges were edges.

Euler's insight was groundbreaking. He demonstrated that the problem could be reduced to a question of whether such a path existed in a graph where each vertex had an even degree (number of connecting edges). In the case of Königsberg, the graph's vertices had odd degrees, and thus, a solution was impossible. This approach led Euler to formulate what is now known as Eulerian paths and circuits—concepts that describe paths in graphs that visit every edge exactly once.

Euler's work established the foundation of graph theory by showing that the nature of a network's structure could be understood through abstract mathematical principles rather than just empirical or geometric observations. His contributions set the stage for future developments in the field, providing tools for analyzing networks, optimizing routes, and solving connectivity problems.

The implications of Euler's work extend far beyond the Königsberg problem. Today, graph theory is a cornerstone of many fields, including computer science, where it underpins algorithms for network analysis, optimization, and data structure design. It also has applications in logistics, biology, social network analysis, and various other areas where relationships and connections are key to understanding complex systems.

Euler's pioneering work in graph theory demonstrated the power of abstract thinking and mathematical modeling in solving real-world problems. His legacy in this field continues to influence how scientists and engineers approach the study and design of networks and systems.

Development of Probability Theory

Leonhard Euler's influence on probability theory is profound and multifaceted. Although Euler did not invent probability theory, his work in the 18th century significantly advanced its formalization and application. His contributions laid critical groundwork that shaped modern probability.

Euler's approach to probability was pioneering in several ways. He was among the first to rigorously formalize the concept of probability as a fraction or ratio. Prior to his work, probability was often treated in a more intuitive and less systematic manner. Euler's rigorous approach involved defining probability as the ratio of favorable outcomes to the total number of possible outcomes. This formalization provided a clearer and more structured foundation for the field.

One of Euler's notable contributions was his work on problems related to games of chance, which was an area of particular interest during his time. He applied mathematical methods to analyze and solve problems in gambling, a popular topic among mathematicians of the era. For example, Euler explored the probabilities involved in dice games, card games, and lotteries. His analyses helped clarify the concept of expected value, which is a fundamental concept in probability theory.

Euler's work also extended to problems related to marriage and other real-world scenarios. One of his famous problems involved calculating the probability of a marriage arrangement where certain conditions must be met. Euler approached these problems with a combination of mathematical rigor and practical insight, applying probability theory to answer questions that were both theoretical and applicable.

By formalizing probability and applying it to a range of problems, Euler made significant strides in establishing the discipline as a rigorous mathematical field. His work helped transition probability theory from a collection of empirical observations and intuitive guesses to a formalized and systematic branch of mathematics. Euler's contributions laid a foundation that would be built upon by future mathematicians, including Pierre-Simon Laplace and Abraham de Moivre, further developing probability theory into the comprehensive field we know today.

Euler's influence in this domain highlights his role in advancing mathematical thought, moving from practical problems and games of chance to a more abstract and generalizable understanding of probability. His formalization of the probability fraction and his approach to solving complex problems remain integral to the field, reflecting his deep and lasting impact on the mathematical sciences.

Contributions to Combinatorics and Enumeration

Leonhard Euler's contributions to combinatorics and enumeration were instrumental in laying the groundwork for modern discrete mathematics and probability theory. His work in these areas provided essential tools and methods that would shape future developments in combinatorial analysis and stochastic processes.

Euler's engagement with combinatorics primarily involved analyzing counting principles and the arrangements of objects. One of his notable contributions was in solving problems related to permutations and combinations, which are fundamental concepts in combinatorial mathematics. Euler approached these problems with a blend of ingenuity and mathematical rigor, offering solutions that often extended beyond the scope of his contemporaries.

A significant aspect of Euler's combinatorial work was his exploration of permutations, which are arrangements of objects in a specific order. Euler investigated how many different ways a set of objects can be arranged and how these arrangements can be systematically counted. His work laid the foundation for what would later become formalized as permutation theory.

Euler's analysis also extended to combinations, where he examined how objects can be selected from a set without regard to order. His methods for counting combinations contributed to the development of binomial coefficients and the binomial theorem, which are crucial in both combinatorics and probability theory.

In addition to permutations and combinations, Euler's work in combinatorics involved analyzing complex arrangements and patterns within sets. For example, he tackled problems related to the arrangement of objects in a grid, the distribution of objects in specific configurations, and the counting of possible outcomes in various scenarios. These analyses provided foundational principles for discrete probability and combinatorial enumeration.

Euler's combinatorial methods laid the groundwork for the development of discrete probability theory and stochastic processes. By formalizing counting principles and arrangements, Euler made it possible to apply these concepts systematically to problems in probability. His contributions helped establish combinatorics as a distinct and vital area of mathematical study, influencing future mathematicians and researchers in both theoretical and applied contexts.

Overall, Euler's work in combinatorics and enumeration represents a critical phase in the development of discrete mathematics. His methods and insights into counting and arrangements not only advanced mathematical theory but also provided essential tools for the analysis of discrete probabilities and stochastic processes, shaping the course of mathematical research and application for centuries to come.

Analytic Advances with Generating Functions

Leonhard Euler's introduction and development of generating functions represent a pivotal advancement in mathematical analysis and combinatorics. Generating functions provide a powerful and versatile tool for solving problems involving sequences and recursive structures, and they continue to be a cornerstone of mathematical research and applications today.

A generating function is a formal power series where the coefficients of the series represent a sequence of numbers. By encoding sequences into power series, Euler and subsequent mathematicians could leverage the algebraic properties of these series to analyze and manipulate sequences in new ways. This approach transforms problems involving sequences into problems involving algebraic functions, simplifying the process of finding solutions.

Euler's early work with generating functions focused on their application to problems in number theory and combinatorics. He used generating functions to solve problems related to partitions of integers, a fundamental concept in combinatorics. For example, Euler employed generating functions to derive results about the number of ways an integer can be expressed as a sum of distinct parts.

One of Euler's significant contributions was the use of generating functions to address recursive structures and relations. Many problems in combinatorics and probability involve sequences that can be defined recursively. Generating functions offer a systematic way to solve these problems by converting recursive relations into algebraic equations that are often easier to handle.

Euler also explored the connection between generating functions and combinatorial identities. By representing combinatorial sequences as generating functions, he was able to derive and prove various identities and relationships, such as those involving binomial coefficients. These results laid the groundwork for many of the identities and theorems used in combinatorics today.

The power of generating functions lies in their ability to simplify complex problems. For instance, problems involving convolutions of sequences, which can be challenging to solve directly, become more tractable when approached through generating functions. Euler's work demonstrated how generating functions could be used to find closed-form solutions and derive new results in a wide range of mathematical contexts.

Even today, generating functions remain a vital tool in mathematics and applied fields. They are extensively used in areas such as probability theory, where they help in analyzing stochastic processes and random variables. In combinatorics, generating functions continue to provide elegant solutions to problems involving counting and arrangements.

In summary, Euler's analytic advances with generating functions revolutionized the approach to solving problems involving sequences and recursive structures. His innovative use of this technique laid the foundation for a wide range of mathematical applications and established generating functions as a powerful and enduring tool in mathematical analysis.

Influence on Later Statisticians and Probability Thinkers

Leonhard Euler's contributions to probability theory and combinatorics had a profound and lasting impact on the field, shaping the development of probability theory and influencing countless statisticians and mathematicians who followed in his footsteps.

Euler's formalization of probability as a fraction and his exploration of generating functions provided a rigorous foundation for the field. His work offered a structured approach to analyzing random events and sequences, laying the groundwork for future developments in probability theory. This foundational work was instrumental in establishing probability as a formal mathematical discipline rather than merely an intuitive concept.

Many later statisticians and probability theorists built upon Euler's pioneering ideas. For instance, Pierre-Simon Laplace, a prominent figure in the development of probability theory, extended Euler's ideas and integrated them into his own work on probability and statistics. Laplace's contributions, including his work on the theory of errors and the Laplace transform, were heavily influenced by the principles Euler had established.

Euler's methods for analyzing combinatorial problems using generating functions also influenced the development of combinatorics. Mathematicians such as George Boole and Arthur Cayley, who made significant advances in combinatorial theory and logic, drew upon Euler's ideas. The use of generating functions became a standard technique for solving complex combinatorial problems and analyzing probabilistic models.

In the 20th century, the field of probability theory continued to evolve, with notable figures such as Andrey Kolmogorov and Richard Feynman further developing the mathematical framework. Kolmogorov's axiomatization of probability theory, for instance, was built upon the rigorous groundwork laid by Euler and others. Kolmogorov's work provided a formal mathematical foundation for probability theory, drawing on the ideas of his predecessors, including Euler.

Euler's influence extended beyond the confines of mathematics into applied fields such as statistics and computer science. The principles of probability theory, as established by Euler and refined by subsequent researchers, became central to the development of statistical methods and algorithms. For example, the use of generating functions in statistical mechanics and algorithmic probability is a testament to Euler's enduring legacy.

Overall, Euler's pioneering work in probability theory and combinatorics set the stage for subsequent developments in the field. His rigorous approach to probability and his innovative use of generating functions provided essential tools and concepts that were adopted, extended, and refined by later mathematicians and statisticians. Euler's contributions remain foundational to modern probability theory and continue to influence the field today.

Lasting Impact Beyond Mathematics

Leonhard Euler's contributions to mathematics, particularly in probability theory and combinatorics, extended far beyond the confines of pure mathematics, influencing a diverse array of scientific disciplines and industries. His pioneering work laid the groundwork for developments in areas ranging from engineering and physics to computer science and economics.

Euler's methods and theories have had a profound impact on various scientific disciplines. In physics, his work on differential equations and graph theory provided critical insights into the behavior of physical systems and networks. For example, Euler's graph theory concepts have been applied to problems in electrical engineering and network design, helping to optimize and analyze complex systems.

In engineering, Euler's principles are embedded in the design and analysis of structures. His early work on elasticity theory, which deals with the deformation of solid objects under stress, remains a fundamental part of structural engineering. The Euler-Bernoulli beam theory, for instance, is a critical component in understanding how beams bend under loads, influencing the design of buildings, bridges, and machinery.

In the realm of computer science, Euler's graph theory has been instrumental in the development of algorithms for network analysis and optimization. Algorithms for searching and sorting, as well as network routing and data structure design, owe much to Euler's foundational work on graphs. His methods for analyzing networks and paths are still used in modern computer algorithms and network theory.

Economics and social sciences have also benefited from Euler's contributions. His work on probability and combinatorics has informed decision theory, game theory, and risk analysis. In finance, Euler's principles help model market behavior and assess financial risks. His methods for calculating probabilities and analyzing combinatorial structures are used in various economic models and statistical analyses.

Euler's influence extends to statistics, where his work laid the groundwork for modern statistical methods and probabilistic models. The principles he developed are central to statistical theory, including techniques used in data analysis and interpretation across various fields.

In recognition of his vast contributions, Euler is universally acclaimed as one of history's most influential scientists. His ability to connect abstract mathematical ideas with practical applications has earned him a lasting legacy in both mathematics and science. Euler's work continues to be a source of inspiration and a foundation upon which much of modern science and technology is built.

Overall, Euler's impact transcends mathematics, as his work has had lasting implications across numerous scientific and industrial fields. His pioneering spirit and innovative approaches have shaped the development of many disciplines, cementing his place as a towering figure in the history of science.

Carl Friedrich Gauss and Least Squares Regression

Early Life and Child Prodigy in Germany

Carl Friedrich Gauss, born on April 30, 1777, in Brunswick, Germany, demonstrated an extraordinary mathematical talent from a remarkably young age. His early prodigious abilities were evident when he solved complex mathematical problems that even the most experienced scholars found challenging. By the age of seven, Gauss had already made a significant mathematical discovery: he found a formula to sum the integers from 1 to 100, a feat that exemplified his innate numerical prowess.

Gauss's early life was marked by a series of impressive accomplishments that foreshadowed his future contributions to mathematics and science. At the age of 9, he was already solving problems involving arithmetic progressions, and by the time he was 15, he had developed his own proof of the fundamental theorem of algebra. His mathematical abilities were so advanced that his teachers and local mathematicians quickly recognized his potential.

The support of local patrons and his own remarkable talent enabled him to pursue higher education in mathematics at the University of Göttingen, where he began his formal academic journey. Gauss's time at Göttingen was transformative, as it allowed him to delve deeper into mathematical theory and engage with the mathematical community.

Throughout his career, Gauss made groundbreaking contributions across numerous fields, including number theory, statistics, astronomy, and physics. His work laid the foundation for many areas of mathematics and science that continue to influence these disciplines today. Gauss's early life and accomplishments reflect not only his exceptional intellect but also the impact he would have on the world of mathematics and beyond.

Foundations of Least Squares Regression

In 1809, Carl Friedrich Gauss made a landmark contribution to the field of statistics with his publication on the method of least squares, which he introduced in his work Theoria Motus Corporum Celestium. This method was a pivotal advancement in statistical analysis, offering a systematic approach to fitting data to a model by minimizing the sum of the squared differences between observed values and the values predicted by the model.

Gauss's approach to least squares regression was grounded in his derivation of the normal equations, which provide a solution to the problem of finding the best-fitting line through a set of data points. This method is used to estimate the parameters of a linear model, minimizing the discrepancies between observed data and the model's predictions. The normal equations are derived from the principle of minimizing the sum of the squared residuals, which are the differences between observed values and the values predicted by the model.

The method of least squares regression proved to be highly effective and versatile, finding applications in various scientific fields such as astronomy, engineering, and economics. Gauss's work was instrumental in enabling more accurate data analysis and prediction, and it laid the foundation for modern statistical methods. His technique was initially used to analyze astronomical data but quickly found broader applications in other disciplines.

Even more than 200 years later, least squares regression remains one of the most fundamental and widely used techniques in statistical analysis and data modeling. Its enduring relevance is a testament to Gauss's profound impact on the field of statistics and his ability to develop methods that continue to be crucial for understanding and interpreting data. The method's robustness and applicability across diverse fields underscore Gauss's significant contribution to statistical science.

Other Contributions to Statistics and Probability

Carl Friedrich Gauss made several other pivotal contributions to the fields of statistics and probability that have had a lasting impact on how data is analyzed and interpreted. His work extended beyond the method of least squares, influencing key concepts that are fundamental to modern statistical theory.

Central Limit Theorem (CLT) and Normal Distribution: One of Gauss's most influential contributions is his work on the normal distribution, also known as the Gaussian distribution. Although the normal distribution was named after Gauss, its significance extends beyond mere nomenclature. In his research, Gauss demonstrated that the normal distribution arises naturally when dealing with errors and measurements that are subject to random variability. This is encapsulated in what is now known as the CLT, which states that the sum of a large number of independent, identically distributed random variables will tend to be distributed normally, regardless of the original distribution of the variables. Gauss's insights into the normal distribution laid the groundwork for many statistical methods and are fundamental to the field of inferential statistics.

Method of Maximum Likelihood: Another major contribution from Gauss is the method of maximum likelihood estimation (MLE). While Gauss did not formally name this technique, his work laid the foundation for it. MLE is a method used to estimate the parameters of a statistical model by maximizing a likelihood function, which measures how likely it is that a given set of parameters would produce the observed data. Gauss's use of this method in the context of astronomical observations demonstrated its power in providing parameter estimates that best fit the observed data. The method of maximum likelihood has become a cornerstone of statistical inference and is widely used in various fields, from economics to genetics, for estimating and testing model parameters.

Gauss's advancements in these areas have profoundly shaped the development of statistical science. His work provided the theoretical underpinnings that have enabled subsequent statisticians to build more sophisticated models and analyses, ensuring his lasting legacy in the field.

Revolutionary Work in Number Theory

Carl Friedrich Gauss's contributions to number theory are among his most profound and transformative. His work in this area not only advanced the field but also laid the groundwork for many modern mathematical theories.

Proof of the Law of Quadratic Reciprocity: One of Gauss's most celebrated achievements in number theory is his proof of the law of quadratic reciprocity. This law, first conjectured by Euler and Legendre, is a fundamental theorem in number theory that describes the solvability of quadratic equations modulo prime numbers. Gauss's proof of this law, which he first presented in his work Disquisitiones Arithmeticae (1801), was groundbreaking. It provided a deeper understanding of the relationship between different prime numbers and their residues. Gauss's work on quadratic reciprocity was not only significant for its own sake but also for the way it influenced subsequent mathematical research. It established Gauss as a leading figure in number theory and set a new standard for rigor and depth in the field.

Advances with Complex Numbers and Modular Arithmetic: In addition to his work on quadratic reciprocity, Gauss made substantial contributions to the theory of complex numbers and modular arithmetic. His work on complex numbers began with the extension of the concept of numbers to include imaginary and complex numbers. Gauss's introduction of complex numbers and their properties, including his geometric interpretation of complex multiplication, was revolutionary. He showed that every polynomial equation with complex coefficients has a root in the complex plane, a result now known as the Fundamental Theorem of Algebra.

Gauss's contributions to modular arithmetic also had a profound impact on mathematics. He developed a systematic theory of congruences, which are equations that describe the equivalence of numbers modulo a given integer. His work on modular arithmetic provided essential tools for solving problems in number theory and laid the foundation for later developments in algebra and cryptography.

Overall, Gauss's revolutionary work in number theory transformed the field, introducing new concepts and methods that have become fundamental to modern mathematics. His insights into quadratic reciprocity, complex numbers, and modular arithmetic continue to influence and inspire mathematicians today.

Pioneering Work in Magnetism and Astronomy

Carl Friedrich Gauss's scientific contributions extended far beyond mathematics, making significant impacts in the fields of magnetism and astronomy. His work in these areas not only demonstrated his versatility as a scientist but also advanced the understanding of natural phenomena through rigorous measurement and analysis.

Gauss's pioneering work in geomagnetism involved the meticulous measurement and analysis of Earth's magnetic field. In the early 19th century, Gauss was instrumental in developing the first precise and systematic method for measuring the Earth's magnetic field. His work led to the creation of the first comprehensive magnetic survey of Europe, providing valuable data on the distribution and variations of the Earth's magnetic field.

One of Gauss's notable contributions was the development of the method of geomagnetic measurements, which involved placing magnetic observatories at different locations to monitor variations in the magnetic field. His detailed analysis of these measurements led to the formulation of mathematical models that described the Earth's magnetic field with unprecedented accuracy. Gauss's work laid the foundation for the field of geomagnetism and significantly contributed to the development of magnetic surveys and the study of magnetic anomalies.

In astronomy, Gauss's contributions were equally groundbreaking. His work in celestial mechanics, particularly in the determination of planetary orbits, was instrumental in improving the accuracy of orbit predictions. Gauss applied his mathematical expertise to the problem of calculating the orbits of celestial bodies based on observational data. His most notable achievement in this area was his work on the orbit of the asteroid Ceres, which had been discovered in 1801 but whose orbit was not well-determined at the time.

Using his method of least squares, Gauss developed a systematic approach to determining the orbit of Ceres from observational data. His calculations were so precise that they allowed for the accurate prediction of the asteroid's position, which was a significant advancement in celestial mechanics. This work demonstrated Gauss's ability to apply mathematical methods to complex astronomical problems and provided a new level of accuracy in the study of celestial bodies.

Gauss's contributions to magnetism and astronomy showcased his exceptional ability to apply mathematical principles to practical scientific problems. His work in these fields not only advanced the understanding of Earth's magnetic properties and celestial mechanics but also had a lasting impact on the development of scientific measurement and analysis techniques.

Later Career and Broader Scientific Pursuits

As Carl Friedrich Gauss advanced in his career, he continued to make significant contributions across a range of scientific fields, cementing his status as one of the most influential scientists of his time.

In 1807, Gauss took on a prominent role as the director of the Göttingen Observatory, a position that allowed him to further his interests in astronomy and observational science. Under his leadership, the observatory became a center for cutting-edge astronomical research. Gauss's work at the observatory involved not only supervising the scientific activities but also implementing improvements in observational techniques and instrumentation.

Gauss's tenure at Göttingen was marked by his focus on the application of mathematical methods to astronomical problems. He continued his work on celestial mechanics, enhancing the precision of planetary and asteroid orbit calculations. His leadership helped to foster an environment of rigorous scientific inquiry and innovation, contributing to the advancement of observational astronomy and reinforcing Göttingen's reputation as a leading institution in the field.

Diverse Works on Optics, Mechanics, and More

Beyond his contributions to astronomy and magnetism, Gauss made substantial contributions to other areas of science, including optics and mechanics. His work in optics involved the development of mathematical theories related to the propagation of light. Gauss's investigations into optical systems led to improvements in understanding image formation and lens design, which had practical implications for optical instruments.

In mechanics, Gauss contributed to the field through his work on the theory of surfaces and the application of mathematical principles to physical phenomena. His research in this area included the study of the curvature of surfaces, which laid the groundwork for later developments in differential geometry. Gauss's approach to mechanics was characterized by his emphasis on mathematical rigor and precision, reflecting his broader commitment to applying mathematical methods to solve complex scientific problems.

Gauss's later career also included diverse explorations in other scientific domains. His contributions extended to number theory, where he continued to make groundbreaking discoveries, and he maintained an active interest in various mathematical and physical sciences throughout his life. His broad scientific pursuits not only showcased his versatility as a scientist but also left a lasting impact on multiple fields of study.

Overall, Gauss's leadership at the Göttingen Observatory and his diverse scientific endeavors exemplify his extraordinary breadth of knowledge and his dedication to advancing science through rigorous mathematical and empirical methods. His work in astronomy, optics, mechanics, and beyond continues to influence scientific research and understanding to this day.

Enduring Legacy as Mathematical Genius

Carl Friedrich Gauss's impact on mathematics and science is profound and far-reaching, earning him a lasting legacy as one of the greatest mathematicians of all time. His work has shaped not only the field of statistics but also physics, astronomy, and various other scientific disciplines.

Gauss's pioneering work in statistics, particularly with least squares regression and the normal distribution, laid the foundation for modern statistical theory and practice. His contributions to the method of least squares revolutionized the way data fitting and error minimization were approached, making it an indispensable tool in statistical analysis and data science.

In physics, Gauss's research on magnetism and the Earth's magnetic field established fundamental principles that are still relevant today. His contributions to the theory of electromagnetism, although not as well known as his other work, were crucial in advancing the understanding of magnetic phenomena and laid the groundwork for future developments in the field.

Gauss's influence extended beyond these fields into areas such as astronomy and number theory. His precise calculations of planetary orbits improved the accuracy of celestial mechanics, and his work on number theory, including his proof of the law of quadratic reciprocity, set new standards for mathematical rigor and insight. His methods and theories continue to be integral to these fields, demonstrating the breadth and depth of his impact.

Gauss's genius is reflected in the wide recognition he has received from the scientific community. Often referred to as the "Prince of Mathematicians," Gauss's contributions are celebrated for their originality, rigor, and lasting influence. His work has been foundational in shaping many areas of mathematics and science, and his innovative approaches have inspired countless researchers and practitioners.

Gauss's legacy is not confined to his lifetime; his methodologies, discoveries, and insights continue to resonate across scientific disciplines. His ability to bridge theoretical concepts with practical applications exemplifies his extraordinary talent and has cemented his status as a central figure in the history of mathematics and science.

In summary, Carl Friedrich Gauss's enduring legacy as a mathematical genius is evident in the profound and lasting impact of his work across various scientific fields. His contributions have shaped modern statistics, physics, and many other disciplines, and his status as one of the greatest mathematicians ever is firmly established through his revolutionary innovations and the continued relevance of his theories.

Karl Pearson and the Foundations of Statistics

Early Life and Education

K arl Pearson, born on March 27, 1857, in London, was raised in an environment that would profoundly shape his future contributions to statistics. His father, William Pearson, was a successful barrister, and his mother, Fanny Smith, was deeply involved in social and educational reform. This combination of legal precision and social consciousness created a fertile ground for young Karl's intellectual development.

Growing up in a household that valued education and social justice, Pearson was encouraged to think critically about the world around him from a very early age.

Pearson's early education took place at University College School, London, where he demonstrated a natural aptitude for mathematics and the sciences. His academic prowess quickly became apparent, and he earned a scholarship to King's College, Cambridge, where he studied mathematics. At Cambridge, Pearson was not only immersed in rigorous academic training but also exposed to a variety of intellectual influences. It was here that he first encountered the works of Charles Darwin, whose theories on evolution and natural selection would later inspire Pearson's own work in biostatistics.

The influence of his parents' social activism also played a crucial role in shaping Pearson's worldview. His mother, in particular, was involved in movements aimed at improving education and welfare for the underprivileged. These early exposures to social issues instilled in Pearson a belief in the power of science and education to drive social progress. This belief would later be reflected in his dedication to applying statistical methods to real-world problems, particularly in the fields of biology and social sciences.

After completing his studies at Cambridge, Pearson traveled extensively across Germany, where he furthered his education in physics, metaphysics, and the history of literature at the University of Heidelberg and the University of Berlin. This period of his life was marked by a deep engagement with philosophical and cultural studies, which broadened his intellectual horizons and influenced his approach to scientific inquiry. Pearson's exposure to German intellectual traditions, particularly the works of philosophers such as Immanuel Kant and Friedrich Schiller, provided him with a unique perspective that he would later integrate into his statistical theories.

Pearson returned to England in the early 1880s, armed with a rich tapestry of knowledge and experiences. He began teaching at University College London (UCL), where he would spend the majority of his career. It was here that he established the first university statistics department in the world and laid the foundations for modern statistics. Pearson's commitment to rigorous scientific inquiry, combined with his desire to address social issues, would drive him to develop statistical methods that remain influential to this day.

Career at UCL

In 1884, Karl Pearson embarked on a significant chapter of his life when he was appointed the first professor of applied mathematics and mechanics at UCL. This position allowed Pearson to merge his profound mathematical knowledge with his passion for scientific inquiry. His innovative thinking and dedication quickly earned him respect among his peers and students. Pearson's teaching style was known for being both rigorous and inspiring, encouraging students to think critically and creatively about mathematical problems. His approach was not merely about imparting knowledge but about cultivating a mindset of inquiry and discovery.

At UCL, Pearson's career took a momentous turn when he became involved in the establishment of the Galton Laboratory for National Eugenics in 1904. Named after his close colleague and influential mentor, Sir Francis Galton, the laboratory was dedicated to the study of anthropometry and human heredity. Pearson, deeply inspired by Galton's work on heredity and statistics, saw the laboratory as a means to advance the understanding of human variation and evolution through the application of statistical methods. Under Pearson's leadership, the Galton Laboratory became a pioneering institution in the field of biometrics, emphasizing the use of statistical analysis to study biological and anthropological data.

Pearson's work at the Galton Laboratory was characterized by his commitment to rigorous scientific standards and his innovative use of statistical techniques. He believed that understanding human traits and behaviors through statistical analysis could contribute to societal improvement. Although some aspects of eugenics and anthropometry are viewed critically today, Pearson's contributions to statistical methodology during his tenure at the laboratory were groundbreaking. He developed methods such as the Pearson correlation coefficient and the chi-square test, which have become fundamental tools in statistics and have applications far beyond their original context.

Throughout his career at UCL, Pearson remained dedicated to advancing the field of statistics. He was instrumental in founding the journal "Biometrika" in 1901, which provided a platform for the dissemination of research in the emerging field of biostatistics. Pearson's editorial work ensured that the journal maintained high standards of scientific rigor, and it quickly became a leading publication in the field. His commitment to both education and research fostered a thriving academic environment at UCL, attracting students and scholars from around the world.

Pearson's tenure at UCL was marked by a harmonious blend of teaching, research, and institutional leadership. His ability to inspire and mentor students, combined with his groundbreaking research, solidified his reputation as a pioneer in the field of statistics. Pearson's legacy at UCL is not only reflected in his contributions to statistical theory and practice but also in the vibrant academic community he helped cultivate, which continues to thrive and evolve to this day.

Development of the Correlation Coefficient

Karl Pearson's motivation to quantify the relationships between two variables stemmed from his profound interest in understanding the natural world through the lens of statistics. Inspired by the work of his mentor, Sir Francis Galton, who had explored the concept of regression to the mean, Pearson sought to develop a more precise measure of association. He believed that by quantifying these relationships, scientists could uncover underlying patterns and connections that were not immediately apparent. This drive to bring clarity and precision to scientific inquiry fueled Pearson's development of the correlation coefficient.

In the late 19th century, Pearson introduced what would become known as the Pearson product-moment correlation coefficient, a groundbreaking statistical tool that provided a measure of the strength and direction of the linear relationship between two variables. This coefficient captures how changes in one variable are associated with changes in another. If two variables tend to increase together, the correlation is positive; if one increases while the other decreases, the correlation is negative. A correlation close to zero suggests no linear relationship between the variables.

Pearson's correlation coefficient has several key properties that make it a versatile and widely used statistical measure. Firstly, the value of the coefficient ranges from -1 to 1. A value of 1 indicates a perfect positive linear relationship, meaning that as one variable increases, the other increases in a perfectly predictable manner.

Conversely, a value of -1 indicates a perfect negative linear relationship, where one variable decreases as the other increases. A value of 0 indicates no linear relationship, suggesting that changes in one variable do not predict changes in the other.

The simplicity and interpretability of the Pearson correlation coefficient have contributed to its widespread adoption in various fields. It allows researchers to easily determine the strength and direction of relationships between variables, facilitating insights and discoveries across disciplines. For example, in psychology, the correlation coefficient can help identify relationships between behaviors and mental health outcomes. In finance, it can be used to understand the relationship between different economic indicators. Pearson's development of this statistical tool has had a lasting impact, providing a foundational method for exploring and interpreting data relationships.

The introduction of the Pearson product-moment correlation coefficient represented a significant advancement in the field of statistics, providing researchers across various disciplines with a reliable tool to quantify relationships between variables. Pearson's work laid the foundation for modern correlation analysis, and his coefficient remains a cornerstone in statistical practice. Its applications are vast, ranging from psychology and social sciences to finance and natural sciences, underscoring the enduring impact of Pearson's contributions to the field of statistics.

Advocacy for Mathematical Statistics

Karl Pearson was not only a pioneer in developing statistical methods but also a fervent advocate for the establishment of statistics as a rigorous mathematical discipline. His efforts to promote mathematical statistics were marked by his rivalry with another giant in the field, Ronald A. Fisher. This rivalry, while contentious, played a crucial role in shaping modern statistical thought and methodology.

Pearson and Fisher had differing views on several key aspects of statistical theory. One significant point of contention was the emphasis on parametric distributions. Pearson was a strong proponent of parametric methods, which involve making assumptions about the underlying distribution of the data. He believed that by fitting data to specific distributions, such as the normal or chi-square distributions, statisticians could derive meaningful inferences about the population being studied. Pearson developed various statistical tools and methods based on these parametric assumptions, including the Pearson distribution system, which provides a comprehensive framework for modeling different types of data distributions.

Fisher, on the other hand, was more focused on the development of non-parametric methods and the concept of MLE, which did not rely as heavily on predetermined distributional assumptions. Despite their differences, the intellectual rivalry between Pearson and Fisher spurred significant advancements in statistical theory and practice. Their debates and contrasting approaches highlighted the importance of both parametric and non-parametric methods, enriching the field and expanding the toolkit available to statisticians.

Pearson's advocacy for statistics extended beyond methodological debates. He was deeply committed to establishing statistics as a theoretical and quantitative discipline in its own right. In an era when statistics was often seen as a branch of mathematics or an auxiliary tool for other sciences, Pearson worked tirelessly to elevate its status. He emphasized the importance of rigorous mathematical foundations and theoretical development in statistics. His work in founding the first statistics department at UCL and the influential journal "Biometrika" were crucial steps in this direction. These institutions provided platforms for advancing statistical research and education, fostering a community of scholars dedicated to the development and dissemination of statistical knowledge.

Pearson's promotion of statistics as a theoretical discipline also involved demonstrating its practical applications across various fields. He showed how statistical methods could be applied to biology, medicine, and social sciences, providing valuable insights and driving progress in these areas. By highlighting the versatility and utility of statistics, Pearson helped to establish its importance as a central tool for scientific inquiry and decision-making.

Through his advocacy and pioneering work, Karl Pearson played a pivotal role in shaping the field of mathematical statistics. His emphasis on parametric distributions, his rivalry with Fisher, and his efforts to promote statistics as a theoretical and quantitative discipline laid the foundations for modern statistical science. Pearson's legacy is reflected in the robust and dynamic field of statistics today, which continues to evolve and expand, building on the foundations he helped to establish.

Later Academic Pursuits

In the later years of his academic career, Karl Pearson shifted his research focus to the study of inheritance, evolution, and eugenics. This transition was a natural extension of his earlier work in biostatistics and his deep interest in applying statistical methods to biological and social phenomena. Pearson was particularly influenced by the ideas of his mentor, Sir Francis Galton, whose work on heredity and natural selection laid the groundwork for the emerging field of eugenics. Pearson believed that statistical analysis could provide valuable insights into the mechanisms of inheritance and the evolutionary processes shaping human populations.

Pearson's work in inheritance and evolution involved the application of statistical techniques to understand the distribution and transmission of genetic traits. He conducted extensive studies on human physical characteristics, such as height and intelligence, aiming to identify patterns of inheritance and the influence of environmental factors. Pearson's research in this area contributed to the development of quantitative genetics, a field that combines principles of genetics and statistics to study the genetic basis of complex traits. His efforts to quantify and analyze variation within populations were instrumental in advancing the understanding of evolutionary processes and the role of natural selection.

However, Pearson's involvement in eugenics remains a controversial aspect of his legacy. He advocated for the use of statistical methods to promote eugenic policies aimed at improving the genetic quality of human populations. Pearson's views on eugenics were shaped by his belief in the potential of science to address social issues, but these views have been widely criticized for their ethical implications and the potential for misuse. The legacy of eugenics as a field is marred by its association with discriminatory practices and human rights abuses, and Pearson's role in promoting eugenic ideas is a complex and troubling part of his history.

Despite the controversies surrounding his later work, Pearson's contributions to the field of statistics remain profound and enduring. One of his most significant achievements was the establishment of statistics as a separate and distinct academic discipline. Prior to Pearson's efforts, statistics was often seen as a branch of mathematics or a tool for other sciences, rather than a field of study in its own right. Pearson's pioneering work in developing statistical methods, coupled with his advocacy for the importance of statistical analysis, helped to elevate the status of statistics.

Pearson's legacy in establishing statistics as a separate field of study is reflected in the institutions and infrastructure he created to support statistical research and education. At UCL, he founded the first university statistics department, providing a dedicated space for the development of statistical theory and practice. Additionally, the journal "Biometrika," which Pearson co-founded, became a leading publication for statistical research, disseminating new ideas and fostering a community of statisticians.

Through his contributions to statistical methodology, his leadership in academic institutions, and his promotion of statistics as a central tool for scientific inquiry, Karl Pearson laid the foundations for the modern field of statistics. His work has had a lasting impact, influencing generations of statisticians and shaping the way we collect, analyze, and interpret data. Despite the complexities and controversies of his later pursuits, Pearson's legacy in the field of statistics remains a testament to his vision and pioneering spirit.

Contribution to Biometrika and Role of Pearson

Karl Pearson's contributions to the journal Biometrika were pivotal in establishing the publication as a cornerstone of statistical research. Founded in 1901, Biometrika was conceived as a platform dedicated to the development and dissemination of statistical theory and methods, with a particular emphasis on their application to biological and medical research. Pearson's vision for the journal was to create a venue where innovative statistical techniques could be presented and discussed, thereby advancing the field and fostering collaboration among statisticians, biologists, and other scientists.

Pearson co-founded Biometrika alongside Walter Weldon, a zoologist and close collaborator, and Francis Galton, a polymath whose work in heredity and statistics greatly influenced Pearson. The first issue of the journal was published in October 1901, marking the beginning of a significant chapter in the history of statistical science. Pearson served as the journal's editor from its inception, a role he held with distinction until his retirement in 1936. His editorial leadership was instrumental in shaping the journal's direction and maintaining high standards of scientific rigor.

Under Pearson's stewardship, Biometrika published numerous groundbreaking papers that introduced and refined key statistical concepts and methods. For instance, Pearson's own work on the chi-square test and the correlation coefficient found a prominent place in the journal. These contributions not only enhanced the theoretical foundations of statistics but also demonstrated their practical utility in addressing real-world problems. Pearson was meticulous in his editorial duties, ensuring that the papers published in Biometrika were both methodologically sound and innovative.

An interesting aspect of Pearson's role at Biometrika was his commitment to fostering interdisciplinary collaboration. He encouraged submissions from a diverse range of fields, including biology, medicine, anthropology, and social sciences, reflecting his belief in the broad applicability of statistical methods. This interdisciplinary approach helped to establish statistics as a vital tool across various scientific domains and facilitated the exchange of ideas between statisticians and practitioners in other fields.

Pearson's tenure at Biometrika also saw the introduction of several special issues and supplements that focused on specific topics or celebrated milestones in the field of statistics. These special editions provided comprehensive overviews of emerging areas of research and highlighted the contributions of leading statisticians. Pearson's ability to curate these issues effectively showcased the dynamic nature of the field and kept the journal at the forefront of statistical research.

In addition to his editorial contributions, Pearson was actively involved in mentoring young researchers and promoting the professional development of statisticians. Through Biometrika, he provided a platform for early-career scientists to publish their work and gain recognition within the academic community. Pearson's dedication to nurturing the next generation of statisticians helped to build a robust and vibrant statistical community that continued to grow and evolve long after his retirement.

Pearson's work with Biometrika also contributed to the internationalization of the field of statistics. The journal attracted submissions from researchers around the world, fostering a global dialogue on statistical methods and their applications. This international perspective helped to standardize statistical practices and encouraged the adoption of new techniques across different countries and scientific disciplines.

Karl Pearson's contributions to Biometrika and his role as its editor were instrumental in establishing the journal as a leading publication in the field of statistics. His vision, editorial rigor, and commitment to interdisciplinary collaboration helped to shape the development of statistical science and ensured that Biometrika remained a vital resource for researchers worldwide. Pearson's legacy in the journal is a testament to his pioneering spirit and his unwavering dedication to advancing the field of statistics.

William Gosset and Practical Statistics

Career at Guinness Brewery

William Sealy Gosset, an English statistician better known by his pseudonym "Student," made significant contributions to statistics while working at the Guinness Brewery in Dublin, Ireland. Gosset's background in chemistry and brewing science was fundamental to his work in statistics, as he applied mathematical principles to solve practical problems in brewing.

Educational Background: Gosset studied at Winchester College and later at New College, Oxford, where he graduated with a degree in chemistry and mathematics. His strong foundation in these disciplines equipped him with the skills needed to address the complex challenges in brewing.

Joining Guinness Brewery: In 1899, after completing his education, Gosset joined the Guinness Brewery as a brewer. The brewery was renowned not only for its beer but also for its innovative approach to production and quality control. Guinness employed scientific methods to improve its brewing processes, making it an ideal environment for Gosset to apply his expertise in chemistry and mathematics.

Focus on Brewing Science: At Guinness, Gosset's primary responsibility was to improve the brewery's production processes and ensure the consistency and quality of its products. This involved a deep understanding of the brewing process, including the selection of raw materials, fermentation, and quality control. Gosset's work required him to conduct experiments and analyze data to identify the factors that influenced the quality of the beer.

Statistical Work to Improve Production Processes

Gosset's role at Guinness Brewery provided him with practical problems that required statistical solutions. His innovative use of statistical methods to improve production processes had a lasting impact on both the brewery and the field of statistics.

Addressing Variability in Brewing: One of the key challenges in brewing was dealing with the inherent variability in the production process. Factors such as the quality of barley and hops, fermentation conditions, and brewing techniques could all affect the final product. Gosset used statistical methods to quantify and control this variability, ensuring that Guinness could produce beer of consistent quality.

Development of the t-Distribution: Gosset's most famous contribution to statistics was the development of the t-distribution, which he published under the pseudonym "Student." The t-distribution is used to estimate population parameters when sample sizes are small, and it provides a way to make inferences about the mean of a normally distributed population. Gosset developed this distribution while working on experiments at Guinness, where sample sizes were often limited. The t-distribution allowed him to make more accurate inferences from small samples, which was crucial for improving the brewing process.

Application of Experimental Design: Gosset applied principles of experimental design to optimize the brewing process. He conducted experiments to test different brewing methods, ingredients, and conditions, using statistical analysis to determine the most effective combinations. This systematic approach to experimentation helped Guinness improve the efficiency and quality of its production.

Impact on Quality Control: Gosset's work at Guinness laid the groundwork for modern quality control methods. By applying statistical techniques to monitor and control the brewing process, he helped the brewery maintain high standards and reduce variability. This approach was pioneering at the time and has since become standard practice in many industries.

Legacy in Industrial Statistics: Gosset's contributions extended beyond brewing to the broader field of industrial statistics. His work demonstrated the practical application of statistical methods to real-world problems, inspiring other statisticians and industries to adopt similar approaches. The principles he developed for quality control and experimental design continue to be used in manufacturing, pharmaceuticals, and other fields.

In summary, William Gosset's career at Guinness Brewery was marked by his innovative use of statistical methods to improve brewing processes. His background in chemistry and brewing science, combined with his application of statistical techniques, enabled him to address variability and enhance the quality of Guinness beer. Gosset's development of the t-distribution and his contributions to experimental design and quality control had a lasting impact on both the brewery and the field of statistics, establishing him as a key figure in the history of practical statistics.

Adoption of Statistics in Industry

William Gosset's motivation for developing skills in data analysis stemmed from his practical experiences at Guinness Brewery, where he encountered complex challenges that required innovative solutions. His work highlighted the necessity of statistical methods in industrial settings, paving the way for the broader adoption of statistics in various industries.

Improving Quality and Efficiency: At Guinness, the primary goal was to produce high-quality beer consistently while maximizing efficiency. Variability in raw materials, brewing processes, and environmental conditions posed significant challenges to achieving this goal. Gosset recognized that traditional methods were insufficient for addressing these issues and saw the potential of statistical analysis to provide more accurate and reliable solutions.

Scientific Approach to Brewing: The culture at Guinness Brewery emphasized scientific rigor and innovation. Encouraged by this environment, Gosset pursued a data-driven approach to problem-solving. He understood that a thorough analysis of data collected from brewing experiments could reveal patterns and relationships that were not immediately apparent. This insight drove him to develop and refine statistical techniques that could be applied to real-world problems.

Educational Background and Curiosity: Gosset's strong foundation in chemistry and mathematics, coupled with his natural curiosity, motivated him to explore the applications of statistics. His academic background provided him with the necessary tools to approach data analysis systematically. Moreover, his desire to understand and control the variability in brewing processes inspired him to seek out and develop new statistical methods.

Early Applications of Experimental Design Concepts

Gosset's early applications of experimental design concepts at Guinness Brewery demonstrated the power of statistical methods to optimize industrial processes. His innovative work laid the foundation for the broader adoption of experimental design in various fields.

Conducting Controlled Experiments: One of Gosset's key contributions was the systematic application of controlled experiments to the brewing process. He designed experiments to test the effects of different variables, such as the type of barley, fermentation temperature, and brewing duration, on the quality of the beer. By controlling these variables and carefully analyzing the resulting data, Gosset was able to identify the optimal conditions for brewing.

Randomization and Replication: Gosset recognized the importance of randomization and replication in experimental design. Randomization helped to ensure that the results were not biased by external factors, while replication allowed for the estimation of variability and the assessment of the reliability of the findings. These principles, now fundamental to experimental design, were pioneering at the time and contributed to the robustness of Gosset's conclusions.

Optimization of Brewing Processes: Through his experiments, Gosset identified ways to optimize various aspects of the brewing process. For example, he developed methods to select the best barley varieties and determine the ideal fermentation conditions. These optimizations not only improved the quality of the beer but also enhanced the efficiency and consistency of production. Gosset's work demonstrated that a systematic, data-driven approach could lead to significant improvements in industrial processes.

Broader Implications for Industry: The success of Gosset's statistical methods at Guinness Brewery highlighted their potential for application in other industries. His work showed that statistical analysis could be used to solve complex problems, optimize processes, and improve quality in a wide range of settings. This realization encouraged other industries to adopt similar approaches, leading to the broader acceptance and integration of statistics in industrial practice.

Influence on Future Developments: Gosset's early applications of experimental design concepts had a lasting impact on the field of statistics. His work inspired subsequent developments in experimental design, quality control, and industrial statistics. The principles he established continue to be applied and expanded upon, influencing modern statistical practices and methodologies.

In summary, William Gosset's motivation for developing skills in data analysis was driven by his desire to improve quality and efficiency at Guinness Brewery. His early applications of experimental design concepts, including controlled experiments, randomization, and replication, demonstrated the power of statistical methods to optimize industrial processes. Gosset's innovative work not only improved brewing at Guinness but also laid the groundwork for the broader adoption of statistics in industry, highlighting the value of a data-driven approach to problem-solving.

Derivation of the Student's t-Distribution

One of the significant challenges William Gosset faced in his work at the Guinness Brewery was the issue of small sample sizes in quality control. Ensuring consistent quality in the brewing process often required testing and analyzing samples that were small in size due to practical constraints. Traditional statistical methods, which were largely based on large sample theory, were not suitable for making reliable inferences from these small samples. This limitation spurred Gosset's innovative work in developing new statistical techniques that could address this issue.

Variability in Small Samples: Small samples are inherently subject to greater variability and uncertainty. In the context of brewing, this meant that small batches of beer or limited quantities of raw materials could produce results that were not representative of the larger population. Gosset needed a method that could account for this increased variability and provide accurate estimates and hypothesis tests.

Limitations of the Normal Distribution: The normal distribution, which is central to many statistical methods, assumes that the sample size is large enough for the CLT to apply. This assumption is not valid for small samples, leading to inaccurate and misleading results. Gosset recognized that relying on the normal distribution for small sample inference was problematic and sought an alternative approach.

Practical Constraints in Quality Control: In industrial settings like Guinness Brewery, it was often impractical to collect large samples due to time, cost, and resource limitations. Quality control processes needed to be efficient and effective, making it essential to develop methods that could work reliably with the available small samples. Gosset's challenge was to derive a statistical method that could provide valid inferences under these constraints.

Finding a Continuous Probability Distribution

In response to these challenges, William Gosset derived what is now known as the Student's t-distribution. This groundbreaking work provided a solution to the problem of small sample inference and has had a profound impact on the field of statistics.

Derivation of the t-Distribution: Gosset's derivation of the t-distribution was based on his work with small samples in quality control experiments at Guinness Brewery. He needed a probability distribution that could accurately model the variability in small samples and provide reliable estimates of population parameters. By considering the ratio of the sample mean to the sample standard deviation, Gosset derived a continuous probability distribution that accounted for the increased uncertainty in small samples.

Characteristics of the t-Distribution: The t-distribution is similar in shape to the normal distribution but has heavier tails, reflecting the greater variability and uncertainty associated with small samples. As the sample size increases, the t-distribution approaches the normal distribution, making it a versatile tool for both small and large sample inference. This characteristic makes the t-distribution particularly useful for hypothesis testing and confidence interval estimation when dealing with small samples.

Application to Hypothesis Testing: Gosset's t-distribution allowed for more accurate hypothesis testing in small sample scenarios. By using the t-distribution, researchers could determine critical values and p-values that appropriately accounted for the increased variability. This improvement enabled more reliable decision-making and inference based on small sample data, which was crucial for quality control and other practical applications.

Publication Under Pseudonym "Student": Gosset published his findings in a 1908 paper titled "The Probable Error of a Mean" under the pseudonym "Student." The use of a pseudonym was necessary due to Guinness Brewery's policy against employees publishing research. Despite this, Gosset's work gained widespread recognition and has since become a fundamental component of statistical theory and practice.

Impact on Statistical Methods: The derivation of the t-distribution was a significant advancement in statistical methods. It provided a robust framework for small sample inference, addressing a critical gap in existing statistical techniques. The t-distribution has since been widely adopted in various fields, including psychology, medicine, and social sciences, where small sample sizes are common.

In summary, William Gosset's derivation of the Student's t-distribution was a response to the challenges of small sample inference in quality control at Guinness Brewery. His innovative work provided a continuous probability distribution that accounted for the increased variability in small samples, enabling more accurate and reliable statistical inference. The t-distribution has had a lasting impact on the field of statistics, becoming an essential tool for hypothesis testing and confidence interval estimation in small sample scenarios.

Collaboration with Karl Pearson

William Gosset, under the pseudonym "Student," made significant contributions to the journal Biometrika, which was co-founded by the prominent statistician Karl Pearson. This collaboration played a crucial role in the development and dissemination of statistical methods during the early 20th century.

Introduction to Karl Pearson: Gosset first became aware of Karl Pearson's work during his time at Guinness Brewery. Pearson was already a well-established figure in the field of statistics, known for his contributions to correlation and regression analysis. Recognizing the potential applications of Pearson's work to his own challenges in quality control, Gosset reached out to Pearson for guidance and collaboration.

Use of the Pen Name "Student": Due to the policies at Guinness Brewery, which prohibited employees from publishing work under their real names to protect proprietary information, Gosset adopted the pseudonym "Student." This allowed him to share his innovative findings with the broader academic community without breaching his employer's rules.

Publishing in Biometrika: Gosset's landmark paper, "The Probable Error of a Mean," was published in Biometrika in 1908. This paper introduced the t-distribution, a major breakthrough for statistical inference with small samples. The choice of Biometrika as the publication venue was strategic, as the journal was a leading outlet for pioneering research in biometry and statistics, co-edited by Pearson himself.

Collaboration with Pearson: Although Gosset and Pearson had different personalities and professional backgrounds, their collaboration was mutually beneficial. Pearson provided a platform for Gosset's ideas through Biometrika, ensuring that Gosset's contributions reached a wide audience of statisticians and researchers. In turn, Gosset's practical insights from his work at Guinness enriched the theoretical developments in statistics that Pearson was advancing.

Recognition Among Academic Statisticians

Gosset's work, published under the pseudonym "Student," gradually gained recognition and respect within the academic community. His contributions had a profound impact on the field of statistics and established him as a key figure despite his relatively modest professional background compared to his academic contemporaries.

Academic Acceptance: Initially, the academic community was cautious about Gosset's findings, given the unconventional pseudonym and the commercial background of his work. However, the robustness and utility of the t-distribution in small sample inference soon became apparent, leading to widespread acceptance and adoption by statisticians.

Influence on Statistical Education: As the t-distribution and the associated t-tests became fundamental tools in statistical analysis, they were incorporated into the curriculum of statistical education. Textbooks and academic courses began to teach these methods, ensuring that generations of statisticians were familiar with Gosset's contributions.

Recognition by Leading Statisticians: Notable statisticians of the time, including Karl Pearson, recognized the significance of Gosset's work. Pearson's support and publication of Gosset's research in Biometrika were instrumental in legitimizing his contributions. Moreover, Ronald A. Fisher, another towering figure in statistics, further developed and popularized the t-distribution in his own work, acknowledging Gosset's foundational contributions.

Lasting Legacy: Over time, the significance of Gosset's work extended beyond academic circles to practical applications in various fields, including agriculture, medicine, psychology, and social sciences. The principles he developed for small sample inference continue to be relevant and widely used today.

In summary, William Gosset's collaboration with Karl Pearson and his contributions to Biometrika under the pen name "Student" were pivotal in the dissemination and acceptance of the t-distribution. His innovative work on small sample inference gained recognition among academic statisticians and had a lasting impact on both the theoretical and practical aspects of statistics. This collaboration not only advanced the field of statistics but also ensured that Gosset's contributions would be remembered and valued by future generations.

Impact on Fields Beyond Brewing

The work of William Gosset, known as "Student," had a profound impact that extended well beyond the brewing industry. Guinness Brewery, recognizing the significance of Gosset's contributions, took measures to preserve his works, ensuring that future generations could benefit from his statistical innovations.

Preservation of Manuscripts and Research: Guinness Brewery maintained detailed records of Gosset's experiments, analyses, and findings. These archives include original manuscripts, correspondence with other statisticians, and internal reports that document his pioneering work in statistical methods. By preserving these documents, Guinness acknowledged the value of Gosset's contributions to both the company and the broader field of statistics.

Access for Researchers: The preservation of Gosset's work in the Guinness archives provided valuable resources for researchers and historians interested in the development of statistical methods. Scholars studying the history of statistics and its applications in industry have been able to access these archives to gain insights into Gosset's innovative approaches and the practical challenges he addressed.

Recognition of Historical Significance: The preservation efforts by Guinness highlighted the historical significance of Gosset's contributions. By maintaining these records, Guinness not only honored Gosset's legacy but also underscored the importance of integrating statistical methods into industrial practices. This recognition helped to cement Gosset's status as a key figure in the history of statistics.

Legacy as a Pioneer of Applied Statistics

William Gosset, known by his pseudonym "Student," is celebrated as a pioneer who effectively bridged the gap between theoretical statistics and practical applications in industry and agriculture. His work demonstrated that rigorous statistical methods could solve real-world problems, thus laying the groundwork for modern applied statistics.

Integration of Statistical Theory in Brewing: At Guinness Brewery, Gosset faced practical challenges that required innovative solutions. By applying statistical theory to improve the quality and consistency of beer production, he showcased how abstract mathematical concepts could have tangible benefits in industrial processes. His work on small sample inference was particularly relevant in brewing, where production constraints often limited the size of data sets.

Development of Practical Statistical Methods: Gosset's ability to derive practical solutions from theoretical principles was instrumental in the creation of the t-distribution. This innovation addressed the specific needs of small sample inference, which was critical for quality control at Guinness. His work proved that statistical methods could be adapted and refined to meet the demands of various industrial contexts.

Influence on Agricultural Research: Gosset's contributions extended beyond brewing to agriculture, where experimental design and statistical analysis are crucial. His methods for small sample inference and controlled experiments provided a robust framework for agricultural research, influencing studies on crop yields, soil treatments, and other vital areas. His work demonstrated the importance of applying rigorous statistical methods to optimize agricultural practices and improve productivity.

Collaboration with Karl Pearson: Gosset's collaboration with Karl Pearson and the publication of his work in Biometrika under the pseudonym "Student" helped disseminate his findings to a broader audience. This partnership not only enhanced the academic credibility of his work but also facilitated the integration of statistical theory into practical applications across various fields.

Enduring Importance of Small Sample Methodology

Gosset's development of the t-distribution and his pioneering work on small sample methodology have had a lasting impact on the field of statistics. These contributions remain vital for statistical analysis in many disciplines, underscoring his legacy as a key figure in applied statistics.

Fundamental Tool for Small Sample Inference: The t-distribution has become a fundamental tool for statistical inference in situations where sample sizes are small. Its ability to provide reliable estimates and hypothesis tests, even with limited data, has made it indispensable in fields such as medicine, psychology, social sciences, and engineering. Gosset's work ensured that researchers could draw meaningful conclusions from small samples, thereby advancing knowledge in these areas.

Widespread Adoption in Statistical Practice: The principles underlying the t-distribution have been widely adopted in statistical practice. Techniques such as the one-sample t-test, paired t-test, and independent samples t-test are now standard methods taught in statistics courses and used by researchers worldwide. Gosset's contributions have thus become integral to the training of new generations of statisticians and researchers.

Applications Across Disciplines: The versatility of the t-distribution has led to its application in diverse scientific disciplines. Whether in clinical trials, psychological experiments, agricultural studies, or quality control processes, the t-distribution provides a robust framework for making inferences from small samples. This cross-disciplinary relevance highlights the enduring importance of Gosset's small sample methodology.

Legacy of Practical Innovation: Gosset's work exemplifies the power of practical innovation driven by theoretical insights. His ability to translate complex statistical concepts into practical solutions for industry and agriculture has inspired subsequent generations of statisticians to pursue applied research. His legacy is a testament to the value of bridging theory and practice to address real-world challenges.

Recognition and Influence: Despite his modest professional background compared to his academic contemporaries, Gosset's work has earned widespread recognition and respect. His contributions have influenced not only the field of statistics but also the broader scientific community. The enduring relevance of his methods attests to his profound impact on statistical thinking and practice.

In summary, William Gosset's legacy as a pioneer of applied statistics is characterized by his successful integration of statistical theory with practical industrial and agricultural applications. His development of the t-distribution and small sample methodology remains critically important for statistical analysis across various disciplines. Gosset's work continues to inspire and influence statisticians and researchers, underscoring his lasting contributions to the field of statistics.

R.A. Fisher and the Beginnings of Modern Statistics

Early Life and Education

Ronald Aylmer Fisher, commonly known as R.A. Fisher, was born on February 17, 1890, in East Finchley, London, England. However, much of his formative years were spent on a farm, which his family moved to after the death of his mother when he was 14. The farm environment provided young Fisher with a unique perspective on nature and agriculture,

fostering a deep interest in the natural world that would later influence his scientific work. The combination of rural life and his inquisitive nature spurred Fisher's early fascination with biology and the principles governing living organisms.

Fisher's academic journey began at Harrow School, one of the leading independent schools in England. Here, he demonstrated exceptional talent in mathematics and science, subjects that quickly became his passion. Despite suffering from poor eyesight, Fisher developed remarkable skills in mental arithmetic and spatial reasoning, often performing complex calculations in his head. His abilities in mathematics were recognized early on, and he won several scholarships that enabled him to pursue higher education.

In 1909, Fisher entered Gonville and Caius College, Cambridge, where he studied mathematics. His time at Cambridge was profoundly influential, exposing him to a wide array of scientific disciplines and rigorous academic training. Fisher thrived in the intellectually stimulating environment, where he was particularly inspired by the works of Charles Darwin and the emerging field of genetics. Under the mentorship of influential mathematicians and scientists, Fisher began to see the potential for applying mathematical principles to biological problems.

At Cambridge, Fisher's interest in statistics began to take shape. He was introduced to the work of Karl Pearson, whose pioneering contributions to the field of statistics laid the groundwork for Fisher's future endeavors. Pearson's focus on the application of statistical methods to biological data resonated with Fisher, who saw the potential for developing more sophisticated and precise tools for scientific analysis. Fisher's exceptional mathematical skills and his deep interest in biology positioned him perfectly to make significant contributions to the field of statistics.

Fisher graduated from Cambridge in 1912 with a degree in mathematics. His time at the university had not only honed his mathematical prowess but also deepened his understanding of biological processes and the importance of statistical analysis in scientific research. Armed with this knowledge and inspired by the intellectual challenges he encountered at Cambridge, Fisher embarked on a career that would revolutionize the field of statistics and establish him as one of the foremost statisticians of the 20th century.

The combination of his upbringing on a farm, his rigorous education at Cambridge, and his natural mathematical talent set the stage for Fisher's groundbreaking work in statistics. His unique background allowed him to bridge the gap between theoretical mathematics and practical scientific applications, paving the way for the development of modern statistical methods that continue to influence research across numerous disciplines today.

Early Career at Rothamsted Experimental Station

In 1919, after serving in World War I and engaging in various teaching positions, R.A. Fisher was appointed as an agricultural statistician at the Rothamsted Experimental

Station in Harpenden, England. This position marked the beginning of a highly productive period in Fisher's career, where he would make some of his most significant contributions to the field of statistics. Rothamsted was one of the oldest agricultural research institutions in the world, and it provided Fisher with a unique opportunity to apply his statistical expertise to real-world agricultural problems.

At Rothamsted, Fisher was tasked with analyzing vast amounts of data from long-term experiments on crop variety studies. The station had been conducting experiments on different crops, fertilizers, and farming techniques for many years, resulting in an extensive collection of data. Fisher's role was to make sense of this data and derive meaningful conclusions that could improve agricultural practices. This work was crucial for developing more efficient and productive farming methods, particularly in the post-war period when food production was a critical concern.

One of Fisher's significant achievements at Rothamsted was the development of the analysis of variance (ANOVA) technique. ANOVA allowed researchers to determine whether there were statistically significant differences between the means of different groups, such as various crop treatments. This method provided a robust and systematic way to analyze experimental data and helped in identifying the most effective agricultural practices. Fisher's introduction of ANOVA was a breakthrough in statistical methodology, and it quickly became a fundamental tool in experimental design and analysis across many scientific disciplines.

Fisher also worked on the design of experiments (DoEs), emphasizing the importance of randomization and replication in agricultural trials. He understood that to draw valid conclusions, it was essential to control for confounding variables and ensure that the experiments were not biased by external factors. Fisher's principles of experimental design laid the groundwork for modern scientific experimentation, promoting rigor and precision in research practices. His work at Rothamsted demonstrated how careful statistical analysis and well-designed experiments could lead to significant advancements in agricultural science.

In addition to ANOVA and experimental design, Fisher contributed to the development of the MLE method, which provided a unified approach to estimating the parameters of a statistical model. This method became a cornerstone of statistical theory and practice, offering a way to make inferences about populations based on sample data. Fisher's work on MLE further solidified his reputation as a leading figure in the field of statistics.

Fisher's tenure at Rothamsted was marked by a blend of theoretical innovation and practical application. His statistical methods transformed agricultural research, enabling scientists to draw more accurate and reliable conclusions from their experiments. By applying his mathematical skills to the challenges of crop variety studies, Fisher demonstrated the power of statistics to solve real-world problems and improve agricultural productivity.

Overall, Fisher's early career at Rothamsted Experimental Station was a period of remarkable productivity and innovation. His contributions to statistical theory and methodology during this time laid the foundations for many of the techniques used in modern statistics. Fisher's work at Rothamsted not only advanced agricultural science but also had a lasting impact on the field of statistics, influencing research practices in diverse areas of study.

Development of Fiducial Inference

R.A. Fisher's development of fiducial inference was motivated by the challenges he encountered while analyzing small sample agricultural experiments at the Rothamsted Experimental Station. Fisher recognized that traditional methods of statistical inference, which relied heavily on large sample sizes and asymptotic properties, were often inadequate for the small sample problems that frequently arose in agricultural research. He sought a new approach that could provide more accurate and reliable inferential procedures for these situations.

Fiducial inference was introduced by Fisher in the 1930s as an innovative method to address the limitations of existing statistical techniques. The concept emerged from Fisher's desire to create a more direct and intuitive form of inference, one that did not rely on subjective prior distributions, as Bayesian methods did, nor solely on long-run frequency properties, as frequentist methods did. Instead, fiducial inference aimed to provide objective probability statements about parameters based on the observed data alone.

The method of fiducial inference begins with the fiducial distribution, which Fisher described as a distribution of the parameter given the observed data. Unlike traditional confidence intervals, which provide a range of values within which the parameter is likely to lie, the fiducial distribution gives a probability distribution over the parameter space. This approach allows for more precise probability statements about the parameter, particularly in the context of small samples where traditional methods may lack precision.

To construct a fiducial distribution, Fisher utilized pivotal quantities, which are functions of both the data and the parameters that have a known probability distribution independent of the parameters. By solving the equation involving the pivotal quantity for the parameter, Fisher derived the fiducial distribution. This process allowed him to transform the observed data into a distribution over the parameter space, effectively bypassing the need for prior distributions or long-run frequency considerations.

One of the key features of fiducial inference is its ability to provide exact distributions for parameters in small sample scenarios. This was particularly useful in agricultural experiments at Rothamsted, where sample sizes were often limited due to practical constraints. Fisher believed that fiducial inference could offer more informative and accurate conclusions in such contexts, enhancing the reliability of statistical analysis and decision-making in experimental research.

Despite its innovative nature, fiducial inference was met with considerable skepticism and debate within the statistical community. Critics argued that the method lacked a solid theoretical foundation and that its interpretations could be ambiguous. The fiducial distribution's status as an objective probability distribution was particularly contentious, as it seemed to blur the line between Bayesian and frequentist approaches.

Nevertheless, fiducial inference had a significant impact on the development of statistical theory. It stimulated discussions about the nature of statistical inference and the roles of probability and uncertainty in parameter estimation. Fisher's work on fiducial inference also inspired further research into alternative inferential methods, including the development of confidence distributions and other approaches that sought to address the limitations of traditional techniques.

In summary, R.A. Fisher's development of fiducial inference was driven by the need for more effective statistical methods for small sample agricultural experiments. Through the method of fiducial distribution, Fisher aimed to provide objective probability statements about parameters based on observed data, offering a novel approach to statistical inference. While fiducial inference faced criticism and debate, its introduction marked an important milestone in the evolution of statistical thought and continues to influence discussions on the nature and methods of statistical inference.

Foundations of Experimental Design

R.A. Fisher's contributions to the foundations of experimental design are among his most enduring and influential achievements. His work established fundamental principles that transformed how scientific experiments, particularly in agriculture, are conducted and analyzed. Fisher's principles of blocking, randomization, and replication provided a systematic framework that enhanced the reliability and validity of experimental results.

Blocking: One of the core principles Fisher introduced was blocking, which involves grouping experimental units that are similar in some way and then randomly assigning treatments within these blocks. The purpose of blocking is to control for known sources of variability that could otherwise confound the results of the experiment. By accounting for these sources of variation, blocking increases the precision of the experiment and helps to isolate the effect of the treatments being tested. In agricultural experiments, for example, blocking might involve grouping plots of land with similar soil characteristics or other environmental factors, ensuring that comparisons between treatments are not biased by these variables.

Randomization: Randomization is another cornerstone of Fisher's experimental design. It involves randomly assigning experimental units to different treatment groups, which helps to eliminate selection bias and ensures that the treatment groups are comparable. Randomization also allows the use of probability theory to make valid inferences about the treatment effects. By randomizing the assignment of treatments, researchers can be more confident that any observed differences between groups are due to the treatments themselves rather than other extraneous factors. This principle is crucial in establishing the internal validity of an experiment.

Replication: Replication involves repeating the experiment or treatment on multiple experimental units to obtain an estimate of the variability in the response. This principle is essential for quantifying the natural variability within the experimental units and providing a more reliable estimate of the treatment effects. Replication enhances the robustness of the experimental results and allows researchers to generalize their findings to a broader population. In agricultural experiments, replication might involve applying the same treatment to multiple plots of land or conducting the experiment in different locations or seasons to account for environmental variability.

Layout of Agricultural Field Experiments

Fisher's principles of experimental design were particularly influential in the layout and analysis of agricultural field experiments. At Rothamsted Experimental Station, Fisher applied these principles to optimize the DoEs aimed at improving crop yields and farming practices.

Field Layout: Fisher devised systematic approaches for arranging experimental plots in agricultural fields to implement blocking, randomization, and replication effectively. One common design he promoted was the randomized complete block design (RCBD), where the field is divided into blocks, and treatments are randomly assigned within each block. This design controls for variability within blocks while maintaining random assignment of treatments.

Latin Square and Factorial Designs: Fisher also developed more sophisticated designs, such as the Latin square design and factorial experiments. The Latin square design is particularly useful when there are two sources of variability that need to be controlled. It involves arranging treatments in a square grid, where each treatment appears exactly once in each row and each column, thus controlling for two dimensions of variability simultaneously. Factorial designs, on the other hand, allow researchers to study the effects of multiple factors and their interactions simultaneously, providing a comprehensive understanding of how different variables influence the outcome.

Analysis of Experimental Data: Alongside the design principles, Fisher advanced methods for analyzing experimental data. He introduced the ANOVA technique, which became a fundamental tool for examining the effects of different treatments and assessing the significance of observed differences. ANOVA helps in partitioning the total variability in the data into components attributable to the treatments, blocks, and random error, facilitating a clear interpretation of the results.

Through these contributions, Fisher revolutionized the conduct of agricultural experiments and scientific research more broadly. His principles of experimental design provided a rigorous framework for planning, executing, and analyzing experiments, ensuring that conclusions drawn from the data were scientifically sound and reliable. The impact of Fisher's work extends beyond agriculture, influencing experimental practices in medicine, psychology, industrial research, and numerous other fields where controlled experimentation is essential.

In summary, R.A. Fisher's foundational work in experimental design, including the principles of blocking, randomization, and replication, along with his innovative approaches to field layout and data analysis, has had a profound and lasting impact on the methodology of scientific research. His contributions continue to underpin the design and interpretation of experiments across a wide range of disciplines, ensuring the robustness and validity of scientific findings.

Contributions to Genetics and Evolution

R.A. Fisher's work in genetics and evolution is a testament to his ability to apply statistical methods to biological problems, significantly advancing the understanding of inheritance, genetic variance, and evolutionary processes. His contributions laid the groundwork for the modern field of population genetics and provided essential tools for studying the genetic basis of traits and the dynamics of evolutionary change.

Application of Statistics to Study Inheritance: Fisher's application of statistical methods to genetics began with his groundbreaking work in the early 20th century. He recognized that the principles of Mendelian genetics, which described how traits are inherited from one generation to the next, could be rigorously analyzed using statistical techniques. Fisher's approach allowed for a more precise and quantitative understanding of genetic inheritance, bridging the gap between Mendelian genetics and the biometric approach championed by Francis Galton and Karl Pearson.

One of Fisher's most notable contributions was his 1918 paper, "The Correlation Between Relatives on the Supposition of Mendelian Inheritance," which introduced the concept of ANOVA to partition genetic and environmental sources of variation in phenotypic traits. This paper provided a mathematical framework for understanding how genes and the environment contribute to the observed variation in traits such as height, intelligence, and disease susceptibility. Fisher's work demonstrated that Mendelian inheritance could explain the continuous variation observed in many traits, which had previously been attributed solely to environmental factors.

Concepts of Heritability, Genetic Variance, and Fitness

Heritability: Fisher introduced the concept of heritability, a measure of the proportion of phenotypic variation in a population that is attributable to genetic differences among individuals. Heritability provides a way to quantify the genetic contribution to traits and predict the response to selection in breeding programs. Fisher's work on heritability laid the foundation for quantitative genetics, a field that studies the inheritance of complex traits controlled by multiple genes. His insights into heritability have had profound implications for agriculture, medicine, and evolutionary biology, guiding the selection and breeding of plants and animals for desired traits.

Genetic Variance: Fisher also made significant contributions to understanding genetic variance, which refers to the diversity of genetic information within a population. He identified different components of genetic variance, including additive variance, dominance variance, and epistatic variance. Additive genetic variance, which arises from the cumulative effect of individual alleles, is particularly important because it determines the potential for a trait to respond to natural or artificial selection. Fisher's decomposition of genetic variance into its components allowed for a more detailed analysis of how genetic factors influence phenotypic traits and the potential for evolutionary change.

Fitness and the Fundamental Theorem of Natural Selection: Fisher's contributions to the concept of fitness and evolutionary theory are epitomized by his Fundamental Theorem of Natural Selection, often compared to the second law of thermodynamics in its importance. The theorem states that the rate of increase in the average fitness of a population is equal to the genetic variance in fitness. In other words, populations evolve over time in response to selection pressures, with the speed of evolutionary change proportional to the amount of genetic variation affecting fitness. Fisher's theorem provided a quantitative framework for understanding how natural selection operates and how it drives the evolution of populations over time.

Fisher's work in genetics and evolution extended beyond theoretical contributions. He was also involved in practical breeding programs and experimental studies, applying his statistical methods to real-world problems in agriculture and biology. His interdisciplinary approach, combining mathematics, statistics, and biology, set a precedent for future research in population genetics and evolutionary biology.

In summary, R.A. Fisher's contributions to genetics and evolution were transformative, applying statistical methods to elucidate the genetic basis of inheritance and the dynamics of evolutionary change. His concepts of heritability, genetic variance, and fitness provided essential tools for studying complex traits and understanding the processes driving evolution. Fisher's work laid the foundation for modern population genetics and continues to influence research in genetics, evolutionary biology, and related fields.

Disagreements with Neyman and Pearson

R.A. Fisher's disagreements with Jerzy Neyman and Egon Pearson centered around the logical foundations of hypothesis testing and the differing approaches and interpretations of statistical inference. These debates were highly influential in shaping the field of statistics, highlighting the contrasting philosophies and methodologies that underpin statistical practice.

Logical Foundations of Hypothesis Testing: Fisher's approach to hypothesis testing was rooted in his concept of significance testing, which he introduced in the 1920s. Fisher's method involved formulating a null hypothesis (H_0), which represents a baseline or default assumption, and then calculating the probability (p-value) of obtaining the observed data, or more extreme results, if the null hypothesis were true. If this p-value was sufficiently small, Fisher argued, the null hypothesis should be rejected, suggesting that the observed data were unlikely to have occurred by chance alone.

Fisher's significance testing emphasized the p-value as a measure of evidence against the null hypothesis. He advocated for using a significance level (e.g., 0.05) as a threshold for rejecting the null hypothesis, but he also emphasized the need for scientific judgment in interpreting results. Fisher saw the p-value as a flexible tool for assessing evidence, rather than a rigid decision rule.

In contrast, Neyman and Pearson developed an alternative framework known as the Neyman-Pearson lemma, which formalized the process of hypothesis testing in a more structured way. Their approach involved comparing two competing hypotheses: the null hypothesis (H_0) and an alternative hypothesis (H_1). They introduced the concepts of Type I error (rejecting H_0 when it is true) and Type II error (failing to reject H_0 when H_1 is true), and emphasized controlling these error rates through the use of predefined significance levels (α) and power ($1 - \beta$).

Neyman and Pearson's method focused on the long-run performance of hypothesis tests, advocating for a more systematic and objective approach to decision-making. They introduced the idea of an acceptance region and a rejection region, and proposed the use of critical values to determine whether the observed data fell within these regions. This framework provided a clear, repeatable procedure for hypothesis testing, designed to minimize errors over repeated trials.

Debates Over Approaches and Interpretations

The debates between Fisher and Neyman-Pearson revolved around several key issues:

Philosophical Differences: Fisher viewed statistical inference as a process of learning from data and assessing evidence, with a focus on the p-value as a measure of evidence against the null hypothesis. He believed in the flexibility and interpretative nature of significance testing. Neyman and Pearson, on the other hand, saw hypothesis testing as a decision-making process, emphasizing the need for pre-specified criteria and long-run error control. They advocated for a more rigid and procedural approach, which they argued would lead to more consistent and reliable decisions.

Role of the Alternative Hypothesis: Fisher criticized Neyman and Pearson's reliance on the alternative hypothesis, arguing that it was often unrealistic or difficult to specify in practice. He believed that focusing on the null hypothesis and assessing the evidence against it was a more practical and meaningful approach. Neyman and Pearson countered that considering the alternative hypothesis was essential for understanding the power of a test and making informed decisions about the trade-offs between Type I and Type II errors.

Interpretation of p-Values and Significance Levels: Fisher's use of p-values as a measure of evidence was at odds with Neyman and Pearson's emphasis on fixed significance levels and decision rules. Fisher argued that p-values provided a nuanced understanding of the data, while Neyman and Pearson contended that pre-specified significance levels offered greater objectivity and clarity in decision-making.

Flexibility vs. Rigidity: Fisher's approach allowed for more flexibility and subjective judgment in interpreting statistical results, which he believed was necessary for scientific research. Neyman and Pearson's method, by contrast, promoted a more structured and objective framework, which they argued would reduce ambiguity and improve the reliability of statistical conclusions.

Despite their disagreements, the contributions of Fisher and Neyman-Pearson collectively advanced the field of statistics. Fisher's work laid the foundation for significance testing and introduced key concepts that remain central to statistical practice. Neyman and Pearson's framework provided a systematic approach to hypothesis testing, emphasizing error control and decision theory.

In summary, the disagreements between R.A. Fisher and Neyman-Pearson over the logical foundations of hypothesis testing and their differing approaches to statistical inference highlight the rich diversity of thought within the field of statistics. Their debates underscored the importance of both flexibility and rigor in statistical practice, and their contributions continue to influence the ways in which statistical methods are developed and applied today.

Later Academic Career

In the latter part of his career, R.A. Fisher accepted a position as a professor at UCL, one of the leading institutions for statistical research. Fisher's tenure at UCL, beginning in 1933, marked a significant phase in his academic journey, allowing him to further his research and influence the next generation of statisticians and scientists.

At UCL, Fisher held the prestigious Galton Chair of Eugenics, succeeding Karl Pearson. This position not only reflected Fisher's stature in the field of statistics but also provided him with a platform to advance his research in genetics and statistical methods. His work during this period continued to bridge the gap between statistical theory and practical applications, particularly in the fields of genetics, agriculture, and medicine.

Fisher's role at UCL involved both teaching and research. He was known for his rigorous and inspiring lectures, which attracted students from diverse academic backgrounds. His ability to convey complex statistical concepts in an accessible manner helped to demystify the subject for many students, fostering a deeper appreciation for the power of statistical analysis. Fisher's influence as a teacher extended beyond the classroom, as his students went on to make significant contributions to the field of statistics and related disciplines.

The Design of Experiments

One of Fisher's most impactful contributions during his time at UCL was the publication of his seminal textbook, *The Design of Experiments*, in 1935. This book systematically outlined the principles of experimental design that Fisher had developed and refined over his career. It became an essential reference for researchers across various fields, providing a comprehensive guide to planning, conducting, and analyzing experiments.

The Design of Experiments introduced key concepts such as randomization, replication, and blocking, which Fisher argued were crucial for obtaining valid and reliable results. The book emphasized the importance of carefully planning experiments to control for sources of variability and ensure that the results could be generalized to broader contexts. Fisher's clear and logical presentation of these principles made the book accessible to a wide audience, from agricultural scientists to medical researchers and industrial engineers.

One of the most influential aspects of the book was Fisher's discussion of the ANOVA, a statistical technique he had developed to partition the variability in data and test the significance of experimental factors. Fisher's ANOVA framework provided researchers with a powerful tool for analyzing complex experimental data and making informed decisions based on the results. The widespread adoption of ANOVA and other techniques outlined in *The Design of Experiments* revolutionized scientific research, enabling more rigorous and systematic investigations across a wide range of disciplines.

Fisher's textbook also highlighted the practical applications of experimental design principles, drawing on examples from his work at Rothamsted Experimental Station and other research contexts. By illustrating the real-world impact of sound experimental design, Fisher underscored the importance of statistical methods in advancing scientific knowledge and improving decision-making processes.

The Design of Experiments had a profound influence on the practice of scientific research worldwide. It established Fisher as a leading authority in the field of experimental design and cemented his legacy as one of the most important figures in the history of statistics. The principles and methods outlined in the book continue to be foundational in the training of researchers and the conduct of experiments across diverse fields.

In summary, R.A. Fisher's later academic career at UCL and the publication of his influential textbook, *The Design of Experiments*, marked significant milestones in his contribution to the field of statistics. His role as a professor at UCL allowed him to inspire and educate future generations of statisticians, while his textbook provided a comprehensive and accessible guide to experimental design that transformed scientific research practices worldwide. Fisher's legacy in statistics remains enduring, reflecting the profound impact of his work on the development of rigorous and effective research methodologies.

Lasting Impact and Statistical Thinking

R.A. Fisher's unique blend of mathematical rigor and practical relevance is one of the key reasons his work has had such a lasting impact on the field of statistics. Fisher was a pioneer in applying mathematical principles to solve real-world problems, and his ability to bridge the gap between theory and practice revolutionized statistical science.

Fisher's mathematical rigor is evident in his development of foundational statistical concepts and methods, such as MLE, ANOVA, and fiducial inference. His work was characterized by a deep understanding of mathematical principles and a commitment to precision and accuracy in statistical analysis. Fisher's contributions to statistical theory provided researchers with robust tools for analyzing data and drawing valid conclusions, setting new standards for rigor in the field.

At the same time, Fisher was acutely aware of the practical applications of statistical methods. His work at the Rothamsted Experimental Station, where he applied statistical techniques to agricultural research, exemplifies his commitment to using statistics to solve practical problems. Fisher's principles of experimental design, including randomization, replication, and blocking, were developed with the practical needs of researchers in mind. These principles have been widely adopted in various fields, demonstrating the practical relevance and utility of Fisher's work.

Legacy as Founder of Modern Statistical Science

R.A. Fisher is widely regarded as one of the founders of modern statistical science. His contributions laid the groundwork for many of the methods and principles that underpin contemporary statistical practice. Fisher's influence extends across numerous fields, including agriculture, biology, medicine, and social sciences, where his methods continue to be essential tools for researchers. Fisher's legacy is evident in several key areas:

Statistical Theory and Methods: Fisher's development of statistical concepts such as MLE, fiducial inference, and ANOVA provided a rigorous mathematical framework for statistical analysis. These methods have become fundamental tools in statistical practice, used by researchers worldwide to analyze data and draw reliable conclusions.

Experimental Design: Fisher's principles of experimental design transformed the way experiments are conducted in scientific research. His emphasis on randomization, replication, and blocking has become standard practice in experimental research, ensuring the validity and reliability of experimental results. Fisher's work in this area has had a profound impact on fields ranging from agriculture to medicine, where well-designed experiments are crucial for advancing knowledge and improving outcomes.

Education and Influence: Fisher's role as a professor and his influential textbooks, such as *Statistical Methods for Research Workers* and *The Design of Experiments*, have educated generations of statisticians and researchers. His clear and accessible presentation of statistical principles has made his work widely accessible, helping to disseminate his methods and ideas across diverse disciplines.

Interdisciplinary Impact: Fisher's ability to apply statistical methods to a wide range of scientific problems exemplifies the interdisciplinary nature of his work. His contributions to genetics, evolutionary biology, and agricultural research highlight the versatility and relevance of statistical science in addressing complex questions across different fields.

Philosophical Contributions: Fisher's debates with Neyman and Pearson over the foundations of hypothesis testing and statistical inference have shaped the philosophical landscape of statistics. These discussions have influenced the development of statistical methodologies and have led to a deeper understanding of the principles underlying statistical analysis.

In summary, R.A. Fisher's lasting impact on statistical thinking is a testament to his blend of mathematical rigor and practical relevance. His legacy as a founder of modern statistical science is evident in the widespread adoption of his methods, the enduring influence of his principles of experimental design, and the continued relevance of his work in educating and guiding researchers. Fisher's contributions have fundamentally shaped the field of statistics, providing a foundation that continues to support and advance scientific research across a multitude of disciplines.

Harold Jeffreys and Bayesian Foundations

Early Life and Education

Harold Jeffreys was born in Fatfield, England, in 1891. His early years in this industrial town laid the foundation for a future distinguished by intellectual rigor and scientific curiosity. Fatfield, though modest in its resources, offered Jeffreys the initial grounding in an environment that would nurture his budding interest in mathematics  in mathematics and science. From an early age, he demonstrated a remarkable aptitude for mathematics, a trait that would define his academic and professional career.

Jeffreys's formal education began at the University of Cambridge, where he pursued studies in both mathematics and physics. Cambridge, renowned for its rigorous academic environment, provided Jeffreys with a rich intellectual backdrop that would shape his future contributions to science. During his time there, Jeffreys engaged deeply with both theoretical and applied aspects of these disciplines. His education at Cambridge was marked by a commitment to understanding complex mathematical concepts and their practical implications.

In 1914, Jeffreys completed his PhD at Cambridge, focusing on topics that bridged mathematics with the physical sciences. His doctoral research involved a detailed exploration of statistical methods, which laid the groundwork for his future work in Bayesian statistics. The early 20th century was a period of significant development in various scientific fields, and Jeffreys's work during this time positioned him as a pioneering figure in the integration of statistical methods with scientific research.

Jeffreys's PhD was a crucial step in his academic journey, equipping him with the tools and knowledge needed to make substantial contributions to statistics and other scientific domains. His education at Cambridge not only provided him with advanced mathematical training but also exposed him to a broader scientific perspective that would influence his approach to Bayesian analysis and statistical inference.

Contributions to Bayesian Foundations

Harold Jeffreys was a towering figure in the development of Bayesian statistical theory, significantly shaping its evolution and application. His work laid the groundwork for much of the modern Bayesian framework, and his influence is still felt across a wide range of disciplines today.

One of Jeffreys's most profound contributions was his 1939 book, *Theory of Probability*. This seminal work provided a comprehensive framework for Bayesian inference, presenting Bayesian methods as a coherent and practical approach to statistical problems. The book offered detailed explanations of Bayesian principles, including how they could be applied to various scientific problems. Its publication marked a pivotal moment in the formalization and acceptance of Bayesian methods.

Jeffreys also introduced the concept of Jeffreys priors, a class of non-informative prior distributions designed to reflect a state of prior ignorance about parameters. These priors are named after him and are particularly significant in Bayesian analysis because they provide a way to incorporate prior knowledge in a manner that is both objective and systematic. Jeffreys priors are used to ensure that the results of Bayesian inference are not unduly influenced by subjective biases.

His advocacy for Bayesian methods extended across various scientific disciplines, including physics, geology, and psychology. Jeffreys demonstrated how Bayesian approaches could be applied to parameter estimation, hypothesis testing, and model selection, offering a robust alternative to classical statistical methods. His work in these areas highlighted the flexibility and utility of Bayesian methods in addressing real-world problems.

In addition to his methodological contributions, Jeffreys tackled several philosophical and conceptual issues in the foundations of probability and statistics. He explored the interpretation of probability and the role of prior information, addressing fundamental questions about how probability should be understood and applied. This philosophical inquiry was crucial in shaping the way Bayesian methods are perceived and utilized in scientific practice.

Overall, Jeffreys's contributions to Bayesian statistics were transformative, providing a rigorous and practical foundation for the field. His work not only advanced statistical theory but also had a lasting impact on how scientific inference is conducted, ensuring his legacy as a key figure in the development of Bayesian analysis.

Harold Jeffreys and Other Achievements

Academic Positions and Contributions: Harold Jeffreys dedicated a significant portion of his career to academia, holding positions at the University of Cambridge. At Cambridge, he was instrumental in shaping the field of Bayesian statistics and mentored numerous students who would go on to become prominent statisticians themselves. His tenure at Cambridge not only solidified his reputation as a leading statistician but also provided a platform for his broader scientific contributions.

Contributions to Science Beyond Statistics: Jeffreys's influence extended well beyond statistics into other scientific domains. He made notable contributions to geophysics, particularly in the area of seismic activity and the theory of tides. His work in geophysics was integral in understanding the Earth's structure and the dynamics of tidal forces, demonstrating his versatility as a scientist. His research in these areas helped bridge the gap between statistical methodology and practical scientific applications, showcasing the utility of statistical thinking in diverse fields.

Honors and Recognitions: Jeffreys's contributions were widely recognized by the scientific community. He was elected to prestigious institutions such as the Royal Society and the Royal Astronomical Society, reflecting his standing among his peers. These honors were a testament to his significant impact on both statistical theory and its application across various scientific disciplines.

Role in the British Interplanetary Society: In addition to his academic and scientific achievements, Jeffreys played a pivotal role in the establishment of the British Interplanetary Society. This organization was founded to promote the exploration of space and the development of space travel, aligning with Jeffreys's interests in scientific advancement and exploration. His involvement in the society underscored his commitment to advancing human knowledge and technology, further illustrating his broad impact on scientific progress.

Overall, Harold Jeffreys's achievements reflect a career marked by a deep commitment to both statistical theory and practical scientific inquiry. His work in Bayesian statistics, combined with his contributions to geophysics and his involvement in space exploration, highlights his exceptional role as a scientist and thinker of the 20th century.

Harold Jeffreys and His Legacy

Pioneering Bayesian Statistics: Harold Jeffreys is widely recognized as one of the pioneering figures in modern Bayesian statistics. His contributions to Bayesian theory and methodology have profoundly influenced the field, establishing him as a central figure in the Bayesian revolution of the 20th century. Jeffreys's work laid the groundwork for many of the Bayesian techniques used today, and his ideas have become fundamental in the practice of statistical inference.

Impact of Jeffreys Priors: One of Jeffreys's most significant contributions is the development of Jeffreys priors, a class of non-informative prior distributions that are central to Bayesian analysis. These priors are designed to provide a neutral starting point for Bayesian inference, minimizing the influence of prior assumptions on the results. Jeffreys priors have become a standard tool in Bayesian statistics, and their application has enabled more robust and objective analysis across a wide range of disciplines.

Conceptual Issues and the Jeffreys-Lindley Paradox: Jeffreys's work also introduced several important conceptual issues in statistics, including the Jeffreys-Lindley paradox. This paradox highlights the challenges of interpreting Bayesian results in the context of frequentist hypothesis testing, raising critical questions about the relationship between Bayesian and frequentist approaches. Discussions of the paradox and other issues raised by Jeffreys continue to be a vibrant area of debate and exploration in the statistical literature, reflecting the ongoing relevance of his ideas.

Influence on Generations of Statisticians: Jeffreys's impact extends to the many statisticians and researchers who have built upon his foundational work. His pioneering efforts in Bayesian methods have inspired generations of statisticians to explore and expand upon his ideas, leading to a rich body of research that continues to shape the field. Jeffreys's influence is evident in the work of numerous scholars who have advanced Bayesian theory and its applications, underscoring his role as a key figure in the development of modern statistics.

Jeffreys-Matérn Distribution and Statistical Models: In addition to his theoretical contributions, Jeffreys's name is associated with several important statistical models, including the Jeffreys-Matérn distribution. This distribution and other models named after him are widely used in various scientific disciplines, including spatial statistics, geostatistics, and environmental science. The continued use of these models highlights the practical impact of Jeffreys's work and its enduring relevance in applied statistics.

In summary, Harold Jeffreys's legacy is marked by his foundational contributions to Bayesian statistics, his development of key concepts such as Jeffreys priors, and his influence on subsequent generations of statisticians. His work has left a lasting imprint on the field, and his ideas continue to be central to the practice and development of statistical methodology.

Jerzy Neyman and Hypothesis Testing

Early Life and Education in Poland

Jerzy Neyman was born on April 16, 1894, in Bendery, a town that was part of the Russian Empire and is now in Moldova. He was raised in a family that valued education and intellectual pursuits. His father, Czesław Neyman, was a lawyer, and his mother, Kazimiera Lutosławska Neyman, came from an aristocratic Polish family. This nurturing environment fostered Neyman's early interest in mathematics and the sciences.

Neyman attended high school in Kharkiv, where he excelled in his studies and developed a passion for mathematics. His enthusiasm for the subject was evident from a young age, and he quickly distinguished himself as a promising student. His early education laid a solid foundation for his later academic achievements and

contributions to statistical science.

After completing high school, Neyman enrolled at the University of Kiev, where he pursued his studies in mathematics. The University of Kiev was a prominent institution in the Russian Empire, known for its rigorous academic programs and distinguished faculty. Neyman's time at the university was marked by intellectual growth and the development of his mathematical skills.

During his studies at the University of Kiev, Neyman was influenced by several prominent mathematicians and statisticians. One of his key mentors was Dmitry Grave, a well-respected mathematician who specialized in number theory and algebra. Grave's guidance and encouragement played a significant role in shaping Neyman's academic trajectory and deepening his interest in mathematical statistics.

Neyman's education at the University of Kiev was interrupted by the outbreak of World War I and the subsequent Russian Revolution. Despite these challenges, Neyman continued to pursue his academic interests, eventually completing his studies and earning a degree in mathematics. His perseverance and dedication to his education during these turbulent times demonstrated his commitment to his field and his resilience in the face of adversity.

Following his graduation, Neyman remained at the University of Kiev to begin his academic career. He worked as a lecturer and researcher, further honing his skills in mathematics and statistics. During this period, Neyman conducted research on various mathematical topics, including probability theory and statistical inference. His early work laid the groundwork for his later contributions to hypothesis testing and the development of statistical methods.

In summary, Jerzy Neyman's early life and education in Poland were characterized by a supportive family environment, a strong foundation in mathematics, and influential mentors at the University of Kiev. These formative experiences shaped Neyman's intellectual development and set the stage for his significant contributions to the field of statistics. His early academic journey demonstrated his passion for mathematics, his dedication to his studies, and his resilience in the face of challenging circumstances.

Move to England and Collaboration with Fisher

Jerzy Neyman's move to England marked a significant turning point in his academic career. In the early 1920s, after a brief period of teaching and research in Poland, Neyman received a fellowship to study in England. This opportunity led him to UCL, a hub for statistical research, where he began his doctoral studies under the supervision of Karl Pearson.

At UCL, Neyman immersed himself in advanced statistical theory and methods. His research was characterized by a rigorous approach to mathematical problems and a keen interest in the practical applications of statistics. During this period, Neyman focused on problems related to probability theory and statistical inference, which laid the groundwork for his later contributions to hypothesis testing.

While at UCL, Neyman was influenced by the work of prominent statisticians, including Karl Pearson and his son, Egon Pearson. These interactions were instrumental in shaping Neyman's thinking and provided a collaborative environment where new ideas in statistics could flourish.

Neyman's collaboration with Egon Pearson, the son of Karl Pearson, proved to be one of the most fruitful partnerships in the history of statistics. Together, they worked on developing the theory of hypothesis testing, a cornerstone of modern statistical inference. Their collaboration began in the late 1920s and extended through the 1930s, during which they published a series of influential papers that fundamentally transformed the field.

One of their key contributions was the formulation of the Neyman-Pearson lemma, which provided a rigorous framework for testing statistical hypotheses. The lemma established the criteria for choosing the most powerful test for a given size, or significance level, of the test. This work introduced the concepts of Type I error (false positive) and Type II error (false negative), which are crucial for understanding the trade-offs involved in hypothesis testing.

The Neyman-Pearson approach emphasized the importance of considering both the null hypothesis (H_0) and the alternative hypothesis (H_1) when designing a test. They advocated for pre-determined significance levels and the use of critical regions to make decisions about rejecting or failing to reject the null hypothesis. This structured and objective methodology contrasted with R.A. Fisher's approach, which focused on the use of p-values and subjective interpretation of evidence.

Neyman and Pearson's work on hypothesis testing also introduced the concept of power, which measures the probability of correctly rejecting the null hypothesis when it is false. Their framework provided a systematic way to evaluate and compare different statistical tests based on their ability to detect true effects.

The collaboration between Neyman and Pearson resulted in several landmark publications, including their 1933 paper "On the Problem of the Most Efficient Tests of Statistical Hypotheses." This paper laid out the formal principles of their hypothesis testing theory and established their reputation as leading figures in the field of statistics.

Their contributions extended beyond theoretical developments. Neyman and Pearson's work had practical implications for scientific research, providing researchers with robust tools for designing experiments and analyzing data. Their methods have been widely adopted in various fields, including agriculture, medicine, engineering, and social sciences, where hypothesis testing is a fundamental part of the research process.

In summary, Jerzy Neyman's move to England and his collaboration with Egon Pearson were pivotal in the development of modern hypothesis testing theory. Neyman's doctoral research at UCL provided a solid foundation for his later work, while his partnership with Pearson led to significant advancements in statistical inference. Their joint contributions established a rigorous framework for hypothesis testing that continues to influence statistical practice and research across numerous disciplines.

Foundations of Hypothesis Testing

The foundation of hypothesis testing lies in the formulation of two competing hypotheses: the null hypothesis (H_0) and the alternative hypothesis (H_1). This approach allows statisticians to assess evidence from data and make informed decisions about the validity of a particular claim or effect.

Null Hypothesis (H_0): The null hypothesis represents a baseline or default assumption that there is no effect or no difference. It is often a statement of no change, no association, or no relationship between variables. For example, in a clinical trial testing a new drug, the null hypothesis might state that the drug has no effect on patient outcomes compared to a placebo.

Alternative Hypothesis (H_1): The alternative hypothesis represents a competing claim that there is an effect, difference, or association. It is what the researcher aims to support or prove. Continuing with the clinical trial example, the alternative hypothesis might state that the drug does have an effect on patient outcomes, either beneficial or harmful.

The formulation of these hypotheses provides a clear framework for statistical testing. Researchers collect data and use statistical methods to determine whether there is enough evidence to reject the null hypothesis in favor of the alternative hypothesis.

In the process of hypothesis testing, two types of errors can occur: Type I errors and Type II errors. Understanding these errors and their implications is crucial for interpreting the results of a hypothesis test.

Type I Error (False Positive): A Type I error occurs when the null hypothesis is rejected when it is actually true.

In other words, it is the incorrect conclusion that there is an effect or difference when none exists. The probability of committing a Type I error is denoted by the significance level (α). Common significance levels are 0.05 or 0.01, indicating a 5% or 1% risk of making a Type I error, respectively. Researchers choose the significance level based on the context and the potential consequences of making a false positive decision. For instance, in medical research, a lower significance level might be chosen to minimize the risk of incorrectly concluding that a treatment is effective.

Type II Error (False Negative): A Type II error occurs when the null hypothesis is not rejected when it is actually false. This means that the test fails to detect an effect or difference that truly exists. The probability of committing a Type II error is denoted by β. The complement of β, $(1 - \beta)$, is known as the power of the test, which represents the probability of correctly rejecting the null hypothesis when the alternative hypothesis is true. High power is desirable because it indicates that the test is effective at detecting true effects. Researchers aim to design studies with sufficient power to minimize the risk of Type II errors.

The significance level (α) and the power of the test are critical considerations in hypothesis testing. They involve a trade-off: reducing the significance level decreases the risk of a Type I error but may increase the risk of a Type

II error, and vice versa. The choice of α and the desired power level (often 0.80 or 80%) depend on the context of the study and the potential impact of making incorrect decisions.

The Neyman-Pearson framework for hypothesis testing emphasizes the importance of these considerations. By defining a significance level and considering the power of the test, researchers can design studies that balance the risks of Type I and Type II errors appropriately. This approach provides a systematic and objective way to make decisions based on statistical evidence.

In summary, the foundations of hypothesis testing, as developed by Jerzy Neyman and Egon Pearson, involve the formulation of null and alternative hypotheses and the careful consideration of Type I and Type II errors and significance levels. This framework allows researchers to assess evidence, make informed decisions, and balance the risks of different types of errors, thereby enhancing the reliability and validity of scientific conclusions.

Contributions to Multivariate Analysis

Jerzy Neyman made significant contributions to the field of multivariate analysis, particularly in the areas of ANOVA and analysis of covariance (ANCOVA). These statistical techniques are essential for understanding the relationships between multiple variables and for making inferences about data in complex experimental designs.

ANOVA: ANOVA is a statistical method used to compare the means of three or more groups to determine if there are any statistically significant differences among them. Neyman's work in this area focused on developing rigorous mathematical foundations for ANOVA, enhancing its theoretical underpinnings and practical applications. He introduced new ways to partition the total variance observed in the data into components attributable to different sources of variation. This method allows researchers to identify and quantify the effects of different factors on the response variable, making it a powerful tool for experimental research.

ANCOVA: ANCOVA extends ANOVA by including one or more covariate variables that account for variance in the dependent variable. This technique adjusts the dependent variable for the effects of covariates, providing a clearer understanding of the primary factors of interest. Neyman's contributions to ANCOVA involved refining the statistical models and developing methods to accurately interpret the results. His work helped in controlling for confounding variables and improved the precision of statistical inferences in complex experimental designs.

Neyman's contributions to ANOVA and ANCOVA provided researchers with robust tools for analyzing data from multifactorial experiments. These methods are widely used in fields such as psychology, medicine, agriculture, and social sciences, where understanding the interplay of multiple variables is crucial.

Beyond his specific work on ANOVA and ANCOVA, Jerzy Neyman played a pivotal role in advancing the field of mathematical statistics more broadly. His contributions helped to establish rigorous theoretical foundations for many statistical methods that are now standard in the field.

Development of Confidence Intervals: Neyman introduced the concept of confidence intervals, a fundamental tool in statistical inference. Confidence intervals provide a range of values within which the true parameter of a population is likely to lie, with a specified level of confidence. This concept has become a cornerstone of inferential statistics, offering a way to quantify the uncertainty associated with parameter estimates.

Non-Parametric Methods: Neyman also made significant contributions to the development of non-parametric statistical methods. These methods do not rely on assumptions about the underlying distribution of the data, making them more flexible and robust in various situations. Neyman's work in this area included the development of distribution-free tests and other techniques that expanded the toolkit of statisticians, enabling them to analyze data that did not fit traditional parametric models.

Sequential Analysis: Neyman's interest in practical applications of statistics led him to develop methods for sequential analysis, a technique used in quality control and clinical trials. Sequential analysis involves evaluating data as it is collected, allowing researchers to make decisions about continuing or stopping an experiment based on interim results. This approach is particularly useful in contexts where timely decisions are critical.

Multivariate Statistical Methods: Neyman contributed to the development of multivariate statistical methods, which are essential for analyzing data involving multiple dependent variables. His work in this area included developing techniques for multivariate hypothesis testing, principal component analysis, and factor analysis. These methods help researchers to uncover complex patterns and relationships in high-dimensional data.

Neyman's contributions to mathematical statistics have had a profound and lasting impact on the field. His rigorous approach to developing statistical methods and his emphasis on practical applications have influenced generations of statisticians and researchers. The methods he developed continue to be integral to modern statistical practice, enabling scientists to analyze complex data, make informed decisions, and advance knowledge across a wide range of disciplines.

In summary, Jerzy Neyman's contributions to multivariate analysis, including his work on ANOVA, ANCOVA, confidence intervals, non-parametric methods, sequential analysis, and multivariate statistical methods, have significantly advanced the field of mathematical statistics. His innovations have provided researchers with powerful tools for understanding complex data and have laid the foundation for many of the statistical techniques used in contemporary research.

Relocation to the United States

In 1938, Jerzy Neyman accepted a position at the University of California, Berkeley, which marked the beginning of a highly influential period in his career. His relocation to the United States provided him with new opportunities to expand his research and impact the development of statistical theory. At Berkeley, Neyman was appointed as a professor of statistics and the head of the newly established Statistical Laboratory, which he founded.

Neyman's role at Berkeley was pivotal in transforming the university into a leading center for statistical research and education. Under his leadership, the Statistical Laboratory attracted talented students and researchers from around the world, fostering a vibrant intellectual community. Neyman's mentorship and guidance helped shape the careers of many prominent statisticians, including David Blackwell and Elizabeth Scott, among others.

During his tenure at Berkeley, Neyman was instrumental in establishing a rigorous and comprehensive curriculum in statistics. He emphasized the importance of both theoretical foundations and practical applications, ensuring that students were well-equipped to tackle real-world problems. Neyman's commitment to education and research excellence significantly contributed to the growth and recognition of the statistics department at Berkeley.

Continued Development of Statistical Theory

Neyman's move to the United States did not slow his prolific contributions to statistical theory. Instead, it provided him with a stimulating environment to continue his groundbreaking work and collaborate with other leading statisticians.

Empirical Processes and Asymptotic Theory: One of Neyman's notable areas of research at Berkeley was the development of empirical processes and asymptotic theory. His work in this field involved the study of the behavior of statistical estimators and test statistics as the sample size increases. Neyman's contributions helped to establish the theoretical foundations for many statistical procedures, providing insights into their properties and limitations.

Decision Theory: Neyman also made significant contributions to decision theory, a branch of statistics that deals with the principles and methods for making optimal decisions under uncertainty. His work in this area included the development of criteria for choosing among different statistical procedures, taking into account the costs and benefits associated with various decisions. Neyman's research in decision theory has had a lasting impact on fields such as economics, finance, and operations research.

Collaborations and Interdisciplinary Research: Neyman's tenure at Berkeley was marked by fruitful collaborations with researchers from various disciplines. He worked with scientists in fields such as biology, medicine, and agriculture, applying statistical methods to address complex problems and advance knowledge in these areas. His interdisciplinary approach demonstrated the versatility and power of statistical techniques in solving diverse scientific challenges.

Publications and Influence: Throughout his career at Berkeley, Neyman continued to publish influential papers and books that advanced the field of statistics. His publications covered a wide range of topics, including hypothesis testing, estimation, experimental design, and multivariate analysis. Neyman's work was widely recognized and respected, earning him numerous accolades and honors from the statistical community.

Legacy and Impact: Neyman's contributions during his time at Berkeley solidified his reputation as one of the foremost statisticians of the 20th century. His rigorous approach to statistical theory and his emphasis on practical applications left a lasting legacy that continues to influence the field. The methods and principles he developed remain fundamental to modern statistics, and his impact can be seen in the work of countless researchers who have built upon his ideas.

In summary, Jerzy Neyman's relocation to the United States and his professorship at the University of California, Berkeley, marked a significant and productive phase in his career. His leadership at Berkeley helped to establish the university as a premier center for statistical research and education, while his continued development of statistical theory advanced the field in profound ways. Neyman's contributions during this period have left an enduring legacy that continues to shape the practice and understanding of statistics today.

Philosophical Differences from Fisher

Jerzy Neyman and Ronald A. Fisher were both pioneering figures in the field of statistics, but they had notable philosophical differences in their approaches to hypothesis testing and statistical inference.

Neyman's Objectivist Approach: Neyman advocated for an objectivist approach to hypothesis testing, which emphasizes pre-determined criteria and objective decision-making. He believed that statistical procedures should be designed to control long-run error rates, such as Type I and Type II errors, rather than relying on subjective interpretation. This approach is characterized by the use of fixed significance levels (α) and the consideration of power ($1 - \beta$) in the DoEs. Neyman's framework, often referred to as the Neyman-Pearson approach, focused on creating a formalized and systematic method for making statistical decisions based on probability theory.

Bayesian Influence: Although Neyman was not a Bayesian statistician, his approach shared some similarities with Bayesian thinking, particularly in its emphasis on probability and the use of prior information. However, Neyman maintained a more frequentist perspective, focusing on long-run frequencies and the performance of statistical procedures over repeated sampling. His objectivist viewpoint sought to minimize subjective elements in statistical inference, favoring a more rigorous and repeatable approach.

Fisher's Subjective P-Value Approach: In contrast, Ronald Fisher's approach to hypothesis testing relied heavily on the use of p-values, which measure the strength of the evidence against the null hypothesis. Fisher advocated for a more flexible and subjective interpretation of p-values, without strict adherence to pre-determined significance levels. He believed that the p-value provided a measure of the evidence, allowing researchers to make nuanced decisions based on the context of the data. Fisher's approach emphasized the importance of scientific judgment and the continuous assessment of evidence, rather than fixed decision rules.

The philosophical differences between Neyman and Fisher have had a lasting impact on the field of statistics, leading to the development of distinct schools of thought and influencing the practice of statistical inference.

Widespread Adoption of Neyman-Pearson Approach: Neyman's objectivist approach to hypothesis testing has been widely adopted in various scientific disciplines, particularly in fields that require rigorous and repeatable decision-making processes. The Neyman-Pearson framework, with its emphasis on controlling error rates and optimizing statistical power, has become the standard for designing and analyzing experiments in medicine, agriculture, psychology, and many other areas. Researchers appreciate the clarity and objectivity of this approach, which provides clear guidelines for making statistical decisions.

Impact on Statistical Education and Practice: Neyman's methods have also had a profound influence on statistical education and practice. The concepts of Type I and Type II errors, significance levels, and power analysis are fundamental components of modern statistical training. Students and practitioners are taught to design experiments and analyze data using these principles, ensuring that their findings are both reliable and valid. Neyman's emphasis on pre-specified criteria and objective decision rules has contributed to the development of robust and reproducible scientific research.

Complementary Roles of Neyman and Fisher's Approaches: While Neyman's approach has been widely adopted, Fisher's contributions to statistical inference have also had a lasting impact. The use of p-values and the emphasis on continuous assessment of evidence remain integral to many areas of research. In practice, researchers often use a combination of Neyman-Pearson and Fisherian methods, drawing on the strengths of both approaches to make informed decisions. This complementary use of methodologies highlights the importance of both objectivity and flexibility in statistical inference.

Enduring Influence on Statistical Theory: Neyman's work has also had a significant impact on the development of statistical theory. His contributions to hypothesis testing, confidence intervals, and experimental design have provided a rigorous foundation for further advancements in the field. The principles and methods he developed continue to be the basis for new statistical techniques and applications, ensuring the ongoing relevance of his ideas.

In summary, Jerzy Neyman's objectivist Bayesian viewpoint on hypothesis testing, characterized by the Neyman-Pearson approach, has had an enduring impact on the field of statistics. His emphasis on pre-determined criteria, error control, and objective decision-making has shaped the practice of statistical inference across various scientific disciplines. While philosophical differences with Ronald Fisher led to distinct schools of thought, the complementary roles of both approaches continue to influence statistical theory and practice. Neyman's legacy is evident in the widespread adoption and lasting relevance of his methods, which remain fundamental to modern statistical analysis.

Summary of Neyman's Innovations

Jerzy Neyman was a transformative figure in the field of statistics, whose contributions brought about significant changes in both statistical thinking and practice. His innovations reshaped the way statisticians approach data analysis, hypothesis testing, and experimental design.

Hypothesis Testing Framework: One of Neyman's most influential contributions was the development of the Neyman-Pearson framework for hypothesis testing. This approach introduced a formalized method for testing statistical hypotheses, emphasizing the importance of controlling error rates (Type I and Type II errors). By defining the null and alternative hypotheses and establishing criteria for rejecting the null hypothesis, Neyman provided a systematic way to make decisions based on statistical evidence. This framework has become a cornerstone of modern statistical practice, widely adopted in scientific research and experimental design.

Significance Levels and Power Analysis: Neyman's work on hypothesis testing highlighted the importance of significance levels (α) and statistical power ($1 - \beta$) in the design and analysis of experiments. By focusing on pre-determined significance levels, Neyman ensured that the probability of making a Type I error was controlled. His emphasis on power analysis helped researchers design studies with sufficient sample sizes to detect true effects, reducing the likelihood of Type II errors. These concepts are now fundamental components of statistical training and practice, guiding researchers in their experimental designs.

Development of Confidence Intervals: Neyman introduced the concept of confidence intervals, which provide a range of values within which the true parameter of a population is likely to lie, with a specified level of confidence. This innovation allowed statisticians to quantify the uncertainty associated with parameter estimates, offering a more informative and interpretable way to report statistical results. Confidence intervals have become a standard tool in statistical analysis, enhancing the transparency and reliability of research findings.

Empirical Processes and Asymptotic Theory: Neyman's contributions to empirical processes and asymptotic theory advanced the understanding of the behavior of statistical estimators and test statistics as sample sizes increase. His work in this area provided the theoretical foundations for many statistical procedures, helping to establish their properties and limitations. These advancements have had a lasting impact on the development of statistical theory and methods.

Sequential Analysis and Decision Theory: Neyman's interest in practical applications led to significant contributions to sequential analysis and decision theory. Sequential analysis involves evaluating data as it is collected, allowing for timely decisions in quality control and clinical trials. Decision theory provides principles and methods for making optimal decisions under uncertainty, considering the costs and benefits of different choices. Neyman's work in these areas has influenced fields such as economics, finance, and operations research, demonstrating the versatility and practical relevance of his innovations.

Legacy as a Leader in Mathematical Statistics

Jerzy Neyman's legacy as a leader in mathematical statistics is profound and far-reaching. His contributions have left an indelible mark on the field, shaping the practice of statistics and influencing generations of statisticians.

Founding of the Statistical Laboratory at Berkeley: Neyman's role in founding and leading the Statistical Laboratory at the University of California, Berkeley, established the university as a premier center for statistical research and education. Under his leadership, the laboratory attracted talented students and researchers from around the world, fostering a vibrant intellectual community. Neyman's mentorship and guidance helped shape the careers of many prominent statisticians, ensuring the continuation of his legacy.

Educational Impact: Neyman's emphasis on rigorous training and education in statistics has had a lasting impact on statistical education. The principles and methods he developed are now fundamental components of statistical curricula, providing students with a solid foundation in hypothesis testing, experimental design, and data analysis. Neyman's commitment to education ensured that future generations of statisticians would be well-equipped to tackle complex problems and advance the field.

Influence on Statistical Theory and Practice: Neyman's contributions to statistical theory and practice have influenced a wide range of disciplines, including medicine, agriculture, psychology, biology, economics, and engineering. His innovations in hypothesis testing, confidence intervals, and experimental design have provided researchers with powerful tools for analyzing data and making informed decisions. The widespread adoption of Neyman's methods in scientific research attests to their enduring relevance and impact.

Recognition and Honors: Neyman's work has been widely recognized and honored by the statistical community. He received numerous awards and accolades for his contributions, reflecting the high regard in which he is held by his peers. Neyman's legacy is celebrated through the continued use and development of the methods he pioneered, ensuring that his influence will endure for generations to come.

In summary, Jerzy Neyman's innovations brought about significant changes in statistical thinking and practice. His development of the Neyman-Pearson framework for hypothesis testing, introduction of confidence intervals, advancements in empirical processes and asymptotic theory, and contributions to sequential analysis and decision theory have profoundly influenced the field of statistics. Neyman's legacy as a leader in mathematical statistics is reflected in the widespread adoption of his methods, his impact on statistical education, and the lasting influence of his work on scientific research and decision-making.

W. Edward Deming and Quality Management

Early Career as a Physicist and Statistician

W. Edward Deming's journey into the realms of physics and statistics began with his academic achievements and early professional experiences, which laid the foundation for his later groundbreaking work in quality management.

Educational Background: Deming earned his Ph.D. from Yale University in mathematical physics and engineering. His rigorous academic training equipped him with a strong foundation in quantitative methods and scientific thinking, which he would later apply to the field of quality management.

Doctoral Research: During his doctoral studies, Deming's research focused on the application of mathematical principles to physical phenomena. This early work honed his analytical skills and deepened his understanding of complex systems, both of which would prove invaluable in his later career.

Early Work Applying Statistics to Industrial Quality Control

Introduction to Statistical Methods: Deming's initial foray into the application of statistics to industrial processes began in the 1920s and 1930s, when he started working with the U.S. Department of Agriculture and later the Bureau of the Census. These roles involved extensive use of statistical techniques to analyze and improve processes, sparking his interest in the potential of statistics for quality control.

Influence of Walter A. Shewhart: One of the pivotal moments in Deming's early career was his encounter with Walter A. Shewhart, a pioneering statistician at Bell Telephone Laboratories. Shewhart's work on statistical process control (SPC) and the development of the control chart greatly influenced Deming. He adopted Shewhart's principles and began advocating for their use in industrial settings.

Consulting and Teaching: By the late 1930s and early 1940s, Deming was actively involved in consulting and teaching statistical quality control methods to various industries. He emphasized the importance of using statistical tools to monitor and improve production processes, aiming to enhance product quality and operational efficiency.

World War II Contributions: During World War II, Deming played a crucial role in training engineers and quality control professionals in the United States. He conducted extensive training sessions, teaching statistical quality control techniques to ensure the production of high-quality war materials. His efforts significantly contributed to the war effort and demonstrated the practical benefits of applying statistical methods to manufacturing.

Post-War Influence in Japan: After the war, Deming's reputation as a quality expert grew internationally. He was invited to Japan by Japanese industrial leaders, where he introduced statistical quality control concepts to Japanese manufacturers. His teachings laid the groundwork for Japan's post-war economic recovery and transformation into a global leader in manufacturing quality.

Legacy in Quality Management: Deming's early career as a physicist and statistician provided him with the expertise to revolutionize quality management. His emphasis on the application of statistical methods to improve industrial processes became the cornerstone of his later work, including the development of the Deming System of Profound Knowledge and the widely recognized Deming Prize for quality.

In summary, W. Edward Deming's early career as a physicist and statistician, marked by his Ph.D. from Yale University and his pioneering work in applying statistics to industrial quality control, set the stage for his transformative contributions to quality management. His foundational experiences and influential encounters shaped his approach to quality improvement, leaving a lasting legacy in both the field of statistics and the world of manufacturing.

Post-War Work in Japan and Quality Renaissance

W. Edward Deming's contributions to quality management took a pivotal turn after World War II, when his expertise in SPC methods played a transformative role in Japan's post-war industrial recovery. This period marked a significant chapter in Deming's career, highlighting his impact on the global stage and solidifying his legacy in quality management.

Initial Invitation to Japan: In the early 1950s, Deming was invited to Japan by the Union of Japanese Scientists and Engineers (JUSE) to provide guidance on quality control methods. Japan, seeking to rebuild its war-torn economy and enhance its manufacturing capabilities, turned to Deming for his expertise in SPC.

Seminars and Training Sessions: Deming conducted a series of seminars and training sessions for Japanese engineers, managers, and executives. He introduced them to the principles of statistical quality control, emphasizing the use of data and statistical tools to monitor and improve manufacturing processes. His teachings focused on reducing variability, improving product quality, and increasing efficiency.

Introduction of the Plan-Do-Check-Act (PDCA) Cycle: One of Deming's key contributions during his time in Japan was the introduction of the PDCA cycle, also known as the Deming Cycle. This iterative process emphasized continuous improvement and became a fundamental concept in Japanese quality management practices.

Cultural Transformation: Deming's influence in Japan went beyond technical training; he instigated a cultural transformation in Japanese industry. He emphasized the importance of management's role in quality improvement and advocated for a systemic approach to problem-solving. His teachings encouraged Japanese companies to foster a culture of continuous improvement and employee involvement.

Rise of Japanese Manufacturing Excellence: Deming's methods contributed significantly to the remarkable rise of Japanese manufacturing excellence. Companies like Toyota, Nissan, and Sony embraced his principles, leading to dramatic improvements in product quality and efficiency. Japan's reputation for producing high-quality goods grew, positioning it as a global leader in manufacturing.

Deming Prize: In recognition of his contributions, the Union of JUSE established the Deming Prize in 1951. This prestigious award honors organizations and individuals who have demonstrated outstanding performance in quality management. The Deming Prize continues to be a highly regarded accolade in the field of quality management.

Legacy and Lasting Impact

Global Influence: Deming's work in Japan had a profound impact on quality management practices worldwide. His teachings on SPC and continuous improvement were widely adopted in industries across the globe. Companies in the United States and Europe began to incorporate Deming's principles, leading to improvements in quality and competitiveness.

Humanizing the Workplace: Beyond the technical aspects of quality control, Deming emphasized the importance of respecting and valuing employees. He believed that empowering workers and fostering a collaborative environment were crucial for achieving long-term success. This humanistic approach to management resonated deeply with Japanese companies and contributed to their sustained growth.

Enduring Legacy: Deming's post-war work in Japan not only transformed the Japanese economy but also left an enduring legacy in the field of quality management. His contributions laid the foundation for modern quality management practices, and his principles continue to influence organizations seeking to improve their processes and achieve excellence.

In summary, W. Edward Deming's post-war work in Japan was instrumental in guiding the country's industrial recovery and establishing its reputation for manufacturing excellence. Through his expertise in SPC and his emphasis on continuous improvement, Deming left an indelible mark on Japanese industry and quality management practices worldwide. His legacy as a pioneer in quality management endures, shaping the way organizations approach process improvement and employee engagement.

Theories of Management and Systems Thinking

W. Edward Deming's theories of management and systems thinking revolutionized the way organizations approached quality and efficiency. His emphasis on continuous improvement, reduction of variation, and the promotion of collaboration and worker empowerment laid the groundwork for modern quality management practices.

Focus on Reducing Variation: Deming believed that reducing variation in processes was essential for achieving consistent quality. He taught that variation is the root cause of many quality issues and that by identifying and minimizing sources of variation, organizations could significantly improve their products and services.

SPC: Deming introduced the use of SPC to monitor and control processes. SPC tools, such as control charts, help organizations detect and address variations in real time. By applying these tools, companies could maintain process stability and predictability, leading to higher quality and reduced waste.

Continuous Improvement (Kaizen): Deming's approach emphasized the concept of continuous improvement, or "Kaizen" in Japanese. He advocated for ongoing, incremental improvements rather than relying on occasional large-scale changes. This philosophy encouraged organizations to constantly seek ways to enhance processes, products, and services.

Promotion of Collaboration and Worker Empowerment

Systemic Approach to Management: Deming viewed organizations as systems composed of interconnected processes. He argued that optimizing individual components without considering the entire system would not lead to sustainable improvements. Instead, he promoted a holistic approach, where all parts of the organization work together harmoniously to achieve common goals.

The Deming System of Profound Knowledge: Deming's System of Profound Knowledge consisted of four key components: appreciation for a system, knowledge of variation, theory of knowledge, and psychology. This framework provided a comprehensive understanding of how organizations function and how to improve them effectively.

Empowering Workers: A cornerstone of Deming's philosophy was the empowerment of workers. He believed that employees at all levels should be involved in the improvement process and encouraged to contribute their ideas and insights. By fostering a culture of trust and collaboration, organizations could harness the collective knowledge and creativity of their workforce.

Elimination of Fear: Deming stressed the importance of eliminating fear within the workplace. He argued that fear stifles innovation and prevents employees from speaking up about problems or suggesting improvements. Creating an environment where employees feel safe to express their concerns and ideas was crucial for achieving continuous improvement.

Lasting Impact on Management Practices

Total Quality Management (TQM): Deming's theories formed the foundation of the TQM movement, which gained widespread adoption in the 1980s and 1990s. TQM principles, such as customer focus, process improvement, and employee involvement, are rooted in Deming's teachings.

Lean Manufacturing: The principles of Lean Manufacturing, which aim to eliminate waste and create value for customers, are heavily influenced by Deming's work. Techniques like value stream mapping, just-in-time production, and continuous improvement align closely with Deming's emphasis on reducing variation and optimizing processes.

Six Sigma: The Six Sigma methodology, which focuses on reducing defects and improving quality through data-driven decision-making, also draws on Deming's principles. The DMAIC (Define, Measure, Analyze, Improve, Control) framework used in Six Sigma is reminiscent of Deming's PDCA cycle.

In summary, W. Edward Deming's theories of management and systems thinking have had a profound and lasting impact on how organizations approach quality and efficiency. His emphasis on continuous improvement, reduction of variation, and the promotion of collaboration and worker empowerment has shaped modern management practices and continues to influence organizations striving for excellence.

The Deming Philosophy and 14 Points

W. Edward Deming's philosophy, encapsulated in his renowned 14 Points, offers a comprehensive framework for achieving quality, productivity, and effective management. These guiding principles profoundly influenced Japanese quality methods post-World War II and have left a lasting legacy in the field of quality management.

Deming's 14 Points provide a roadmap for transforming management practices and organizational culture. They emphasize long-term thinking, continuous improvement, and a systemic approach to quality and productivity.

1. **Create Constancy of Purpose for Improvement:** Organizations should focus on long-term planning rather than short-term gains. This involves investing in innovation, research, and continuous improvement to remain competitive and meet future challenges.

2. **Adopt the New Philosophy:** Embrace a culture of quality and continuous improvement. Organizations must adapt to the modern business environment by adopting new management

philosophies that prioritize quality and customer satisfaction.

3. **Cease Dependence on Inspection:** Quality should be built into processes from the beginning rather than relying solely on inspection to catch defects. Preventing defects through robust processes is more effective than detecting and correcting them later.

4. **End the Practice of Awarding Business on Price Alone:** Focus on the total cost of ownership rather than just the initial price. Establish long-term relationships with suppliers based on quality and mutual trust, ensuring consistent and reliable supply chains.

5. **Improve Constantly and Forever the System of Production and Service:** Continuous improvement should be an ongoing effort in all aspects of production and service. This involves using statistical tools and methods to identify areas for improvement and implementing changes systematically.

6. **Institute Training on the Job:** Provide employees with the necessary training and education to perform their tasks effectively. Continuous learning and skill development are crucial for maintaining high-quality standards.

7. **Adopt and Institute Leadership:** Leadership should focus on helping employees do their jobs better. Leaders should guide, support, and empower employees rather than simply supervising them.

8. **Drive Out Fear:** Create an environment where employees feel safe to express their ideas, concerns, and suggestions without fear of retribution. Eliminating fear encourages open communication and innovation.

9. **Break Down Barriers Between Departments:** Foster collaboration and teamwork across different departments and functions. Silos hinder communication and efficiency; breaking them down leads to a more integrated and effective organization.

10. **Eliminate Slogans, Exhortations, and Targets:** Avoid using slogans and targets that place the blame on employees for systemic issues. Instead, focus on improving processes and systems to achieve quality and productivity goals.

11. **Eliminate Numerical Quotas for the Workforce and Management by Objectives:** Numerical quotas and management by objectives can create pressure and lead to suboptimal behaviors. Emphasize quality and continuous improvement over meeting arbitrary numerical targets.

12. **Remove Barriers to Pride in Workmanship:** Ensure that employees can take pride in their work by providing them with the right tools, resources, and support. Recognize and value their contributions to the organization's success.

13. **Institute a Vigorous Program of Education and Self-Improvement:** Encourage continuous learning and self-improvement at all levels of the organization. Investing in education and development helps build a knowledgeable and skilled workforce.

14. **Put Everybody in the Company to Work Accomplishing the Transformation:** Quality and improvement are the responsibility of everyone in the organization, not just a select few. Engage all employees in the effort to transform the organization and achieve long-term success.

Enduring Influence on Japanese Quality Methods

Post-War Industrial Recovery: Deming's 14 Points played a crucial role in Japan's post-war industrial recovery. His teachings helped Japanese companies achieve remarkable improvements in quality and productivity, leading to their dominance in global markets.

TQM: The principles of TQM, widely adopted in Japan, are deeply rooted in Deming's philosophy. TQM focuses on customer satisfaction, continuous improvement, and involving all employees in the quality process.

Kaizen: The Japanese concept of Kaizen, or continuous improvement, aligns closely with Deming's emphasis on ongoing, incremental improvements. Kaizen has become a fundamental part of Japanese business culture.

Lean Manufacturing: Lean principles, which aim to eliminate waste and improve efficiency, also draw heavily from Deming's teachings. Techniques like just-in-time production and value stream mapping are inspired by his focus on process optimization and reducing variation.

In summary, W. Edward Deming's 14 Points provide a timeless framework for achieving quality, productivity, and effective management. His principles have had a profound and enduring impact on Japanese quality methods and continue to influence organizations worldwide striving for excellence and continuous improvement.

Later Career in the United States

After his influential work in Japan, W. Edward Deming returned to the United States and continued his advocacy for quality practices in both manufacturing and service industries. Despite initial resistance from traditional management approaches, his teachings eventually gained significant traction and led to substantial improvements in American business practices.

Upon his return to the U.S., Deming tirelessly promoted the principles of statistical quality control and continuous improvement. He emphasized that the same practices that had revolutionized Japanese industry could be applied to American businesses. Deming's message was clear: quality should be the driving force behind management decisions, not just an afterthought.

Resistance from Traditional Management Approaches

Despite his successes abroad, Deming faced significant resistance from traditional management approaches in the U.S. Many American executives were skeptical of his methods, viewing them as too radical or impractical. There was a strong adherence to hierarchical, top-down management styles, which clashed with Deming's principles of worker empowerment and systemic thinking.

Challenges Encountered: Short-Term Focus: American businesses were often focused on short-term financial results, which conflicted with Deming's emphasis on long-term planning and investment in quality.

Resistance to Change: Many managers were reluctant to abandon established practices and adopt new methodologies that required a fundamental shift in organizational culture.

Lack of Understanding: There was a general lack of understanding of statistical methods and their application to quality control among American managers, leading to skepticism and slow adoption of Deming's ideas.

Breakthrough and Recognition

Despite initial resistance, Deming's persistence began to pay off in the 1980s. The success of Japanese companies, many of which attributed their quality improvements to Deming's teachings, served as a wake-up call for American industry. As U.S. businesses struggled to compete, they increasingly turned to Deming's principles for solutions.

NBC Documentary: The 1980 NBC documentary "If Japan Can... Why Can't We?" brought widespread attention to Deming's work, highlighting the success of Japanese companies that had implemented his methods. This documentary played a pivotal role in changing American perceptions of quality management.

Adoption by Major Corporations: Leading American companies, such as Ford and General Motors, began to adopt Deming's principles. These corporations saw significant improvements in quality and efficiency, further validating his approach.

Awards and Honors: Deming received numerous awards and accolades for his contributions to quality management, including the National Medal of Technology in 1987.

In summary, Deming's later career in the United States was marked by his relentless advocacy for quality practices in the face of traditional management resistance. His teachings eventually gained recognition and led to substantial improvements in American manufacturing and service industries, solidifying his legacy as a pioneer in quality management.

Lasting Impact and Recognition

W. Edward Deming's profound contributions to quality management and his relentless pursuit of excellence have left an enduring legacy in the fields of business and management. His principles have shaped modern quality practices and inspired countless leaders and organizations to prioritize continuous improvement and systemic thinking.

In recognition of Deming's transformative impact on quality management, the Union of JUSE established the Deming Prize in 1951. This prestigious award honors individuals and organizations that have demonstrated exceptional commitment to quality control and management.

Key Aspects of the Deming Prize:

Criteria: The prize evaluates applicants based on their implementation of quality management principles, focusing on aspects such as innovation, employee involvement, and customer satisfaction.

Global Influence: Initially aimed at Japanese companies, the Deming Prize has since expanded to include international organizations, underscoring the global relevance of Deming's teachings.

Encouraging Excellence: The prize has played a significant role in promoting best practices in quality management and encouraging organizations worldwide to strive for excellence.

Deming's influence extended far beyond the realm of quality management. He was widely recognized as one of the most influential American businessmen of the 20th century. His innovative ideas and unwavering dedication to improving organizational performance have left an indelible mark on business practices globally.

Accolades and Recognition:

National Medal of Technology: In 1987, Deming was awarded the National Medal of Technology, one of the highest honors bestowed by the U.S. government for technological innovation and contributions to the nation's economic competitiveness.

Honorary Degrees: Deming received numerous honorary degrees from prestigious institutions, acknowledging his significant contributions to education and industry.

Legacy in Business Education: His principles are now integral to business education curricula worldwide, ensuring that future generations of leaders are well-versed in the importance of quality management and continuous improvement.

Enduring Influence on Business Practices

Deming's legacy continues to influence modern business practices, with his principles being adopted across various industries and sectors. His teachings have become foundational to methodologies such as Lean, Six Sigma, and TQM.

Continuous Improvement: Deming's emphasis on continuous improvement (Kaizen) has become a cornerstone of modern management practices, driving organizations to seek incremental enhancements in processes and products.

Systemic Thinking: His advocacy for viewing organizations as interconnected systems has helped businesses understand the importance of collaboration and holistic problem-solving.

Customer Focus: Deming's focus on meeting and exceeding customer expectations has driven organizations to prioritize customer satisfaction and loyalty as key drivers of success.

In summary, W. Edward Deming's lasting impact and recognition reflect his pivotal role in transforming quality management and business practices. The establishment of the Deming Prize and his ranking among the most influential American businessmen are testaments to his enduring legacy. Deming's principles continue to inspire and guide organizations worldwide, ensuring that his contributions to quality and excellence remain relevant for generations to come.

Integrating Statistics with Management Strategies

W. Edward Deming's groundbreaking approach to quality management was rooted in the integration of statistical methods with strategic decision-making. His philosophy emphasized the use of data to understand processes, make informed decisions, and drive continuous improvement. This integration of statistics with management strategies has had a transformative impact on organizations worldwide.

Deming championed the idea that effective management decisions should be based on data and statistical evidence rather than intuition or guesswork. He believed that by understanding processes through data, organizations could identify areas for improvement and make strategic decisions to enhance quality and efficiency.

SPC: Deming introduced SPC as a method for monitoring and controlling processes through statistical techniques. By using control charts and other tools, organizations could detect variations, identify root causes of problems, and implement corrective actions.

Data Collection and Analysis: Deming advocated for systematic data collection and rigorous analysis to understand process performance. This approach enabled organizations to make data-driven decisions that were grounded in empirical evidence.

Informed Decision-Making: By relying on statistical analysis, managers could make more informed decisions, reducing the risk of errors and improving overall process outcomes. This data-driven mindset helped organizations achieve higher levels of quality and efficiency.

Transformative Impact on Organizations

Deming's integration of statistics with management strategies led to a quality revolution in organizations around the world. His methods were instrumental in transforming industries such as manufacturing, healthcare, and services, leading to significant improvements in quality, efficiency, and customer satisfaction.

Japanese Manufacturing: Deming's work with Japanese industries after World War II played a crucial role in their post-war economic recovery. By adopting his statistical methods and management principles, Japanese companies achieved unprecedented levels of quality and efficiency, gaining a competitive edge in global markets.

Healthcare Quality Improvement: In healthcare, Deming's principles have been applied to improve patient outcomes and operational efficiency. Hospitals and healthcare organizations have used SPC and data-driven decision-making to reduce errors, streamline processes, and enhance patient care.

Service Industries: Deming's methods have also been adopted by service industries, where data-driven approaches have led to improved customer experiences, reduced costs, and enhanced service delivery.

In summary, W. Edward Deming's integration of statistics with management strategies has had a profound and lasting impact on organizations worldwide. His data-driven approach to process understanding and strategic decision-making, combined with his holistic quality principles, has revolutionized industries and set new standards for excellence. Deming's legacy continues to inspire organizations to embrace data, foster continuous improvement, and achieve sustainable success.

Abraham Wald and Statistical Decision Theory

Early Life and Education in Europe

Abraham Wald's early life and education were marked by a strong foundation in mathematics and a remarkable journey that led him to become a pivotal figure in statistical decision theory.

Studied Mathematics in Prague and Berlin: Born in 1902 in what was then Austria-Hungary, Wald pursued his studies in mathematics at the German University in Prague. There, he demonstrated exceptional aptitude and interest in the field, which propelled him to further his education at the University of Berlin. At Berlin, Wald worked under the mentorship of  prominent mathematicians and became involved in the vibrant academic community that was at the forefront of mathematical research in Europe.

Rise of the Nazi Regime and Escape to the USA: The political climate in Europe took a dramatic turn with the rise of the Nazi regime, leading to increasing persecution of Jewish intellectuals and scholars. In response to these growing threats, Wald, who was of Jewish descent, faced the difficult decision to leave Europe. In 1938, he emigrated to the United States, seeking refuge from the escalating dangers in his home continent. His move to the U.S. marked a significant turning point in his career, setting the stage for his future contributions to statistical theory and decision-making.

Wald's early education and his subsequent escape from Europe not only reflect the challenges he faced but also underscore his resilience and determination. His experiences during this tumultuous period shaped his academic career and led to groundbreaking work in statistical decision theory, which has had a lasting impact on both theoretical and applied statistics.

Work at Columbia University

Abraham Wald's tenure at Columbia University was a highly productive period in his career, marked by significant contributions to applied mathematics and a focus on economics. His work at Columbia not only advanced mathematical theory but also addressed practical problems in economic and decision-making contexts.

Applied Mathematics Research: Wald's role at Columbia University involved applying mathematical methods to solve complex problems across various domains, with a particular emphasis on economics. His research extended beyond pure mathematics, encompassing practical applications that bridged the gap between theory and real-world issues. Wald's ability to apply advanced mathematical concepts to economic problems was instrumental in developing innovative solutions and approaches.

Economic Applications: At Columbia, Wald worked on problems related to economic theory and decision-making. His research included developing mathematical models to understand economic phenomena and make informed decisions based on statistical analysis. His work in this area contributed to a deeper understanding of economic behavior and provided tools for analyzing economic systems and policies.

Development of Statistical Decision Theory Concepts

One of Wald's most significant achievements at Columbia University was the development of statistical decision theory, a field that has had a profound impact on both theoretical and applied statistics.

Foundations of Statistical Decision Theory: Wald's work laid the groundwork for statistical decision theory, a framework for making decisions under uncertainty. He introduced key concepts such as decision rules, loss functions, and the minimization of expected loss, which provided a systematic approach to decision-making in the presence of uncertainty. Wald's contributions helped formalize how decisions can be optimized based on statistical information and the potential outcomes of different choices.

Minimax Theorem: Wald is well-known for his development of the minimax theorem, which provides a strategy for minimizing the maximum possible loss in decision-making problems. This theorem, a cornerstone of statistical decision theory, addresses how to choose the best decision rule when faced with uncertainty and varying outcomes. The minimax approach has been widely applied in fields such as economics, game theory, and operations research.

Impact on Modern Statistics: Wald's innovations in statistical decision theory have had a lasting impact on the field of statistics and its applications. His methods and concepts have influenced various areas, including finance, engineering, and policy analysis. The principles of statistical decision theory are now integral to modern statistical practice, providing a foundation for making informed and rational decisions based on data and uncertainty.

In summary, Abraham Wald's work at Columbia University was marked by significant contributions to applied mathematics and the development of statistical decision theory. His research not only advanced mathematical understanding but also provided practical tools and methods for decision-making in economic and uncertain environments. Wald's legacy in statistical decision theory continues to influence a wide range of disciplines, reflecting the enduring impact of his work.

Wartime Contributions on Aircraft Survivability

During World War II, Abraham Wald made significant contributions to the field of aircraft survivability by applying statistical decision theory to analyze bomber maintenance data. His work was instrumental in improving the effectiveness and safety of military operations, particularly in the context of aircraft design and maintenance.

Analysis of Bomber Data: Wald was tasked with analyzing data related to bomber aircraft that had returned from missions. The data included information on the locations of bullet holes and damage sustained by the aircraft. Wald applied his statistical expertise to this data to gain insights into how aircraft could be better protected and how resources should be allocated for reinforcement.

Theoretical Approach: Wald used statistical decision theory to interpret the patterns of damage observed in the bombers. By analyzing the distribution and frequency of damage across different parts of the aircraft, he aimed to determine which areas were most vulnerable and how best to reinforce them. His approach involved evaluating the data to identify critical insights that could improve the design and protection of bomber aircraft.

Counterintuitive Insights on Armor Reinforcement

One of Wald's most notable contributions during the war was his counterintuitive recommendation regarding armor reinforcement based on his analysis of the bomber data.

Survivability Analysis: Wald's analysis revealed that the areas of the aircraft that were most frequently damaged were not necessarily the most critical to reinforce. Contrary to initial expectations, the aircraft's surviving planes showed damage patterns that indicated that certain parts of the aircraft were less likely to be hit if they were critical to the plane's operation. This insight was based on the observation that planes with damage to non-critical areas were more likely to return from missions, while those with damage to critical areas were less likely to survive.

Recommendation for Armor Placement: Based on this analysis, Wald recommended reinforcing the parts of the aircraft that were least damaged in the data—areas that were not showing damage but were crucial for the aircraft's operation. His reasoning was that reinforcing the most frequently hit areas would not be as effective as protecting the critical components that were essential for the aircraft's survival but less frequently damaged. This recommendation was aimed at improving overall survivability by addressing the weaknesses that were not immediately apparent from the damage data alone.

Impact on Aircraft Design: Wald's insights led to a change in how armor reinforcement was approached in bomber design. By focusing on the protection of critical components, the military was able to improve the effectiveness and safety of its aircraft, ultimately contributing to more successful missions and reduced losses.

In summary, Abraham Wald's wartime contributions to aircraft survivability involved applying statistical decision theory to analyze bomber maintenance data and providing counterintuitive yet highly effective recommendations for armor reinforcement. His work demonstrated the power of statistical analysis in making critical decisions and optimizing resources in complex and high-stakes environments. Wald's contributions had a lasting impact on military strategy and aircraft design, reflecting his profound influence on the application of statistical methods in practical situations.

Foundations of Statistical Inference

Abraham Wald's work laid important groundwork for the field of statistical inference, particularly through his contributions to the principles of MLE and sufficiency.

MLE: Wald was instrumental in formalizing the method of MLE, which is a fundamental approach in statistical inference. MLE involves finding the parameter values that maximize the likelihood function, which represents the probability of observing the given data under different parameter values. Wald's work demonstrated how MLE provides estimates that are consistent and efficient under certain conditions, making it a powerful tool for statistical inference.

Sufficiency Principle: Wald also contributed to the concept of sufficiency, which is a key idea in statistical theory. The sufficiency principle states that a statistic is sufficient for a parameter if it captures all the information about that parameter contained in the sample data. In other words, once the value of a sufficient statistic is known, no additional information about the parameter can be gained from the data. Wald's contributions helped formalize this principle and showed how sufficiency can simplify the process of statistical inference by reducing the dimensionality of the data.

Frequentist Perspective on Estimation

Wald's work is closely associated with the frequentist perspective on statistical estimation, which contrasts with Bayesian approaches by focusing on the long-run frequency properties of estimators.

Frequentist Estimation: The frequentist approach to estimation is concerned with the properties of estimators as the sample size grows to infinity. It evaluates estimators based on criteria such as unbiasedness, consistency, and efficiency. Wald's work emphasized these frequentist principles, particularly in the context of developing and evaluating statistical procedures that perform well in large samples.

Properties of Estimators: Wald's frequentist perspective focused on ensuring that estimators have desirable properties such as unbiasedness (the expectation of the estimator equals the true parameter value), consistency (the estimator converges to the true parameter value as the sample size increases), and efficiency (the estimator achieves the lowest possible variance among unbiased estimators). His contributions helped establish a rigorous framework for evaluating and comparing different estimation methods based on these properties.

Impact on Statistical Theory: Wald's work in statistical inference solidified the foundations of the frequentist approach and contributed to the development of various statistical techniques and methodologies. His contributions have influenced the design and analysis of experiments, hypothesis testing, and the development of statistical models that are widely used in research and practice.

In summary, Abraham Wald's contributions to the foundations of statistical inference, including MLE and the sufficiency principle, have had a profound impact on the field. His work from a frequentist perspective has shaped how estimators are developed, evaluated, and applied, providing essential tools and principles for statistical analysis and inference. Wald's insights continue to be foundational in the practice of statistics and the development of statistical theory.

Sequential Analysis Methods

Abraham Wald's development of sequential analysis methods marked a significant advancement in statistical theory and practice. Sequential analysis involves evaluating data and making decisions at various stages throughout the data collection process, rather than waiting until all data is collected.

Sequential Sampling: Wald introduced the concept of sequential sampling, where data is collected and analyzed in stages, allowing decisions to be made before the entire sample is observed. This approach enables more efficient data collection by potentially reducing the number of observations needed to reach a decision. Sequential sampling can be particularly advantageous when data collection is costly or time-consuming.

Stopping Rules: In conjunction with sequential sampling, Wald developed stopping rules that dictate when data collection should be terminated. These rules are based on the information gathered up to that point and are designed to maximize the efficiency of the sampling process while controlling for error rates. Wald's stopping rules are used to determine when enough data has been collected to make a reliable decision or to halt the process if the desired level of precision has been achieved.

Applications: Wald's techniques for sequential analysis are built on the principles of statistical decision theory and involve the use of likelihood ratios and other criteria to make decisions at each stage of the analysis. These methods provide a structured approach to data collection and decision-making, enhancing the ability to draw conclusions efficiently.

Military and Industrial Applications

Wald's sequential analysis methods had important applications in both military and industrial contexts, demonstrating their practical value in real-world scenarios.

Military Applications: During World War II, Wald's sequential analysis techniques were employed to address various military problems, such as evaluating the effectiveness of different strategies and optimizing resource allocation. The methods proved useful in contexts where timely decisions were crucial, and where traditional analysis methods might have been too slow or resource-intensive. For instance, sequential analysis helped in determining when to stop testing new aircraft designs or when to adopt new strategies based on ongoing results.

Industrial Applications: In industrial settings, Wald's methods were applied to improve quality control and decision-making processes. Sequential analysis allowed companies to monitor production processes more effectively, make adjustments based on early data, and reduce the number of defective products. The ability to make decisions based on interim results enabled industries to optimize their operations, minimize waste, and enhance overall efficiency.

Impact on Research and Development: Beyond military and industrial applications, Wald's sequential analysis techniques have influenced research and development across various fields. The ability to make decisions with ongoing data has facilitated advancements in clinical trials, product testing, and other areas where real-time analysis and decision-making are critical. The principles of sequential analysis continue to be applied in modern research methodologies, reflecting their enduring relevance.

In summary, Abraham Wald's development of sequential analysis methods introduced techniques for sequential sampling and stopping rules that have had significant applications in military and industrial contexts. His contributions have enhanced decision-making processes and efficiency in data collection, demonstrating the practical impact of statistical theory on real-world problems. Wald's sequential analysis methods remain a valuable tool in various fields, illustrating the practical benefits of his pioneering work.

Lasting Impact

Abraham Wald's work has had a profound and lasting impact on the fields of econometrics and operations research, shaping how economic data is analyzed and how decisions are made in complex systems.

Econometrics: Wald's contributions to statistical inference and decision theory provided a foundation for econometrics, the application of statistical methods to economic data. His development of techniques such as MLE and sequential analysis has influenced how economists model economic relationships, estimate parameters, and test hypotheses. Wald's work has enabled more accurate and efficient analysis of economic data, contributing to advancements in economic forecasting, policy evaluation, and financial analysis.

Operations Research: Wald's methods also significantly impacted operations research, a field focused on optimizing decision-making in complex systems. His sequential analysis techniques, in particular, have been applied to problems in resource allocation, inventory management, and production planning. The principles of statistical decision theory that Wald developed have been used to design and implement strategies for improving operational efficiency and effectiveness in various industries.

Enduring Influence Through Decision-Theoretic Models

Wald's development of decision-theoretic models has had a lasting influence on how decisions are approached in both theoretical and practical contexts.

Decision-Theoretic Models: Wald's work on statistical decision theory provided a framework for understanding and formalizing decision-making under uncertainty. His models, which include concepts like loss functions, decision rules, and the minimax criterion, have been widely adopted in economic and financial decision-making. These models help economists and analysts make informed decisions by evaluating trade-offs and optimizing outcomes based on available data.

Policy and Strategy Development: The principles of decision theory that Wald introduced have been instrumental in shaping policy and strategy development across various domains. By applying decision-theoretic models, policymakers and business leaders can assess the potential impacts of different decisions, weigh risks and benefits, and develop strategies that align with their objectives. Wald's influence is evident in areas such as risk management, strategic planning, and resource allocation.

Ongoing Research and Application: Wald's impact continues to be felt in contemporary research and application. The techniques and models he developed are still used in modern econometrics and operations research, and his decision-theoretic approach remains a cornerstone of statistical practice. Researchers and practitioners continue to build upon Wald's work, exploring new applications and refining existing methods to address evolving challenges in economics and beyond.

In summary, Abraham Wald's lasting impact on economics is evident in the fields of econometrics and operations research, where his contributions have shaped how data is analyzed and decisions are made. His decision-theoretic models have provided valuable frameworks for understanding and optimizing decision-making under uncertainty, influencing policy, strategy, and ongoing research. Wald's work continues to be foundational in these areas, reflecting the enduring relevance of his pioneering contributions.

Summary of Wald's Methodological Innovations

Abraham Wald's methodological innovations have had a profound and lasting impact on the field of statistics, introducing pioneering concepts that have become integral to statistical modeling and testing.

Statistical Decision Theory: Wald's development of statistical decision theory revolutionized how decisions are made under uncertainty. His introduction of concepts such as loss functions, decision rules, and the minimax criterion provided a structured framework for evaluating and optimizing decisions based on statistical information. These concepts laid the groundwork for modern decision-making processes in a wide range of fields.

MLE: Wald's formalization of MLE provided a powerful method for parameter estimation. MLE involves finding parameter values that maximize the likelihood function, and Wald's work demonstrated the effectiveness of this approach in producing consistent and efficient estimates. MLE remains a fundamental technique in statistical inference and modeling.

Sequential Analysis: Wald's pioneering work on sequential analysis introduced techniques for evaluating data and making decisions at various stages of the data collection process. His development of sequential sampling and stopping rules allowed for more efficient data collection and decision-making, reducing costs and improving the effectiveness of analysis in various applications.

Sufficiency Principle: Wald's contributions to the principle of sufficiency helped simplify statistical inference by identifying statistics that capture all relevant information about parameters. This principle has been crucial in reducing data complexity and focusing analysis on key information.

Interdisciplinary Legacy in Many Applied Domains

Wald's methodological innovations have left an interdisciplinary legacy, influencing a diverse range of applied domains and continuing to shape research and practice.

Economics and Finance: Wald's work has significantly impacted econometrics and financial analysis, providing tools and models for analyzing economic data, optimizing decision-making, and developing effective strategies. His methods are widely used in economic forecasting, policy evaluation, and financial risk management.

Military and Industrial Applications: During World War II, Wald's contributions to sequential analysis and decision theory were applied to military operations, improving aircraft design and resource allocation. In industrial contexts, his techniques have enhanced quality control, production planning, and operational efficiency.

Operations Research: Wald's methods have influenced operations research, aiding in the optimization of complex systems and decision-making processes. His techniques for resource allocation and inventory management have been widely adopted in various industries.

Statistical Research and Application: Wald's innovations continue to be foundational in modern statistical research and practice. His concepts and methods are taught in statistical courses, applied in research studies, and used in practical applications across many fields.

In summary, Abraham Wald's methodological innovations in statistical modeling and testing have had a transformative impact on the field of statistics. His pioneering concepts, including statistical decision theory, MLE, sequential analysis, and the sufficiency principle, have shaped both theoretical and applied statistics. Wald's interdisciplinary legacy extends across economics, finance, military and industrial applications, operations research, and beyond, reflecting the enduring relevance and influence of his contributions.

Andrey Kolmogorov and Probability Theory

Early Life and Education

Andrey Kolmogorov was born in 1903 in Tambov, a city in Russia.

From a young age, Kolmogorov exhibited exceptional talent in mathematics. His early education was marked by a strong aptitude for mathematical problem-solving, which set the stage for his future contributions to the field.

Academic Excellence: In 1920, Kolmogorov enrolled at Moscow State University, where he quickly distinguished himself as a prodigious talent in mathematics. His academic journey at the university was characterized by rapid progress and an impressive grasp of complex mathematical concepts. Under the guidance of leading mathematicians, Kolmogorov's early work laid the foundation for his future contributions to various fields, including probability theory and information theory.

Rapid Ascendancy: Kolmogorov's early education was marked by an unusual blend of rigorous training and innovative thinking. His rapid ascent in the academic world of mathematics was fueled by both his innate talent and the supportive academic environment at Moscow State University. By the time he completed his studies, Kolmogorov had established himself as a leading figure in mathematics, setting the stage for his groundbreaking work in information theory and other areas.

Kolmogorov's early achievements and his educational background were instrumental in shaping his subsequent contributions to mathematics and information theory. His education at Moscow State University provided him with the foundational knowledge and intellectual environment necessary for his pioneering work in probability theory, which later influenced the development of information theory.

Major Contributions to Statistics and Probability Theory

Modern Axiomatic Approach to Probability Theory: In 1933, Andrey Kolmogorov revolutionized the field of probability theory with his development of the modern axiomatic approach. Prior to Kolmogorov's work, probability theory lacked a rigorous mathematical foundation, relying on intuitive and often imprecise definitions. Kolmogorov's axiomatization provided a clear and formal framework for probability, which was based on three fundamental axioms:

1. **Non-Negativity:** The probability of any event is a non-negative real number.
2. **Normalization:** The probability of the entire sample space is equal to one.
3. **Additivity:** For any two mutually exclusive events, the probability of their union is equal to the sum of their individual probabilities.

This axiomatic system not only formalized probability theory but also provided a solid basis for further developments in statistical theory and applications. Kolmogorov's approach is now considered the standard framework for probability theory and has had profound implications across various scientific disciplines.

Markov Chains and Stochastic Processes: Kolmogorov made significant advancements in the theory of Markov chains and stochastic processes. His work in this area includes the development of fundamental results regarding the long-term behavior of Markov processes, such as stationary distributions and ergodic theorems. These contributions laid the groundwork for the analysis of systems that evolve over time according to probabilistic rules.

Kolmogorov's research on stochastic processes extended beyond Markov chains to include more general types of random processes. His work has had extensive applications in fields such as economics, finance, and engineering, where the modeling of random phenomena is essential.

Kolmogorov Scaling Laws in Turbulence: In addition to his work in probability theory, Kolmogorov made groundbreaking contributions to the study of turbulence in fluid dynamics. He developed the Kolmogorov scaling laws, which describe the statistical properties of turbulence in fluids. These laws provide a theoretical framework for understanding the distribution of energy in turbulent flows and have been instrumental in advancing the field of fluid mechanics.

Kolmogorov's scaling laws are based on the idea that turbulence can be characterized by a set of universal statistical properties, which apply to a wide range of turbulent systems. This work has had a lasting impact on both theoretical and applied fluid dynamics.

Applications to Information Theory, Game Theory, and Algorithmic Complexity: Kolmogorov's influence extended into several other areas of applied mathematics. In information theory, his work on the entropy of random variables contributed to the development of information measures and data compression techniques. His contributions to game theory include the formalization of strategies and solutions for games involving randomness and uncertainty.

In algorithmic complexity, Kolmogorov introduced the concept of algorithmic randomness and complexity, which studies the computational aspects of random sequences and data. This area of research has had significant implications for theoretical computer science and the understanding of computational processes.

Kolmogorov's contributions to these diverse fields underscore his role as a pioneering mathematician whose work has shaped modern scientific understanding across multiple disciplines. His rigorous approach to probability theory, combined with his innovative research in related areas, has left a lasting legacy in mathematics and its applications.

Other Accomplishments

Career at the Steklov Institute of Mathematics: Andrey Kolmogorov spent the majority of his career at the Steklov Institute of Mathematics in Moscow, one of the leading centers for mathematical research in Russia. His tenure at the Institute was marked by prolific research and significant contributions to various fields of mathematics and applied sciences. The Steklov Institute provided a collaborative environment where Kolmogorov's groundbreaking work in probability theory, stochastic processes, and other areas could flourish.

Mentorship and Influence on Future Generations: Kolmogorov was also a dedicated mentor, supervising over 50 doctoral students throughout his career. Many of his students went on to become prominent mathematicians and researchers in their own right. His guidance and support played a crucial role in shaping the careers of these individuals, contributing to the continued advancement of mathematical research and theory.

Awards and Honors: Kolmogorov received numerous prestigious awards in recognition of his outstanding contributions to mathematics. Among these, the Stalin Prize was awarded to him for his achievements in the field of mathematics. Additionally, he was honored with the Fields Medal in 1966, one of the highest accolades in mathematics, which recognized his pioneering work and significant impact on the discipline. These awards underscored the importance of Kolmogorov's contributions to both theoretical and applied mathematics.

Leadership in the International Mathematical Union (IMU): Kolmogorov served as the president of the IMU from 1986 until his death in 1987. His leadership in this role highlighted his influence on the global mathematical community and his commitment to advancing the field on an international scale. Under his presidency, the IMU continued to promote mathematical research and foster international collaboration among mathematicians.

Kolmogorov's career and achievements reflect his profound impact on mathematics and his enduring legacy as one of the field's most influential figures. His work continues to inspire and inform contemporary research across a wide range of mathematical disciplines.

Legacy and Impact

Influence on Modern Statistics and Probability Theory: Andrey Kolmogorov is widely regarded as one of the most influential mathematicians of the 20th century, particularly in the realms of probability theory and statistics. His development of the axiomatic approach to probability theory, articulated in his 1933 work Foundations of the Theory of Probability, provided a rigorous mathematical framework that underpins much of modern statistical theory. This axiomatic approach revolutionized the field, transforming probability theory into a well-defined mathematical discipline and laying the groundwork for contemporary statistical methods.

Contributions to Multiple Mathematical Disciplines: Kolmogorov's impact extended beyond probability theory into various branches of mathematics, including stochastic processes, ergodic theory, and turbulence. His pioneering work on Markov chains and stochastic processes has been instrumental in developing models that describe random phenomena, which are essential in fields such as finance, engineering, and computer science. In addition, his Kolmogorov scaling laws have had a lasting influence on the study of turbulence in fluid dynamics, contributing significantly to the understanding of complex fluid behavior.

Influence on Physics and Computer Science: Kolmogorov's work also permeated other scientific disciplines, including physics and computer science. His ideas on algorithmic complexity laid the groundwork for what would become a significant area of research in theoretical computer science. His contributions helped establish a deeper understanding of randomness and complexity, which are crucial in various computational and theoretical applications.

Mentorship and Inspirational Impact: Throughout his career, Kolmogorov supervised over 50 doctoral students, many of whom went on to become leading figures in mathematics and related fields. His mentorship fostered the development of a new generation of mathematicians, who have continued to advance and build upon his foundational work. Kolmogorov's intellectual curiosity and broad interests also served as an inspiration, motivating researchers to explore new areas of mathematical inquiry and application.

Enduring Reputation: Kolmogorov is remembered not only for his exceptional mathematical abilities but also for his broad intellectual pursuits and curiosity. His contributions have left a lasting mark on multiple fields, and his legacy continues to influence contemporary research. The depth and breadth of his work demonstrate his remarkable versatility and his profound impact on both theoretical and applied mathematics.

Kolmogorov's legacy is a testament to his extraordinary contributions to mathematics, and his work remains central to various areas of research and application. His influence spans generations of mathematicians and scientists, affirming his status as a towering figure in the history of mathematics.

Kolmogorov's contributions to probability theory, statistics, and other areas of mathematics were truly groundbreaking and have had a lasting impact on the field.

John von Neumann and Computational Statistics

Early Life and Education

John von Neumann, one of the most influential mathematicians of the 20th century, demonstrated prodigious talent in mathematics and logic from a young age. His early life and education laid the groundwork for his groundbreaking contributions to computational statistics and various other fields.

Prodigious Talent in Mathematics and Logic: Born in Budapest in 1903, von Neumann exhibited extraordinary intellectual abilities from an early age. His keen interest in mathematics and logic became evident when he began solving complex problems that were well beyond the typical scope for someone of his age. von Neumann's remarkable aptitude for abstract thinking and mathematical reasoning earned him recognition as a child prodigy, setting the stage for his future achievements.

Studies at Universities in Budapest and Berlin: von Neumann's formal education began at the University of

Budapest, where he pursued studies in mathematics. His academic prowess quickly became apparent, and he soon moved to Berlin to further his education at the University of Berlin. During his time in Berlin, von Neumann worked with prominent mathematicians and expanded his knowledge in various areas of mathematics and logic. His time at these prestigious institutions allowed him to refine his skills and develop a deep understanding of the mathematical principles that would later underpin his contributions to computational statistics and other scientific fields.

von Neumann's early life and education were characterized by a combination of innate talent and rigorous academic training. His exceptional abilities in mathematics and logic, coupled with his studies at leading universities, provided a strong foundation for his future contributions to computational statistics and other areas of science and technology.

Work in Mathematical Logic and Foundations

John von Neumann made groundbreaking contributions to the field of mathematical logic, establishing himself as a leading figure in the development of formal logic and abstract theory. His work in these areas not only advanced mathematical understanding but also laid the groundwork for future developments in computational statistics and computer science.

Formal Logic: von Neumann's contributions to formal logic include his work on the foundations of mathematical theory. He explored various aspects of logic, including the formalization of mathematical proofs and the structure of logical systems. His insights into the nature of logical reasoning and proof theory helped refine the understanding of how mathematical statements can be rigorously proven and systematically analyzed.

Abstract Theory: In addition to formal logic, von Neumann made significant advances in abstract theory, particularly in the context of algebra and topology. His work on abstract algebraic structures and the development of new theoretical frameworks contributed to the broader understanding of mathematical systems and their properties. These contributions were instrumental in shaping modern mathematical theory and influenced various fields beyond pure mathematics.

Development of Axiomatic Set Theory

One of von Neumann's most notable achievements in mathematical logic was his development of axiomatic set theory, which has had a profound impact on both mathematics and computational theory.

Axiomatic Set Theory: von Neumann's axiomatic set theory provided a formal foundation for understanding sets and their properties. His approach to set theory was grounded in the development of a set of axioms that define the basic properties and operations of sets. This axiomatic framework allowed for a more rigorous and structured approach to set theory, addressing issues and inconsistencies that had been present in earlier formulations.

von Neumann-Bernays-Gödel (NBG) Set Theory: In collaboration with other mathematicians, von Neumann developed the NBG set theory, an extension of his original axiomatic set theory. The NBG system introduced a more comprehensive and refined set of axioms that addressed various foundational issues in set theory. This system has become an important part of modern set theory and has influenced the development of mathematical logic and theoretical computer science.

Impact on Computational Statistics: von Neumann's work in axiomatic set theory also laid the groundwork for advances in computational statistics. By providing a formal framework for understanding mathematical structures, his set theory contributed to the development of algorithms and computational methods that rely on rigorous mathematical foundations. This influence extends to various areas of computer science, including algorithms, data structures, and theoretical computer science.

In summary, John von Neumann's work in mathematical logic and foundations was marked by his significant contributions to formal logic, abstract theory, and the development of axiomatic set theory. His rigorous approach to these areas provided a solid foundation for future developments in mathematics and computational statistics, shaping the way mathematical concepts and systems are understood and applied.

Collaboration at the Institute for Advanced Study (IAS)

John von Neumann's tenure at the IAS in Princeton was a pivotal period in his career, during which he made significant contributions to the development of early electronic computing machines. His collaboration with other leading scientists at the IAS helped shape the future of computing technology.

Early Computing Machines: von Neumann was deeply involved in the design and development of early electronic computers during his time at the IAS. His work included collaborating with pioneers such as Alan Turing and others who were instrumental in advancing the field of computing. von Neumann's expertise in mathematical logic and abstract theory contributed to the practical aspects of computing machine design, including the implementation of algorithms and problem-solving techniques.

Key Contributions: von Neumann's contributions to early electronic computing machines included designing systems that could perform complex calculations and handle a variety of tasks. His work focused on improving the efficiency and capabilities of these machines, paving the way for future developments in computer technology. von Neumann's influence extended to the design of hardware and the formulation of algorithms that would become fundamental to computing.

Formulation of the von Neumann Architecture

One of von Neumann's most enduring contributions to computing was the formulation of the von Neumann architecture, a fundamental design framework for electronic computers that has become a cornerstone of modern computing.

von Neumann Architecture: The von Neumann architecture, proposed by von Neumann and his colleagues in the late 1940s, introduced a new way of structuring electronic computers. The architecture is based on a design that includes a central processing unit (CPU), memory, and input/output devices, all interconnected through a system bus. This design allows for the sequential execution of instructions and the storage of data and programs in the same memory unit, a concept that was revolutionary at the time.

Impact on Computing: The von Neumann architecture has had a profound impact on the development of electronic computers. Its principles form the basis of most modern computer systems, influencing the design of hardware and software. The architecture's emphasis on a stored-program concept, where programs are stored in memory and executed sequentially, has been fundamental to the evolution of computing technology.

Legacy: von Neumann's formulation of the architecture has become a standard reference in computer science and engineering. It has guided the design and development of countless computing systems and continues to be a key concept in the study of computer organization and architecture. The architecture's influence extends to various fields, including software development, computer engineering, and computational theory.

In summary, John von Neumann's collaboration at the IAS was marked by his significant contributions to early electronic computing machines and the formulation of the von Neumann architecture. His work during this period played a crucial role in shaping the future of computing technology and established principles that continue to underpin modern computer systems. von Neumann's legacy in this area reflects his profound impact on the field of computing and his lasting influence on technological innovation.

Early Stochastic Modeling Techniques

John von Neumann made significant contributions to the field of stochastic modeling, particularly in the development of Markov processes and the theory of random walks. These concepts are foundational in the study of random phenomena and have had a lasting impact on various areas of science and engineering.

Markov Processes: Markov processes, named after the mathematician Andrey Markov, are a class of stochastic processes that exhibit the *memoryless* property. This means that the future state of the process depends only on the current state and not on the sequence of events that preceded it. von Neumann's work in this area helped formalize the mathematical framework for analyzing and predicting the behavior of systems governed by such processes.

Application of Markov Processes: von Neumann's exploration of Markov processes included studying their applications in areas such as queueing theory, economics, and genetics. His contributions provided a rigorous foundation for understanding how random systems evolve over time and how their behavior can be modeled and analyzed using probabilistic methods.

Random Walks Theory: The theory of random walks, which involves analyzing paths that consist of a sequence of random steps, is closely related to Markov processes. von Neumann's work on random walks contributed to the development of mathematical models for understanding various types of random motion and diffusion processes. This theory has applications in fields such as statistical mechanics, finance, and computer science.

Modeling Growth and Uncertainty Mathematically

von Neumann's contributions to stochastic modeling extended to the mathematical modeling of growth and uncertainty, addressing how to quantify and analyze random processes and their impacts on various phenomena.

Modeling Growth: von Neumann applied stochastic modeling techniques to understand and predict growth processes in different contexts. This included studying the mathematical properties of growth models and how random variations can affect growth rates and patterns. His work provided insights into how randomness influences growth and how to model these effects mathematically.

Uncertainty Quantification: Understanding and quantifying uncertainty is a critical aspect of stochastic modeling. von Neumann's work included developing methods for analyzing and managing uncertainty in mathematical models. This involved creating frameworks for assessing the impact of random variables and uncertainties on model outcomes, which is essential for making informed decisions and predictions in uncertain environments.

Impact on Modern Techniques: von Neumann's early work in stochastic modeling laid the groundwork for modern techniques used in various fields, including economics, finance, and operations research. His methods for analyzing random processes and modeling uncertainty continue to be relevant and widely used in contemporary statistical and computational methods.

In summary, John von Neumann's early contributions to stochastic modeling techniques, including Markov processes, random walks theory, and mathematical modeling of growth and uncertainty, were foundational in advancing the understanding of random phenomena. His work provided a rigorous framework for analyzing and predicting the behavior of stochastic systems and has had a lasting impact on various scientific and engineering disciplines.

Invention of Simulation and Monte Carlo Methods

John von Neumann, along with his colleagues, made pioneering contributions to the development of simulation techniques and Monte Carlo methods, which have become essential tools in computational statistics and various scientific applications.

Simulation Techniques: The concept of simulation as a method for experimental computation involves creating models that replicate the behavior of complex systems through computational experiments. von Neumann and his collaborators recognized that traditional analytical methods were insufficient for solving problems with intricate, stochastic, or high-dimensional characteristics. They developed simulation techniques to explore these systems by generating and analyzing multiple scenarios to understand their behavior under different conditions.

Monte Carlo Methods: The Monte Carlo method is a statistical technique that involves using random sampling to estimate mathematical functions and simulate the behavior of complex systems. Named after the Monte Carlo Casino due to its reliance on random sampling, this method provides a way to approximate solutions to problems that are otherwise analytically intractable. von Neumann's work laid the foundation for these methods by demonstrating how randomness and statistical sampling could be used to tackle complex computational problems.

Applications to Neutron Transport and Population Growth

von Neumann's development of simulation and Monte Carlo methods had significant applications in various fields, including neutron transport and population growth. These applications highlighted the practical utility of these techniques in solving real-world problems.

Neutron Transport: One of the early applications of Monte Carlo methods was in neutron transport, a critical area in nuclear physics and engineering. The Monte Carlo method was used to simulate the behavior of neutrons as they interact with materials, such as in nuclear reactors. By modeling the random paths of neutrons and their interactions, researchers could better understand neutron diffusion, scattering, and absorption processes. This application was instrumental in improving the design and safety of nuclear reactors.

Population Growth: Monte Carlo methods were also applied to model population growth and dynamics. In this context, the techniques allowed for the simulation of various factors influencing population changes, such as birth rates, death rates, and migration. By running multiple simulations with different random inputs, researchers could analyze the potential outcomes and variability in population growth, providing valuable insights for planning and policy-making.

Broader Impact: The impact of Monte Carlo methods extends beyond neutron transport and population growth to numerous other fields, including finance, engineering, and AI. These methods have become essential tools for simulating complex systems and estimating probabilities in various applications, from risk assessment in financial markets to optimization in engineering design.

In summary, John von Neumann's invention of simulation and Monte Carlo methods revolutionized the way complex problems are approached and solved. By developing techniques for experimental computation and sampling, von Neumann provided powerful tools for analyzing and understanding complex systems. His applications of these methods to neutron transport and population growth demonstrated their practical value and set the stage for their widespread use in various scientific and engineering disciplines.

Foundations for Theoretical Computer Science

John von Neumann's later work on self-replicating automata represents a significant contribution to theoretical computer science and the study of complex systems. His exploration of self-replicating machines laid the groundwork for various fields, including computer science, biology, and AI.

Concept of Self-Replicating Automata: von Neumann's research on self-replicating automata involved theoretical models of machines capable of constructing copies of themselves. This concept, initially explored through mathematical and logical frameworks, addresses fundamental questions about the nature of computation and self-reproduction. von Neumann's models provided insights into how complex systems can achieve replication and adaptation through computational processes.

Theoretical Foundations: von Neumann's work on self-replicating automata helped establish key principles in theoretical computer science, including the idea of automata as computational systems that can perform tasks based on predefined rules. His research contributed to the development of formal languages, automata theory, and the understanding of how complex behaviors can emerge from simple computational rules. These foundational ideas have influenced the study of algorithms, computation, and system design.

Influence Extending Well Beyond Statistics

von Neumann's contributions to the theory of self-replicating automata extended beyond statistics to have a profound impact on various fields of science and technology.

Biology and Artificial Life: The concept of self-replicating automata has inspired research in biology and artificial life, where scientists study self-replicating systems and their potential applications in synthetic biology and robotics. von Neumann's ideas about replication and self-organization have influenced the development of artificial life models and the exploration of self-replicating systems in biological and artificial contexts.

Computer Science and Robotics: In computer science, von Neumann's work laid the groundwork for the development of self-replicating and adaptive algorithms. His ideas have been applied to areas such as autonomous systems, robotics, and ML, where concepts of self-replication and adaptation are central to the design of intelligent systems. The principles derived from his research continue to inform the development of algorithms and systems that exhibit adaptive and self-organizing behaviors.

Philosophy and Cognitive Science: von Neumann's exploration of self-replicating automata also has implications for philosophy and cognitive science, particularly in understanding the nature of consciousness and self-replication. His work raises questions about the nature of intelligence, self-replication, and the potential for artificial systems to exhibit behaviors akin to living organisms. These questions continue to be relevant in discussions about the philosophy of mind and the future of AI.

Cultural Impact: The concept of self-replicating automata has had a cultural impact, influencing science fiction and popular imagination. von Neumann's ideas about self-replicating machines and their potential applications have been explored in literature, film, and other media, reflecting the broader fascination with the possibilities of intelligent and autonomous systems.

In summary, John von Neumann's later work on self-replicating automata significantly advanced theoretical computer science and had a lasting influence on various scientific and technological fields. His research established foundational principles for understanding computation, self-replication, and complex systems, with implications extending to biology, artificial life, computer science, philosophy, and popular culture. von Neumann's legacy in this area reflects his profound impact on our understanding of intelligent and adaptive systems.

Lasting Impact on Computing and Data Science

John von Neumann's contributions to computing have had a profound and lasting impact on how complex modeling is approached and executed. His innovations in computer architecture and simulation techniques have facilitated efficient computation and enabled advancements across various scientific and engineering domains.

von Neumann Architecture: The introduction of the von Neumann architecture, with its stored-program concept, revolutionized the design and functionality of computers. This architecture, which integrates memory, processing units, and input/output systems, allows for efficient execution of complex models and algorithms. The architecture's ability to handle a wide range of tasks and store both data and programs in memory has been fundamental to the development of modern computing systems.

Computational Power: von Neumann's work laid the foundation for the computational power needed to tackle complex modeling problems. The development of electronic computers based on his architectural principles has enabled scientists and engineers to simulate and analyze intricate systems, from climate models to molecular structures. The efficiency and versatility of these systems have made it possible to perform computations that were previously infeasible or impractical.

Algorithmic Efficiency: von Neumann's contributions to algorithms and computational methods have also played a crucial role in improving the efficiency of complex modeling. His work on simulation techniques, including the Monte Carlo methods, has provided powerful tools for exploring and analyzing complex systems. These methods have become standard practices in fields such as finance, engineering, and operations research, where efficient computation is essential.

Statistical Simulation as a Ubiquitous Tool

Statistical simulation, a field significantly influenced by von Neumann's work, has become an indispensable tool in modern data science. His pioneering contributions to simulation methods have shaped how data is analyzed, models are validated, and predictions are made.

Monte Carlo Methods: The Monte Carlo method, developed with von Neumann's contributions, is a widely used technique for statistical simulation. By leveraging random sampling to estimate complex probabilities and model behaviors, Monte Carlo methods have become a cornerstone of data analysis and simulation. These methods are applied across diverse fields, including risk assessment, optimization, and scientific research.

Simulation in Data Science: In contemporary data science, simulation techniques are employed for various purposes, including model validation, uncertainty quantification, and scenario analysis. Statistical simulation allows data scientists to explore different scenarios, assess the robustness of models, and make informed decisions based on simulated outcomes. von Neumann's innovations have made it possible to handle complex data and systems with greater accuracy and efficiency.

Impact on Research and Industry: The impact of statistical simulation extends to research and industry, where it is used to address real-world problems and drive innovation. From financial modeling to healthcare analytics, simulation techniques enable researchers and practitioners to gain insights into complex systems and make data-driven decisions. The widespread adoption of these techniques reflects the enduring influence of von Neumann's work on modern data science.

Educational Influence: von Neumann's contributions to computing and simulation have also shaped educational curricula in computer science, statistics, and related fields. His principles and methods are taught in academic programs, influencing how students and professionals approach computational and statistical challenges. The educational impact underscores the lasting relevance of his work in shaping the future of computing and data science.

In summary, John von Neumann's lasting impact on computing and data science is evident in the efficient computation of complex models and the ubiquitous use of statistical simulation techniques. His innovations in computer architecture and simulation methods have enabled significant advancements in scientific research, industry applications, and data analysis. von Neumann's legacy continues to influence the field, highlighting his profound contributions to modern computing and data science.

Samuel Wilks and Order Statistics

Early Life and Education

Samuel Shapiro Wilks was born on November 30, 1906, in Meridian, Mississippi, USA. His early years were marked by a natural aptitude for mathematics and an insatiable curiosity about the subject. Growing up in the American South during the early 20th century, Wilks demonstrated exceptional academic abilities from a young age, setting the stage for a distinguished career in mathematics and statistics.

Wilks pursued higher education with a focus on mathematics, enrolling at Princeton University, which was renowned for its strong mathematics program. At Princeton, he was mentored by some of the leading mathematicians of the time. He completed his PhD in mathematics in 1931, under the guidance of the influential mathematician and statistician John W. Tukey. His doctoral research laid the groundwork for his future contributions to the field of statistics, particularly in the areas of order statistics and multivariate analysis.

Contributions to Order Statistics

Samuel Shapiro Wilks made groundbreaking advancements in the field of order statistics, a branch of statistics that studies the properties and applications of ordered random variables. Order statistics are derived by sorting a sample of random variables and then analyzing their distributions and relationships. Wilks' work provided a deeper understanding of these statistics, contributing significantly to both theoretical and applied statistics.

Influential 1948 Book *Order Statistics*: In 1948, Wilks authored the seminal book titled *Order Statistics*, which became a cornerstone reference in the field. This book systematically presented the theory and applications of order statistics, making complex concepts accessible and providing a comprehensive treatment of the subject. It covered various aspects, including the distribution functions of order statistics, asymptotic properties, and applications in statistical inference. The book has been highly influential, shaping the study and application of order statistics for generations of statisticians.

Theoretical Results on Order Statistics: Wilks' contributions included significant theoretical results concerning the distribution of order statistics. His work provided important insights into the behavior of the order statistics and their sampling distributions, which are crucial for various statistical applications. For example, his research helped clarify how the distribution of the k-th order statistic in a sample relates to the underlying distribution of the population, enhancing understanding of how these statistics can be used in practice.

Wilks' Lambda Statistic: One of Wilks' notable contributions is the Wilks' lambda statistic, which is used in multivariate analysis of variance (MANOVA). The Wilks' lambda is a test statistic that measures the ratio of the determinant of the error variance-covariance matrix to the determinant of the total variance-covariance matrix. This statistic is used to assess whether there are significant differences between groups in a multivariate setting, making it a valuable tool in many statistical analyses.

Order Statistics in Hypothesis Testing and Estimation: Wilks was a pioneer in applying order statistics to hypothesis testing and estimation. His work demonstrated how order statistics could be used to derive more robust and effective methods for statistical inference. This includes using order statistics for constructing confidence intervals, hypothesis tests, and estimation procedures that are less reliant on strong parametric assumptions.

Tolerance Intervals and Prediction Intervals: Wilks also contributed to the development of tolerance intervals and prediction intervals based on order statistics. Tolerance intervals provide a range within which a specified proportion of the population is expected to fall, while prediction intervals are used to predict the range in which future observations will fall. These intervals are essential for understanding the variability and uncertainty in statistical models and have practical applications in quality control, reliability analysis, and other fields.

Overall Impact

Samuel Wilks' contributions to order statistics have had a profound and lasting impact on the field of statistics. His theoretical advancements and practical applications have enriched statistical methodology and provided essential tools for researchers and practitioners. His work remains highly relevant in modern statistical practice, reflecting his enduring influence on the discipline.

Academic Positions: Samuel Shapiro Wilks held prestigious academic positions at two of the most respected institutions in the United States: Princeton University and Yale University. At Princeton, he was a faculty member in the Department of Mathematics and played a pivotal role in developing the university's statistical programs. His tenure at Yale University further cemented his reputation as a leading statistician, where he continued to contribute to the field and mentor students. These positions allowed him to influence the academic landscape of statistics profoundly.

Presidency of the American Statistical Association (ASA): In 1955, Samuel Wilks served as the president of the ASA. This role underscored his leadership and prominence in the field of statistics. As president, Wilks contributed to the advancement of statistical practice and the strengthening of the ASA as a professional organization. His presidency was marked by efforts to promote statistical science and its applications across various disciplines.

Honors and Recognition: Wilks received numerous honors throughout his career, reflecting his significant contributions to the field of statistics. He was elected to the National Academy of Sciences, one of the highest distinctions a scientist can achieve, recognizing his substantial impact on scientific research and statistical theory. His election to this prestigious academy highlighted his standing as a leading figure in statistics and his contributions to advancing the discipline.

Contributions to Multivariate Analysis and Time Series Analysis: Beyond his work on order statistics, Wilks made important contributions to multivariate analysis and time series analysis. His work in multivariate analysis, including the development of statistical techniques for analyzing multiple variables simultaneously, was crucial for understanding complex data structures and relationships. In time series analysis, Wilks contributed to methods for analyzing and modeling time-dependent data, which is essential for forecasting and understanding temporal patterns in various fields.

Legacy and Impact

Influence on Statistical Theory and Practice: Samuel Shapiro Wilks is widely regarded as one of the most influential statisticians of the 20th century. His groundbreaking work in order statistics significantly advanced the field of statistics, providing essential theoretical insights and practical methodologies that have shaped modern statistical practice. His research laid the groundwork for many statistical techniques and concepts that are fundamental to the discipline today.

Enduring Relevance of Wilks' Contributions: Wilks' contributions to order statistics, including his development of the Wilks' lambda statistic, have had a profound and lasting impact on statistical theory and applications. The Wilks' lambda statistic, a key tool in MANOVA, continues to be widely used in various fields of research. Its application in hypothesis testing and the analysis of multivariate data has become a standard approach in statistical practice, demonstrating the enduring relevance of Wilks' work.

Mentorship and Influence on Future Generations: Throughout his career, Wilks was dedicated to mentoring and inspiring the next generation of statisticians. His role as a teacher and advisor had a lasting effect on his students and colleagues, many of whom went on to become prominent figures in the field of statistics. His influence extended beyond his direct contributions, as his guidance and support helped shape the careers of numerous researchers who continued to advance statistical science.

Recognition and Lasting Impact: Wilks' legacy is marked by his significant contributions to statistical theory and his role in advancing statistical methodology. His work in order statistics and multivariate analysis remains foundational in the field, and his methodologies continue to be applied in diverse areas of research. Wilks' impact on the field of statistics is reflected in the continued use and development of his techniques and in the recognition he received from the statistical community. His contributions have left a lasting imprint on the discipline, solidifying his place as a leading figure in the history of statistics.

Samuel Wilks' achievements extended far beyond his pioneering work in order statistics. His contributions to multivariate analysis, time series analysis, and his leadership roles in professional organizations underscore his broader impact on the field of statistics. His work continues to influence statistical methodology and practice, and he is remembered as a key figure who shaped the development of modern statistical science.

Samuel Wilks made fundamental contributions to the theory and applications of order statistics, which have had a lasting impact on the development of statistical methods and their use in various scientific and practical domains.

Jacob Wolfowitz and Coding Theory

Early Life and Education in Poland

Jacob Wolfowitz, a prominent figure in coding theory and mathematical statistics, began his journey in Poland. Born into a milieu rich in intellectual and academic pursuits, his early education laid the foundation for a distinguished career in mathematics.

Studied Mathematics at Warsaw University: Wolfowitz's academic journey began at Warsaw University, where he studied mathematics. During this period, he was immersed in a rigorous mathematical environment that honed his analytical and problem-solving skills. The intellectual atmosphere at Warsaw University, known for its strong emphasis on mathematical rigor and theory, played a crucial role in shaping Wolfowitz's early academic development.

Immigration to the US after WWII: Following the tumultuous period of World War II and the impact of the war on Europe, Wolfowitz immigrated to the United States.

His move was driven by both the challenging post-war conditions in Europe and the opportunities available in the U.S. academic and research communities. Upon arriving in the U.S., he continued his academic career with a focus on applied mathematics and statistics.

Work at Cornell: After his immigration, Wolfowitz joined Cornell University, where he further developed his expertise in mathematics and statistics. At Cornell, he collaborated with other leading mathematicians and statisticians, contributing significantly to the field of coding theory. His work at Cornell established him as a leading figure in the mathematical community, and he became known for his contributions to both theoretical and applied aspects of coding theory.

In summary, Jacob Wolfowitz's early education in Poland and his subsequent work in the United States set the stage for his significant contributions to coding theory and mathematical statistics. His foundational studies at Warsaw University and his impactful work at Cornell University highlight the key stages of his academic and professional development.

Contributions to Approximation Theory

Jacob Wolfowitz made significant contributions to approximation theory, particularly in the area of best polynomial approximation. His work in this field laid a crucial foundation for numerical analysis and related applications.

Theory of Best Approximation: Wolfowitz's research in approximation theory focused on the problem of best polynomial approximation. This involves finding polynomial functions that approximate a given function as closely as possible, according to a specified norm. His work provided important theoretical results on how to achieve the best approximation within certain constraints, advancing the understanding of polynomial approximation in mathematical analysis.

Key Results and Theorems: One of Wolfowitz's notable contributions was to the development of methods for determining the best polynomial approximation in various settings. His results helped establish criteria for evaluating the quality of approximations and provided insights into how different types of approximations can be achieved under different conditions. These results are fundamental for solving practical problems where approximation is necessary, such as in numerical simulations and algorithm design.

Impact on Numerical Analysis: The theoretical advancements made by Wolfowitz in polynomial approximation have had a significant impact on numerical analysis. Numerical methods often rely on polynomial approximations to solve complex mathematical problems, and Wolfowitz's contributions have provided a rigorous basis for developing and analyzing these methods. His work has influenced the development of algorithms and techniques used in various computational applications.

Basis for Numerical Analysis Applications

Algorithm Development: The principles and results from Wolfowitz's research in approximation theory are integral to the development of numerical algorithms. For instance, polynomial interpolation and approximation methods are widely used in numerical computing to estimate values, solve equations, and perform data fitting. Wolfowitz's contributions provided the theoretical underpinnings necessary for designing efficient and accurate algorithms in these areas.

Application to Engineering and Science: The techniques developed from Wolfowitz's research have been applied across various fields, including engineering, physics, and computer science. For example, in engineering, polynomial approximation is used in signal processing and control systems. In scientific computing, it helps in solving differential equations and modeling complex systems. The broad applicability of his work underscores its importance in both theoretical and practical contexts.

In summary, Jacob Wolfowitz's contributions to approximation theory, especially in best polynomial approximation, have had a lasting impact on numerical analysis and computational methods. His theoretical results have provided a solid foundation for the development of algorithms and applications that rely on polynomial approximations, highlighting the significance of his work in both mathematical theory and practical applications.

Founding of Coding Theory

Jacob Wolfowitz played a pioneering role in the development of coding theory, a field dedicated to ensuring the integrity and reliability of data transmission and storage through error-correcting codes. His foundational work in this area has had a profound impact on telecommunications, data storage, and information theory.

Introduction to Error-Correcting Codes: The core idea behind error-correcting codes is to add redundancy to transmitted information so that errors introduced during transmission can be detected and corrected. This concept is crucial for maintaining the integrity of messages sent over noisy communication channels, where errors can occur due to interference, signal degradation, or other factors.

Impact on Communication Systems: Wolfowitz's work in coding theory addressed the need for reliable data transmission by developing methods to detect and correct errors. Error-correcting codes make it possible to reconstruct original messages accurately even when errors are present, which is essential for the reliability of digital communication systems, including telecommunication networks and data storage devices.

Binary Synchronous Codes and Linear Block Codes

Binary Synchronous Codes: One of Wolfowitz's contributions was the development of binary synchronous codes. These codes are used in digital communication systems where data is transmitted in binary form, and synchronization between the sender and receiver is crucial. Binary synchronous codes are designed to detect and correct errors in such systems, ensuring that data is accurately received despite potential transmission issues.

Linear Block Codes: Wolfowitz also made significant contributions to the theory of linear block codes. Linear block codes are a class of error-correcting codes that use linear algebra to encode data. These codes work by dividing the data into blocks and adding redundancy in a way that allows for error detection and correction. The principles of linear block codes have become fundamental in coding theory and are widely used in various applications, including computer memory, data transmission, and storage systems.

In summary, Jacob Wolfowitz's founding contributions to coding theory, including the development of error-correcting codes, binary synchronous codes, and linear block codes, have had a profound impact on the field of information theory and communication systems. His work laid the groundwork for ensuring the integrity and reliability of data transmission and storage, making significant advances in how errors are managed in digital communication.

Minimum Distance and Coding Bounds

Jacob Wolfowitz made essential contributions to understanding the properties of error-correcting codes, particularly through his work on minimum distance and coding bounds. These concepts are fundamental to the design and evaluation of codes used in various communication systems.

Distance Metrics in Coding Theory: In coding theory, the minimum distance of a code is a crucial metric that measures the smallest Hamming distance between any two distinct codewords in a code. The Hamming distance quantifies the number of positions at which the corresponding symbols in two codewords differ. Wolfowitz's work helped formalize and analyze this concept, which is vital for determining the error-correcting capability of a code. A larger minimum distance implies a greater ability to detect and correct errors.

Capacity Limits and Bounds: Wolfowitz also contributed to proving capacity limits for error-correcting codes. He investigated the theoretical bounds on how efficiently codes can be designed, given constraints such as code length, alphabet size, and minimum distance. These bounds, often referred to as coding bounds, provide limits on the performance of codes and help guide the construction of optimal codes. Wolfowitz's work in this area provided critical insights into the trade-offs between code efficiency and error-correcting capability.

Fundamental Tools in Code Construction

Code Construction: The minimum distance and capacity limits are fundamental tools in the construction and evaluation of error-correcting codes. Understanding the minimum distance allows engineers to design codes that can handle specific levels of noise and interference. Capacity bounds help in determining the maximum achievable performance for a given set of parameters, guiding the development of codes that are both practical and efficient.

Applications: Wolfowitz's contributions have had a broad impact on various applications involving data transmission and storage. The principles of minimum distance and coding bounds are applied in designing codes for digital communication systems, including cellular networks, satellite communications, and data storage devices. These concepts ensure that data can be transmitted and stored reliably, even in the presence of errors.

In summary, Jacob Wolfowitz's work on minimum distance and coding bounds provided essential tools for understanding and constructing error-correcting codes. His contributions to defining distance metrics and proving capacity limits have been fundamental in advancing the field of coding theory, enabling the development of more efficient and reliable communication systems.

Collaborations in Information Theory

Jacob Wolfowitz's collaborations in the field of information theory, particularly his joint work with Claude Shannon, were instrumental in advancing the understanding of source coding and solidifying his reputation as a foundational figure in the field.

Collaboration with Claude Shannon: One of Wolfowitz's most notable collaborations was with Claude Shannon, often regarded as the father of information theory. Together, they explored key concepts related to source coding, which is concerned with the efficient representation and compression of information. This collaboration helped to develop a deeper theoretical understanding of how information can be encoded to minimize redundancy while preserving its integrity.

Source Coding Theorems: In their joint work, Wolfowitz and Shannon contributed to the development of source coding theorems that laid the groundwork for modern data compression techniques. These theorems address how to represent data in the most efficient manner possible, which is crucial for reducing the amount of data required for transmission or storage. Their work in this area has influenced a wide range of applications, from data compression algorithms used in digital media to efficient coding schemes in telecommunications.

Foundational Contributions: Wolfowitz's contributions to information theory, including his work on coding theory and collaborations with Shannon, have earned him recognition as one of the key figures in the establishment of the field. His work has provided foundational insights into how information can be quantified, transmitted, and compressed effectively, making significant contributions to both theoretical and practical aspects of information theory.

Impact and Legacy: The impact of Wolfowitz's work extends beyond his direct contributions to coding theory and source coding. His research has helped shape the development of various information processing technologies and communication systems. The principles and methods developed through his collaborations are now integral to modern information systems, influencing everything from error correction in digital communications to data compression in multimedia applications.

In summary, Jacob Wolfowitz's collaborations in information theory, particularly with Claude Shannon, were pivotal in advancing the field. Their joint work on source coding and related concepts has had a lasting impact on information theory, earning Wolfowitz recognition as one of its foundational figures. His contributions continue to influence the design and implementation of information processing and communication systems.

Later Career at the University of Buffalo

Jacob Wolfowitz's later career at the University of Buffalo was marked by a continuation of his influential research and a commitment to education. During this period, he further solidified his impact on the fields of statistics, economics, and optimization while mentoring the next generation of scholars.

Statistics: At the University of Buffalo, Wolfowitz continued his pioneering work in statistics, focusing on various aspects of statistical theory and applications. His research contributed to the development of advanced statistical methods and techniques, furthering the understanding of statistical inference, estimation, and hypothesis testing. His work during this period helped to refine existing theories and explore new areas within statistical research.

Economics: Wolfowitz also extended his research interests to economics, applying his statistical expertise to economic theory and analysis. His work in this area involved the development and application of mathematical models to address economic problems, contributing to the broader field of econometrics. His research provided valuable insights into economic dynamics and helped bridge the gap between statistical theory and economic practice.

Optimization: Another significant area of focus for Wolfowitz was optimization, particularly in the context of decision theory and mathematical programming. His contributions to optimization theory included developing methods for solving complex optimization problems and applying these techniques to various practical scenarios. His research in this area was instrumental in advancing the theoretical and practical aspects of optimization.

Training the Next Generation of Theorists

Mentorship and Education: Wolfowitz's role at the University of Buffalo also involved training and mentoring students and young scholars. He was dedicated to fostering the development of the next generation of theorists and researchers, providing guidance and support to his students. His teaching and mentorship helped shape the careers of many students who went on to make significant contributions to statistics, economics, and related fields.

Academic Leadership: In addition to his research and teaching, Wolfowitz played a key role in academic leadership at the University of Buffalo. He contributed to the development of the university's research programs and helped establish a strong foundation for future research in his areas of expertise. His efforts in building and supporting the academic community were essential to the continued growth and success of the university's research initiatives.

In summary, Jacob Wolfowitz's later career at the University of Buffalo was marked by continued research contributions in statistics, economics, and optimization. His work during this period not only advanced these fields but also played a crucial role in training and mentoring the next generation of scholars, ensuring the ongoing development and evolution of theoretical research.

Legacy and Lasting Impact of Coding Theory

Jacob Wolfowitz's contributions to coding theory have had a profound and lasting impact on digital communication and data management. His work laid the groundwork for modern error-correcting codes and has influenced various applications in communication systems and data storage.

Error Correcting Codes: One of the most significant impacts of Wolfowitz's work is the development of error-correcting codes, which are crucial for reliable digital communication. These codes are designed to detect and correct errors that occur during data transmission over noisy channels. By adding redundancy to the transmitted information, error-correcting codes ensure that messages can be accurately reconstructed even when errors are introduced, making them essential for the reliability of digital communication systems.

Advancements in Communication Technology: Wolfowitz's work contributed to the development of advanced communication technologies, including cellular networks, satellite communications, and internet protocols. Error-correcting codes are integral to these technologies, enabling high-speed and high-quality data transmission. His contributions helped improve the robustness and efficiency of communication systems, allowing for the widespread adoption of digital technologies in everyday life.

Ubiquitous Use of Codes in Data Storage and Transmission

Data Storage: The principles of coding theory, including those developed by Wolfowitz, are applied extensively in data storage systems. Error-correcting codes are used in hard drives, flash memory, and other storage media to protect against data corruption and ensure data integrity. This application is critical for maintaining the reliability of digital storage devices and safeguarding valuable information.

Data Transmission: In addition to communication systems, error-correcting codes are employed in various data transmission scenarios, such as in wireless networks, optical communication, and digital broadcasting. These codes enhance the quality of data transmission by mitigating the effects of noise and interference, ensuring that transmitted data remains accurate and complete.

Impact Across Industries: The influence of coding theory extends to numerous industries, including telecommunications, computing, and media. Error-correcting codes are used to improve the performance and reliability of various technologies, from streaming services to satellite communication systems. Wolfowitz's contributions have thus had a broad and enduring impact on how data is managed and transmitted across different domains.

In summary, Jacob Wolfowitz's legacy in coding theory has fundamentally shaped the field of digital communication and data storage. His development of error-correcting codes has enabled reliable and efficient communication systems and is now an integral part of modern technology. The widespread application of these codes underscores the lasting impact of his work and its importance in ensuring the accuracy and reliability of digital information.

John Tukey and EDA

Early Life and Education

John Wilder Tukey was born on June 16, 1915, in New Bedford, Massachusetts. His early academic journey was marked by a keen interest in mathematics, which he pursued with dedication and enthusiasm.

Early Academic Inclinations: From a young age, Tukey exhibited a strong aptitude for mathematics. Encouraged by his parents, who were both educators, he developed a deep appreciation for numbers and problem-solving.  This early exposure to intellectual pursuits set the stage for his future academic achievements.

Education at Princeton: Tukey's passion for mathematics led him to Princeton University, where he enrolled as an undergraduate. He quickly distinguished himself as a brilliant student, earning his bachelor's degree in 1936 and a master's degree in 1937. His talent and dedication did not go unnoticed, and he continued his studies at Princeton, eventually earning his Ph.D. in mathematics in 1939. His doctoral thesis, supervised by Solomon Lefschetz, focused on topology, showcasing his prowess in advanced mathematical theory.

Career at Princeton and Bell Labs

After completing his education, Tukey embarked on a remarkable career that spanned academia and industry, making significant contributions to both fields.

Princeton University: Tukey joined the faculty at Princeton University, where he initially focused on pure mathematics. However, his interests soon expanded to include statistics, a field in which he would make groundbreaking contributions. At Princeton, he collaborated with other leading mathematicians and statisticians, fostering an environment of intellectual rigor and innovation. His work at the university laid the foundation for many of his later achievements in statistics and data analysis.

Bell Telephone Laboratories: In addition to his academic role at Princeton, Tukey began working at Bell Telephone Laboratories (Bell Labs) in the early 1940s. Bell Labs was renowned for its cutting-edge research in telecommunications and technology, and Tukey's involvement there allowed him to apply his mathematical expertise to practical problems. His work at Bell Labs was instrumental in developing new statistical methods and tools, including the Fast Fourier Transform (FFT), which revolutionized digital signal processing.

Interdisciplinary Approach: Tukey's career was characterized by an interdisciplinary approach, blending theoretical mathematics with practical applications. At Bell Labs, he collaborated with engineers, scientists, and other researchers, addressing complex problems in telecommunications, quality control, and data analysis. This collaborative environment nurtured Tukey's innovative spirit and led to the development of many of his most influential ideas.

Mentorship and Influence: Throughout his career, Tukey was a dedicated mentor to students and colleagues. At Princeton, he supervised numerous doctoral students who would go on to make their own significant contributions to the field of statistics. His teaching and mentorship were highly regarded, and he played a pivotal role in shaping the next generation of statisticians and mathematicians.

In summary, John Tukey's early life and education were marked by a deep passion for mathematics, which he pursued with distinction at Princeton University. His career at Princeton and Bell Labs allowed him to bridge the gap between theoretical mathematics and practical applications, making significant contributions to statistics and data analysis. Tukey's interdisciplinary approach and collaborative spirit were hallmarks of his career, leaving a lasting impact on the fields of mathematics and statistics.

Coining of New Statistical Terms

John Tukey was not only a brilliant statistician and mathematician but also a prolific coiner of terms that have become integral to the language of modern computing and statistics. His ability to create and popularize new terminology has had a lasting impact on the fields of computer science and data analysis.

'Bit': One of Tukey's most famous contributions to the lexicon is the term "bit," which stands for "binary digit." The word "bit" is fundamental to the field of computer science, representing the basic unit of information in digital systems. Tukey coined this term in 1946 while working on early computer technology, encapsulating the concept of binary data in a simple and memorable way.

'Software': Tukey also introduced the term "software" to describe the programs and instructions that run on computers. Before this, there was a tendency to focus on the hardware aspects of computing. By coining "software," Tukey emphasized the importance of the non-physical components of computing systems. This term has since become ubiquitous, highlighting his foresight in understanding the evolving nature of technology.

'Database': The term "database" is another example of Tukey's ability to capture complex concepts with a single, descriptive word. As the storage and retrieval of data became increasingly important, the need for a term to describe organized collections of data was clear. Tukey's introduction of "database" provided a precise and useful term that has become central to the field of data management and analysis.

Emphasis on Visual and Intuitive Understanding

Beyond his contributions to terminology, Tukey was a strong advocate for making statistical concepts more accessible through visual and intuitive methods. He believed that statistical analysis should be both understandable and practical, leading to the development of new approaches that emphasized clarity and insight.

EDA: Tukey's most notable contribution in this regard was the development of EDA. EDA is a philosophy and set of techniques that prioritize visual methods and direct interaction with data to uncover patterns, spot anomalies, and test hypotheses. Tukey emphasized that EDA should precede formal statistical modeling, allowing analysts to gain a deep understanding of their data.

Box Plots and Stem-and-Leaf Plots: Tukey invented several visual tools that have become standard in statistical practice. The box plot, also known as the box-and-whisker plot, provides a concise summary of data distribution, highlighting the median, quartiles, and potential outliers. The stem-and-leaf plot is another of Tukey's innovations, offering a way to visualize data while retaining the original values. These tools make it easier for statisticians and researchers to understand and communicate data insights.

Promoting Intuitive Insights: Tukey's approach to data analysis was grounded in the belief that intuition and visual inspection could reveal important insights that might be missed by more formal statistical methods alone. He encouraged statisticians to engage directly with their data, using simple, effective visualizations to guide their analysis. This philosophy has influenced many subsequent developments in data visualization and has become a foundational principle in the field.

Broadening the Scope of Statistics: Tukey's emphasis on visual and intuitive understanding helped to broaden the scope of statistics, making it more accessible to practitioners in various fields. His work showed that statistical methods could be both rigorous and user-friendly, bridging the gap between theoretical statistics and practical application.

In summary, John Tukey's contributions to the lexicon of statistics and computing, including terms like "bit," "software," and "database," reflect his ability to encapsulate complex ideas in simple, descriptive language. His emphasis on visual and intuitive understanding through EDA and the development of tools like box plots and stem-and-leaf plots has had a profound impact on the practice of statistics, making it more accessible and insightful for researchers and analysts across diverse disciplines.

Scrutable Modeling of Tukey

John Tukey's approach to statistical modeling was grounded in the principle of using the simplest adequate models to explain data. This philosophy emphasized clarity and interpretability over complex mathematical optimization, reflecting Tukey's commitment to making statistical methods practical and accessible.

Principle of Parsimony: Tukey championed the principle of parsimony, which advocates for selecting the simplest model that sufficiently explains the data. This approach, often referred to as *Occam's Razor* in statistical modeling, suggests that among competing models, the one with the fewest parameters should be preferred if it provides an adequate explanation. By focusing on simplicity, Tukey aimed to make models more comprehensible and easier to communicate to non-specialists.

Avoiding Overfitting: One of Tukey's concerns was avoiding overfitting, where a model becomes too complex and captures noise rather than the underlying data patterns. Simplest adequate models help mitigate this risk by avoiding unnecessary complexity. Tukey's approach aimed to balance model accuracy with interpretability, ensuring that models were both practical and robust.

Emphasis on Transparency: Tukey's emphasis on using the simplest adequate models was also about ensuring transparency in statistical analysis. By opting for models that are straightforward and easy to understand, analysts can more effectively communicate their findings to stakeholders and decision-makers. This transparency helps build trust in the results and supports more informed decision-making.

Focus on Understanding Over Complex Optimization

Tukey's modeling philosophy prioritized understanding the data and the relationships within it over the pursuit of complex optimization techniques. His approach reflected a pragmatic view of statistics, where the goal was to derive meaningful insights rather than achieve the highest level of mathematical precision.

EDA Influence: Tukey's development of EDA reinforced his focus on understanding data through intuitive methods.

EDA encourages analysts to explore data visually and interactively, uncovering patterns and insights before applying formal statistical models. This exploratory approach aligns with Tukey's belief that understanding the data is crucial for effective modeling.

Simplicity in Model Choice: Rather than relying on intricate and computationally demanding models, Tukey advocated for choosing models that were conceptually simple yet sufficient to capture the essential features of the data. This approach allowed analysts to focus on interpreting results and drawing practical conclusions without being overwhelmed by complex calculations.

Practical Application: Tukey's focus on understanding over complex optimization was also influenced by his work in applied settings, such as his time at Bell Labs. In practical applications, the goal is often to derive actionable insights rather than pursue theoretical perfection. Tukey's modeling philosophy reflects this practical perspective, emphasizing the importance of models that are useful and relevant in real-world contexts.

Educational Impact: Tukey's approach to modeling has had a lasting impact on statistical education. By teaching the value of simplicity and clarity in modeling, Tukey's methods have influenced how statistics is taught and applied. His emphasis on understanding and interpretability has become a cornerstone of effective statistical practice.

In summary, John Tukey's scrutable modeling approach was centered around using the simplest adequate models to explain data and focusing on understanding rather than complex optimization. His commitment to clarity, transparency, and practical application reflects a pragmatic view of statistics, where the goal is to derive meaningful insights and communicate them effectively. This philosophy has had a significant influence on both statistical practice and education, highlighting Tukey's enduring impact on the field.

Robust Methods of Tukey

John Tukey was a pioneer in developing robust statistical methods designed to handle outlying observations without distorting the overall analysis. His focus on robustness emphasized the importance of creating techniques that could provide reliable results even in the presence of anomalous data points.

Robust Statistics: Robust statistics are methods that remain effective even when certain assumptions about the data are violated, such as the presence of outliers or deviations from normality. Tukey's work in this area aimed to create techniques that would not be overly influenced by extreme values, which can disproportionately affect the results of traditional statistical methods.

Resistance to Outliers: Tukey's robust methods were designed to resist the impact of outliers, ensuring that the analysis provided a more accurate representation of the central tendency and variability of the data. This resistance is crucial in many real-world scenarios where outliers are common, such as in economic data, environmental measurements, or clinical studies.

Trimmed Means and Medians Preserving Overall Shape

Tukey developed several robust statistical techniques that are particularly effective in mitigating the impact of outliers. Two notable methods he introduced are trimmed means and medians, which preserve the overall shape of the data distribution while minimizing the influence of extreme values.

Trimmed Means: The trimmed mean is calculated by removing a specified proportion of the smallest and largest values from the data set and then computing the mean of the remaining values. This approach reduces the impact of extreme observations on the average, providing a more robust estimate of central tendency. For example, a 10% trimmed mean removes the lowest and highest 10% of data points before calculating the mean. This technique balances robustness with maintaining an overall understanding of the data distribution.

Medians: The median is a robust measure of central tendency that is less sensitive to outliers than the mean. Tukey promoted the use of the median as a summary statistic because it represents the middle value of a data set when ordered, thereby providing a more stable measure of central tendency in the presence of outliers. The median preserves the overall shape of the data distribution while being robust to extreme values.

Box Plots and Visual Robustness: Tukey's introduction of box plots further exemplifies his commitment to robustness. The box plot, also known as a box-and-whisker plot, visually represents the distribution of data, including the median, quartiles, and potential outliers. This graphical method allows analysts to quickly assess the spread and center of the data while identifying any unusual values that might affect the analysis.

Influence on Statistical Practice: Tukey's robust methods have had a profound impact on statistical practice, especially in fields where outliers can significantly affect results. By incorporating robust techniques into statistical analysis, researchers can achieve more reliable and valid conclusions, even when faced with imperfect data. These methods have become standard tools in EDA and robust statistical modeling.

In summary, John Tukey's robust methods, including trimmed means and medians, were designed to handle outlying observations effectively. His focus on creating techniques that are insensitive to extreme values has greatly enhanced the reliability of statistical analysis. By emphasizing robustness, Tukey provided valuable tools for preserving the overall shape of the data distribution and ensuring that statistical conclusions are more accurate and reflective of the true underlying patterns.

Contributions Beyond Statistics of Tukey

John Tukey's influence extended far beyond traditional statistics into diverse fields such as real-time signal processing and computer graphics. His interdisciplinary contributions highlight his ability to apply statistical principles to a wide range of technological and scientific challenges.

Real-Time Signal Processing: Tukey's work in signal processing, particularly his development of the FFT, had a transformative impact on the field. The FFT algorithm, which he co-developed with James Cooley, is a method for efficiently computing the discrete Fourier transform (DFT) of a signal. This innovation allows for the analysis and processing of signals in real-time, which is crucial for various applications, including telecommunications, audio processing, and image analysis.

Applications of FFT: The FFT has become a cornerstone in real-time signal processing, enabling faster and more efficient computations compared to previous methods. This advancement has made it possible to analyze complex signals and perform operations such as filtering, compression, and spectral analysis with unprecedented speed and accuracy. Tukey's contributions to FFT have had lasting effects on modern technology, from mobile phones to digital media.

Computer Graphics: Tukey's influence also reached the field of computer graphics, where his work on data visualization and EDA contributed to the development of graphical techniques and tools. His emphasis on visual understanding and intuitive data representation helped shape the way data is presented and interacted with in computer graphics. This impact is evident in the design of software and algorithms that prioritize user-friendly visualizations.

Interdisciplinary Application of Ideas Across Fields

Tukey's interdisciplinary approach demonstrated his ability to apply statistical and mathematical concepts across various domains, integrating them into practical solutions for diverse challenges.

Integration of Statistics with Engineering and Computing: Tukey's work bridged the gap between theoretical statistics and practical engineering applications. His development of the FFT algorithm exemplifies this integration, as it applied statistical techniques to solve engineering problems related to signal processing. This cross-disciplinary application of ideas has influenced numerous fields that rely on signal analysis and computational methods.

Influence on Scientific Research: Tukey's ideas extended into scientific research, where his statistical techniques and methodologies have been applied to a wide range of disciplines, including biology, economics, and social sciences. His emphasis on robust methods, visual data analysis, and exploratory techniques has helped researchers across various fields better understand and interpret their data.

Educational Impact: Tukey's interdisciplinary contributions also had a significant impact on education. His innovative approaches to data analysis and visualization have been incorporated into educational curricula, influencing how statistics and related fields are taught. His methods encourage students to approach problems from multiple perspectives and apply statistical principles to real-world scenarios.

Legacy of Innovation: Tukey's legacy of interdisciplinary innovation reflects his belief in the practical application of statistical ideas. His work has inspired subsequent generations of researchers and practitioners to explore new ways of applying statistical methods and mathematical concepts to solve complex problems across various fields.

In summary, John Tukey's contributions beyond statistics encompass his pioneering work in real-time signal processing, including the development of the FFT, and his influence on computer graphics and data visualization. His interdisciplinary approach and innovative ideas have had a profound impact on technology, scientific research, and education, highlighting his ability to apply statistical principles to diverse and practical challenges.

Tukey's Legacy and Impact on Modern Data Science

John Tukey's pioneering work in EDA has left a lasting legacy on the field of data science, particularly in the realm of data pre-processing and initial analysis. His innovative approach to data exploration fundamentally transformed how statisticians and data scientists interact with and understand data.

Introduction of EDA: Tukey introduced EDA as a crucial phase in the data analysis process, emphasizing the importance of examining data visually and interactively before applying formal statistical models. EDA focuses on uncovering patterns, identifying anomalies, and generating hypotheses through intuitive methods such as graphical displays and summary statistics. This approach contrasts with traditional methods that often start with hypothesis testing and model fitting.

Tools and Techniques: Tukey developed several tools and techniques that are now standard in data pre-processing, including stem-and-leaf displays, box plots, and the concept of robust statistics. These tools enable data scientists to visualize the distribution of data, identify outliers, and understand the underlying structure of the data set. By promoting these methods, Tukey emphasized the value of understanding data before diving into complex analysis.

Impact on Data Cleaning: The principles of EDA have become integral to data cleaning and preparation processes. Modern data science practices emphasize the importance of exploring data to identify and address issues such as missing values, inconsistencies, and outliers. Tukey's focus on thorough initial analysis has influenced how data scientists approach data cleaning, ensuring that the data is accurate and reliable before applying advanced analytical techniques.

Influence on Exploratory Techniques in Analytics

Tukey's influence on exploratory techniques has shaped the way data is analyzed and interpreted across various domains. His emphasis on exploratory methods has contributed to the development of modern data analytics and visualization practices.

Visual Data Analysis: Tukey's work laid the foundation for the widespread use of visual data analysis in modern analytics. Techniques such as scatter plots, histograms, and heatmaps are now common tools for exploring data and gaining insights. By highlighting the importance of visual methods, Tukey's approach has enhanced the ability of analysts to communicate findings and make data-driven decisions.

Interactive Data Exploration: The principles of EDA have influenced the development of interactive data exploration tools and software. Modern data visualization platforms often incorporate features that allow users to interact with and manipulate data visually, facilitating a deeper understanding of complex data sets. Tukey's emphasis on hands-on exploration and intuitive analysis has inspired the design of these tools, which prioritize user engagement and insight generation.

Data Science Methodologies: Tukey's approach to data analysis has become a core component of contemporary data science methodologies. The practice of starting with exploratory analysis to inform subsequent modeling and hypothesis testing reflects Tukey's belief in the importance of understanding data before applying formal techniques. This methodology is now widely adopted in data science workflows, emphasizing the value of exploration in guiding analytical processes.

Educational Impact: Tukey's contributions to EDA and exploratory techniques have also had a significant impact on education in data science and statistics. His methods are taught in academic programs and training courses, shaping how students and professionals approach data analysis. Tukey's legacy in education reflects his commitment to making statistical methods accessible and practical.

In summary, John Tukey's legacy in modern data science is marked by his pioneering approach to EDA and his influence on exploratory techniques. His emphasis on visual and intuitive data exploration has transformed how data is pre-processed, analyzed, and interpreted. Tukey's contributions have shaped contemporary data science practices, influencing tools, methodologies, and education in the field. His impact continues to be felt as data scientists and analysts build upon his foundational ideas to explore and understand complex data sets.

John Kendall and Queuing Theory

Early Life and Background

John Kendall was born in London, England, in 1916. His early life in the vibrant and historically rich city of London provided a stimulating environment for intellectual growth. From a young age, Kendall demonstrated a strong aptitude for mathematics and science, interests that would shape his future career.

Kendall's academic journey began at the University of London, where he pursued studies in mathematics and statistics. The University of London, renowned for its rigorous academic standards, provided Kendall with a solid foundation in these disciplines. His education was characterized by a deep engagement with mathematical theory and statistical methods, laying the groundwork for his future contributions to the field.

In 1940, Kendall completed his PhD at the University of London. His doctoral research, conducted during a period of significant global upheaval due to World War II, focused on various aspects of statistical theory. The completion of his PhD marked the beginning of a distinguished career in statistics, characterized by groundbreaking contributions to probability theory and statistical methodology.

Academic and Professional Foundations

During his time at the University of London, Kendall developed a strong theoretical background in statistics, which he would later apply to a range of innovative statistical problems. His education equipped him with the analytical skills and theoretical knowledge that would underpin his future research and professional achievements.

Kendall's early academic experiences were crucial in shaping his approach to statistical problems and his eventual contributions to the field. His rigorous training in mathematics and statistics prepared him for a career that would see significant advancements in probability theory and the development of new statistical methods.

Contributions to Statistics and Queuing Theory

Advancements in Mathematical Modeling: John Kendall made groundbreaking contributions to the mathematical modeling and analysis of queuing systems. Queuing theory, which studies the behavior and performance of queues (waiting lines), is essential in various fields such as operations research, telecommunications, and computer science. Kendall's work provided critical insights into how systems can be designed and managed to optimize performance and efficiency.

***A/B/c* Notation for Queuing Models:** One of Kendall's most enduring contributions is the introduction of the *A/B/c* notation for classifying queuing models. This notation became the standard in queuing theory and is still widely used today. In this notation:

- *A* denotes the arrival process (e.g., Poisson process, which describes the time between arrivals).
- *B* denotes the service time distribution (e.g., exponential, which describes the time taken to serve a customer).
- *c* denotes the number of servers in the system.

This classification system allows researchers and practitioners to categorize and analyze a wide range of queuing scenarios systematically, facilitating the comparison and application of theoretical results to practical problems.

Kendall's Equation: Kendall developed the Kendall equation, a fundamental formula for calculating the expected waiting time in a queuing system. This equation is crucial for understanding the performance of queuing systems and helps in predicting various performance metrics such as average wait times and queue lengths. The equation reflects the interplay between arrival rates, service rates, and the number of servers, providing a valuable tool for both theoretical analysis and practical applications.

Pioneering Use of Stochastic Processes: Kendall was a pioneer in applying stochastic processes, particularly Markov chains, to the analysis of queuing problems. Stochastic processes involve systems that evolve over time in a probabilistic manner, and Markov chains are a specific type of stochastic process where future states depend only on the current state and not on the sequence of events that preceded it. By applying these concepts, Kendall was able to model and analyze complex queuing systems with greater accuracy and insight.

Applications in Operations Research, Telecommunications, and Computer Science: Kendall's work in queuing theory extended to practical applications in various fields. In operations research, his methods helped optimize resource allocation and improve efficiency in systems involving waiting lines. In telecommunications, Kendall's theories were used to analyze and design systems for managing data traffic and communication networks. In computer science, queuing theory provided insights into system performance and resource management in computing environments. Kendall's contributions thus had a broad impact, influencing both theoretical research and practical applications across multiple disciplines.

Other Achievements

Work as a Statistician During World War II: During World War II, John Kendall served as a statistician for the UK government. His role involved applying statistical methods to various wartime problems, including those related to military operations, logistics, and resource allocation. This experience not only contributed to the war effort but also provided Kendall with practical insights that would later influence his academic research in queuing theory and other areas of statistics.

Academic Positions: After the war, Kendall held significant academic positions that allowed him to shape the field of statistics. He was a faculty member at the University of Cambridge, where he contributed to the development of the statistical curriculum and mentored numerous students.

Later, he joined the University of North Carolina, where his influence extended to the American statistical community. His roles at these prestigious institutions provided him with platforms to advance his research and collaborate with other leading statisticians.

Presidency of the Institute of Mathematical Statistics (IMS): John Kendall served as the president of the IMS from 1961 to 1962. The IMS is a major organization dedicated to the advancement and dissemination of mathematical statistics. Kendall's presidency was a period of growth and increased recognition for the field, and his leadership helped to promote statistical research and foster collaboration among statisticians.

Election to the Royal Society of London: In recognition of his significant contributions to statistics and queuing theory, Kendall was elected to the Royal Society of London, one of the highest honors a scientist in the UK can receive. The Royal Society is an esteemed scientific institution that recognizes outstanding achievements in scientific research. Kendall's election underscored the impact and importance of his work in advancing statistical theory and its applications.

Legacy and Impact

Pioneering Modern Queuing Theory: John Kendall is widely recognized as a pioneer in the field of queuing theory.

His foundational work laid the groundwork for the mathematical analysis and modeling of queuing systems. His contributions provided the theoretical underpinnings necessary for understanding complex systems involving waiting lines and service processes, which are prevalent in numerous real-world scenarios.

Foundation for Mathematical Analysis of Queuing Systems: Kendall's innovations in queuing theory, including the introduction of the $A/B/c$ notation and the development of the Kendall equation, established a rigorous framework for analyzing a broad range of queuing systems. These contributions enabled researchers and practitioners to model and understand the behavior of systems involving queues, such as telecommunications networks, customer service operations, and computer systems.

Influence Across Disciplines: Kendall's work has had a profound impact on various fields that rely on queuing models. In operations research, his methods have been used to optimize resource allocation and improve system efficiency. In computer science, queuing theory has been applied to network design and performance analysis. Additionally, his contributions have influenced fields such as telecommunications, manufacturing, and logistics, where understanding and managing queuing processes are crucial.

Enduring Tools in Queuing Theory: The Kendall notation, which he introduced, remains a standard way to classify and describe different types of queuing systems. The Kendall equation, another of his key contributions, is still widely used for calculating performance metrics such as waiting times and system utilization. These tools are integral to the practice of queuing theory and continue to be referenced in both academic research and practical applications.

Establishing Queuing Theory as a Respected Field: Kendall's work played a critical role in establishing queuing theory as a respected and influential branch of applied mathematics and statistics. His contributions not only advanced the theoretical aspects of the field but also demonstrated its practical relevance across various industries. This helped to elevate queuing theory from a niche area of study to a core component of modern applied mathematics and operations research.

Overall, Kendall's legacy is marked by his profound influence on the development of queuing theory and its applications. His work has shaped the field and continues to guide researchers and practitioners in analyzing and optimizing complex systems involving queues.

John Kendall's contributions to the mathematical foundations of queuing theory have had a profound and lasting impact on the field, enabling the development of more sophisticated models and analysis techniques for a wide range of practical applications.

Jimmie Savage and Bayesian Statistics

Early Life and Education

Jimmie Savage's early life and education set the stage for his influential contributions to Bayesian statistics and the broader field of decision theory.

Studied Mathematics at University of Virginia: Jimmie Savage was born in 1917 and pursued his undergraduate studies in mathematics at the University of Virginia. His time at this institution provided him with a strong foundation in mathematical theory and problem-solving. The rigorous mathematical training

he received during this period was instrumental in shaping his future research and contributions to statistical theory.

Early Exposure to Logical Philosophy: During his academic career, Savage was also exposed to logical philosophy, which had a significant impact on his approach to statistical theory. His interest in logical and philosophical aspects of decision-making led him to explore how formal methods could be applied to solve practical problems. This exposure to logical philosophy influenced Savage's perspective on statistics and contributed to his development of Bayesian methods, which emphasize the role of prior beliefs and subjective probability in decision-making.

Savage's early education and philosophical influences provided him with a unique perspective that informed his groundbreaking work in Bayesian statistics and decision theory. His academic background in mathematics, combined with his engagement with logical philosophy, enabled him to develop innovative approaches to statistical analysis and decision-making.

Reinterpretation of Probability in Personalistic Terms

Jimmie Savage's work fundamentally redefined the concept of probability by introducing subjective, or personalistic, interpretations that emphasized individual beliefs and personal judgment.

Subjective Probability: Savage proposed that probability should be interpreted as a measure of personal belief or confidence about uncertain events, rather than as a frequency or objective measure. This subjective approach to probability acknowledges that individuals may have different beliefs about the likelihood of an event based on their personal experiences, information, and reasoning. By framing probability in personalistic terms, Savage emphasized the role of individual perspectives in decision-making and statistical inference.

Personalistic Framework: Savage's reinterpretation of probability was rooted in the idea that probabilities are subjective assessments made by individuals. This personalistic framework allowed for a more flexible and nuanced understanding of uncertainty, where probabilities reflect personal beliefs rather than objective frequencies. This perspective was a significant departure from classical interpretations of probability and paved the way for the development of Bayesian statistics, which incorporates personal beliefs and prior knowledge into the analysis.

Work Developing Bayesian Decision Theory

Jimmie Savage's contributions to Bayesian decision theory were instrumental in formalizing and advancing the field. Bayesian decision theory integrates subjective probability with decision-making, providing a framework for making rational choices under uncertainty.

Bayesian Decision Theory: Savage developed Bayesian decision theory by combining subjective probability with decision-making processes. The theory provides a systematic approach to making decisions based on prior beliefs (subjective probabilities) and observed data. Savage's work emphasized that decisions should be made by evaluating the expected utility of different choices, considering both the probabilities of outcomes and the subjective preferences of the decision-maker.

Savage's Theorem: One of Savage's key contributions was his formulation of the *Savage Theorem*, which formalizes the idea that rational decision-making under uncertainty can be understood through Bayesian principles. The theorem provides a foundation for using subjective probabilities and utility functions to guide decision-making. Savage's theorem shows that if an individual's preferences satisfy certain axioms, then their decisions can be represented using Bayesian probabilities and expected utility.

Impact on Bayesian Statistics: Savage's development of Bayesian decision theory had a profound impact on Bayesian statistics, influencing how statistical inference and decision-making are approached. The Bayesian framework, which incorporates prior beliefs and updates them with new data, has become a fundamental approach in statistical analysis. Savage's work demonstrated the practical applicability of Bayesian methods in a wide range of fields, from economics to medicine.

In summary, Jimmie Savage's reinterpretation of probability in personalistic terms and his development of Bayesian decision theory were groundbreaking contributions that transformed the understanding of uncertainty and decision-making. By emphasizing subjective beliefs and integrating them with decision-making processes, Savage's work laid the foundation for modern Bayesian statistics and provided a robust framework for rational decision-making under uncertainty.

Exchanges Shaping Modern Bayesian Foundations

Jimmie Savage's collaboration with other subjectivist statisticians, particularly Bruno de Finetti, played a crucial role in shaping the foundations of modern Bayesian statistics.

Collaboration with Bruno de Finetti: Savage and de Finetti were prominent figures in the development of subjective probability and Bayesian statistics. Their collaboration and exchanges helped refine and solidify the theoretical underpinnings of Bayesian methods. De Finetti, an Italian statistician known for his work on subjective probability, shared with Savage a commitment to understanding probability in terms of personal beliefs rather than objective frequencies. Their discussions and writings contributed significantly to the formalization of subjective probability and Bayesian decision theory.

Theoretical Contributions: The work of Savage and de Finetti complemented each other in advancing Bayesian foundations. De Finetti's emphasis on the coherence of subjective probabilities and the concept of betting odds as a measure of belief resonated with Savage's approach to decision-making under uncertainty. Their collaboration helped integrate subjective probability with formal decision theory, reinforcing the validity of Bayesian methods as a coherent framework for statistical inference and decision-making.

Focus on Quantifying Expert Beliefs Over Frequencies

The collaboration between Savage, de Finetti, and other subjectivists emphasized a shift from traditional frequency-based approaches to focusing on quantifying expert beliefs and personal judgments.

Subjective Probability as Belief: Savage and his colleagues argued for the use of subjective probability as a way to quantify expert beliefs. Rather than relying on long-run frequencies or objective measures, subjective probability allows individuals to express their uncertainty and beliefs about specific events based on their knowledge and experience. This approach acknowledges that different individuals may have different beliefs about the same event, reflecting their unique perspectives and information.

Expert Beliefs and Decision Making: The emphasis on quantifying expert beliefs rather than relying solely on frequencies has significant implications for decision-making. Bayesian methods, supported by the work of Savage and de Finetti, provide a framework for incorporating expert judgments into statistical models and decision processes. This approach enables more flexible and personalized analyses, allowing decision-makers to use their knowledge and experience to inform their decisions.

Influence on Bayesian Practice: The focus on subjective probability and expert beliefs has influenced modern Bayesian practice, where prior distributions are often based on expert knowledge and subjective assessments. This shift has allowed Bayesian methods to be applied to a wide range of problems where objective frequencies are not readily available, making Bayesian statistics a valuable tool in various fields, including finance, medicine, and engineering.

In summary, Jimmie Savage's collaboration with Bruno de Finetti and other subjectivists was instrumental in shaping the foundations of modern Bayesian statistics. Their focus on subjective probability and expert beliefs over traditional frequency-based approaches contributed to the development of a coherent and flexible framework for statistical inference and decision-making. This collaborative effort has had a lasting impact on Bayesian practice, enabling the integration of personal judgments and expert knowledge into statistical analyses.

Contributions to Statistical Decision Theory

Jimmie Savage made significant contributions to statistical decision theory by applying his ideas to various domains, including scientific and economic inferences. His work helped formalize and advance methods for making rational decisions under uncertainty, influencing how data and decisions are approached in these fields.

Scientific Inferences: Savage's decision theory provided a structured framework for scientific inference, enabling researchers to make informed decisions based on uncertain or incomplete data. By applying Bayesian methods and subjective probability, Savage's approach allowed scientists to quantify their beliefs about hypotheses and update them as new evidence emerged. This methodology facilitated more rigorous and rational decision-making in experimental design, hypothesis testing, and data interpretation.

Economic Inferences: In economics, Savage's contributions were equally impactful. His decision theory helped economists model uncertainty and make decisions about investments, policy, and resource allocation. The principles of Bayesian decision theory allowed economists to incorporate prior knowledge and expert judgments into their analyses, improving the accuracy and relevance of economic forecasts and evaluations. Savage's work on expected utility and risk assessment became fundamental tools for economic decision-making.

Publishing Influential Textbooks in the 1950s-60s

Savage's contributions were also disseminated through his influential textbooks, which played a crucial role in shaping the field of statistical decision theory and Bayesian statistics.

***The Foundations of Statistics* (1954):** One of Savage's most significant works, this book introduced and formalized many of his ideas on subjective probability and decision theory. It provided a comprehensive treatment of Bayesian methods and statistical inference, presenting a clear and systematic approach to decision-making under uncertainty. The book was widely regarded as a seminal text in Bayesian statistics, influencing both theoretical developments and practical applications.

The Foundations of Statistics: The textbook's impact extended beyond academia, affecting how statistical methods were taught and applied in practice. By presenting Bayesian decision theory in a rigorous yet accessible manner, Savage's book helped to establish Bayesian methods as a mainstream approach in statistics and decision-making. It also contributed to the broader acceptance of subjective probability as a valid and valuable framework for statistical analysis.

Further Publications: In addition to his seminal textbook, Savage published numerous papers and articles that expanded on his ideas and applications. These works addressed various aspects of statistical decision theory, including utility theory, sequential analysis, and Bayesian inference. His publications contributed to the ongoing development of the field and provided practical guidance for researchers and practitioners.

In summary, Jimmie Savage's contributions to statistical decision theory were marked by his application of Bayesian methods to scientific and economic inferences, as well as his influential textbooks published in the 1950s and 1960s. His work provided a solid foundation for decision-making under uncertainty and helped to establish Bayesian statistics as a central approach in both theoretical and applied contexts. Through his research and publications, Savage significantly shaped the development and dissemination of statistical decision theory.

Promotion of Bayesian Approaches

Jimmie Savage was a staunch advocate for Bayesian approaches, particularly the personalistic viewpoint on probability, which emphasizes the role of individual beliefs and subjective judgments in statistical analysis.

Personalistic Probability: Savage championed the idea that probability should be interpreted as a measure of personal belief or confidence rather than an objective frequency. This personalistic viewpoint recognizes that different individuals may have varying degrees of belief about uncertain events based on their own experiences and information. Savage argued that subjective probability provides a more flexible and realistic framework for dealing with uncertainty, allowing for the incorporation of personal judgments and expert opinions into statistical models.

Theoretical Foundations: By promoting personalistic probability, Savage helped to formalize and legitimize the Bayesian approach to statistics. His work demonstrated that subjective probabilities could be used in a coherent and rational manner, leading to the development of Bayesian decision theory. This approach considers the probability of events as personal beliefs that can be updated in light of new evidence, providing a systematic method for making decisions under uncertainty.

Persuading Other Statisticians and Beyond

Savage's advocacy for Bayesian approaches extended beyond theoretical contributions; he actively worked to persuade other statisticians and professionals of the value and applicability of Bayesian methods.

Influence on the Statistical Community: Savage's efforts to promote Bayesian approaches included engaging with the broader statistical community through conferences, publications, and personal interactions. He actively communicated the advantages of Bayesian methods and personalistic probability, working to address skepticism and build support for these approaches. His influential textbook, *The Foundations of Statistics*, was a key tool in spreading Bayesian ideas and demonstrating their practical utility.

Persuading Non-Statisticians: Savage also aimed to reach professionals in fields outside of statistics, including economics, decision theory, and various applied disciplines. By showcasing the benefits of Bayesian methods for decision-making and inference in real-world applications, he helped to broaden the appeal of Bayesian approaches and encourage their adoption in diverse areas.

Educational Impact: Through his teaching and writing, Savage played a significant role in educating a new generation of statisticians and decision theorists about Bayesian methods. His emphasis on personalistic probability and Bayesian decision theory influenced many students and researchers, contributing to the growing acceptance and use of Bayesian approaches in both academic and practical contexts.

In summary, Jimmie Savage's promotion of Bayesian approaches was characterized by his strong advocacy for personalistic probability viewpoints and his efforts to persuade both statisticians and professionals in other fields of the value of Bayesian methods. His work in formalizing Bayesian decision theory, engaging with the statistical community, and educating others played a crucial role in advancing the acceptance and application of Bayesian approaches across various domains.

Later Academic Career

Jimmie Savage's later academic career was marked by prestigious positions and continued contributions to the field of statistics, particularly Bayesian theory.

University of Michigan: In the early 1960s, Savage took up a position at the University of Michigan, where he continued to advance his research and teaching in statistical theory. His tenure at Michigan provided him with an opportunity to influence a new generation of statisticians and to collaborate with colleagues in various fields. During this period, Savage's work in Bayesian statistics continued to gain recognition and respect, and his influence helped shape the development of statistical methods at the university.

Yale University: Later in his career, Savage moved to Yale University, where he held a professorship and continued to make significant contributions to the field. His time at Yale was marked by ongoing research in Bayesian statistics and decision theory, as well as his involvement in academic and professional activities. Savage's role at Yale further solidified his reputation as a leading figure in statistics, and his work continued to impact both theoretical and applied aspects of the field.

Continued Research and Exposition of Bayesian Logic

Throughout his later career, Savage remained deeply engaged in research and exposition of Bayesian logic, furthering the development and application of Bayesian methods.

Ongoing Research: Savage's research during this period continued to explore and refine Bayesian approaches to statistics. He worked on various aspects of Bayesian theory, including the application of subjective probability to complex decision-making problems and the development of new methods for statistical inference. His research contributed to the ongoing evolution of Bayesian statistics and maintained its relevance in both theoretical and practical contexts.

Exposition and Teaching: Savage was also dedicated to educating and mentoring students and colleagues in Bayesian logic. His teaching and publications during this period emphasized the principles of Bayesian theory and its applications. Savage's ability to clearly articulate and explain Bayesian concepts helped to promote their understanding and adoption among statisticians and researchers.

Influence and Legacy: Savage's later career was marked by continued influence in the field of statistics. His work at both the University of Michigan and Yale, along with his ongoing research and teaching, contributed to the enduring impact of Bayesian methods. Savage's legacy is reflected in the widespread use of Bayesian approaches in statistical analysis and decision-making, as well as in the continued respect and recognition he received from the academic community.

In summary, Jimmie Savage's later academic career was distinguished by his professorships at the University of Michigan and Yale, where he continued to advance Bayesian logic and statistical theory. His ongoing research, teaching, and exposition of Bayesian concepts reinforced his influence in the field and contributed to the broader acceptance and application of Bayesian methods. Savage's legacy as a leading figure in statistics is evident in the continued relevance and impact of his work.

Enduring Impact on Statistics

Jimmie Savage's contributions have had a profound and lasting impact on the field of statistics, particularly in shaping modern Bayesian practices and integrating subjectivism into statistical thinking.

Advancement of Bayesian Methods: Savage's advocacy for Bayesian approaches transformed how statisticians and researchers approach data analysis and decision-making. By emphasizing subjective probability and Bayesian decision theory, he introduced a framework that integrates prior beliefs with observed data to make informed decisions under uncertainty. His work laid the foundation for many contemporary Bayesian practices, including the use of prior distributions and updating them with new evidence.

Influence on Computational Techniques: Savage's contributions extended to the development of computational techniques for Bayesian statistics. His work in formalizing Bayesian decision theory and subjective probability provided a theoretical basis for computational methods such as Markov Chain Monte Carlo (MCMC) and other algorithms used in Bayesian inference. These techniques have become essential tools in modern statistics, enabling complex Bayesian models to be implemented and analyzed efficiently.

Educational Impact: Through his teaching and influential textbooks, Savage educated a generation of statisticians about Bayesian methods. His clear exposition of Bayesian principles helped to establish them as fundamental components of statistical practice, shaping how Bayesian statistics is taught and applied in various fields.

Embedded Subjectivism into Statistical Thinking

Personalistic Probability: Savage's emphasis on personalistic probability introduced a paradigm shift in how probability is understood and applied. By framing probability as a measure of personal belief, he challenged the traditional frequency-based interpretations and encouraged statisticians to consider subjective judgments in their analyses. This approach has become a core aspect of Bayesian statistics, influencing how uncertainty and risk are assessed in various contexts.

Integration into Decision Theory: Savage's work in Bayesian decision theory has embedded subjectivism into the broader field of decision theory. His development of expected utility theory and the application of subjective probabilities to decision-making problems provided a framework for understanding how individuals make rational choices under uncertainty. This integration has had lasting implications for fields such as economics, finance, and policy analysis, where decision-making often involves subjective assessments of risk and uncertainty.

Legacy in Applied Statistics: The principles championed by Savage have permeated various applied fields, including medicine, engineering, and social sciences.

Bayesian methods, driven by his ideas on subjective probability, are now widely used for making predictions, estimating parameters, and guiding decisions in complex and uncertain environments. Savage's impact is evident in the continued growth and application of Bayesian approaches across diverse disciplines.

In summary, Jimmie Savage's enduring impact on statistics is reflected in his role in shaping modern Bayesian practices and embedding subjectivism into statistical thinking. His contributions have influenced both the theoretical development and practical application of Bayesian methods, leaving a lasting legacy in the field of statistics and beyond.

Oscar Kempthorne and Experimental Design

Early Life and Education

Oscar Kempthorne was born in Christchurch, New Zealand, in 1919. Growing up in this city, he was exposed to a rich academic environment that nurtured his early interests in mathematics and science. His formative years in Christchurch provided a solid foundation for his future academic pursuits. He enrolled at the University of Canterbury, where he

pursued studies in mathematics and statistics. Kempthorne's academic prowess was evident early on, and his keen interest in statistical theory and its applications guided his educational trajectory.

After completing his undergraduate studies, Kempthorne continued his academic journey at the University of Canterbury. His commitment to the field of statistics was demonstrated through his doctoral research, which culminated in his PhD in 1945. His dissertation, focused on statistical methods and experimental design, set the stage for his future contributions to the field. This period of intense study and research not only honed his technical skills but also sparked his lifelong passion for improving and developing statistical methodologies.

Kempthorne's educational background provided him with a strong theoretical foundation in mathematics and statistics. His work during this period laid the groundwork for his subsequent contributions to experimental design and statistical theory, marking the beginning of a distinguished career that would significantly impact the field of statistics.

Contributions to Experimental Design

Oscar Kempthorne made groundbreaking contributions to the theory and practice of experimental design, significantly shaping the field and influencing modern statistical methodology.

Kempthorne's work revolutionized experimental design by refining and expanding the methods used to design and analyze experiments. His approach emphasized the importance of rigorous statistical techniques to ensure the reliability and validity of experimental results. His contributions were instrumental in providing a structured framework for researchers to follow, leading to more accurate and interpretable findings.

In 1952, Kempthorne published the seminal book, *The Design and Analysis of Experiments*, which quickly became a cornerstone reference in the field of experimental design. This book introduced a comprehensive methodology for designing experiments and analyzing data, covering various design principles and statistical techniques. The work offered practical guidance for implementing experimental designs and has been widely cited and used in both academic and applied research settings.

Kempthorne played a pivotal role in the development and formalization of the ANOVA, a statistical technique used to assess the differences among group means in an experiment. ANOVA is crucial for determining whether observed differences in experimental outcomes are statistically significant, making it an essential tool in experimental research. Kempthorne's contributions helped establish ANOVA as a foundational method in statistical analysis, widely adopted across various scientific disciplines.

Kempthorne was a key proponent of randomization as a fundamental principle in experimental design. Randomization involves the random assignment of treatments or conditions to experimental units, which helps eliminate bias and ensures that the results are representative of the true effects of the treatments. By incorporating randomization into experimental design, Kempthorne advanced the reliability and validity of experimental outcomes, setting a standard for future research practices.

Kempthorne's work on factorial designs and fractional factorial designs introduced efficient methods for conducting experiments involving multiple factors. Factorial designs allow researchers to study the effects of several factors simultaneously, while fractional factorial designs enable experimentation with fewer trials by examining only a subset of possible combinations. These designs are highly effective in understanding complex interactions between factors and optimizing experimental resources.

Kempthorne also contributed to the development of response surface methodology (RSM), a statistical technique used to model and analyze the relationships between input variables and response variables in industrial experimentation. RSM helps in optimizing processes and improving product quality by identifying the optimal levels of input variables. Kempthorne's advancements in RSM have been widely adopted in industrial and scientific research, facilitating more efficient and effective experimentation.

Integration of Statistical Methods with Subject-Matter Knowledge

One of Kempthorne's notable contributions was advocating for the integration of statistical methods with subject-matter knowledge in the design and analysis of experiments. He emphasized that effective experimental design requires collaboration between statisticians and subject-matter experts to ensure that the experiments address relevant research questions and yield meaningful results. This interdisciplinary approach has been influential in improving the applicability and impact of experimental research across various fields.

Other Achievements

Academic Positions at Iowa State University and the University of North Carolina: Oscar Kempthorne held prominent academic positions at two leading institutions: Iowa State University and the University of North Carolina. At Iowa State University, he was instrumental in shaping the department of statistics and experimental design, fostering an environment of innovation and research excellence. His tenure at the University of North Carolina further solidified his reputation as a leading figure in experimental design, where he continued to advance the field through teaching, research, and collaboration.

President of the ASA: In 1965, Kempthorne was honored with the presidency of the ASA, a testament to his significant contributions and leadership within the statistical community. The ASA presidency is one of the highest accolades in the field, recognizing individuals who have made outstanding contributions to the development and application of statistical methods. Kempthorne's term as president underscored his influence and dedication to advancing statistical practice and promoting the discipline.

Awards and Honors: Kempthorne received numerous awards and honors throughout his career, reflecting his exceptional contributions to experimental design and statistics. Among these, the prestigious Samuel S. Wilks Memorial Medal stands out. This medal, awarded by the ASA, is given to individuals who have made outstanding contributions to statistical theory and practice. Receiving this honor was a testament to Kempthorne's lasting impact and excellence in his field.

Mentorship and Influence: Beyond his formal achievements, Kempthorne's influence extended through his role as a mentor to many students and junior researchers. His guidance and support helped shape the careers of numerous individuals who went on to become prominent leaders in the field of experimental design. Kempthorne's mentorship was characterized by a commitment to nurturing talent and fostering intellectual curiosity, leaving a lasting legacy through the success of his protégés. His impact on the next generation of statisticians and researchers is a testament to his dedication to the advancement of the field.

Legacy and Impact

Oscar Kempthorne is widely regarded as one of the most influential figures in the development of modern experimental design. His contributions laid the foundation for many of the core principles and methodologies used in experimental research today. Through his innovative approaches and rigorous analytical techniques, Kempthorne helped to transform experimental design from a specialized practice into a central component of statistical methodology.

Kempthorne's work on ANOVA, randomization, and factorial designs has become foundational in the field of experimental design. The development and refinement of ANOVA provided researchers with a powerful tool for analyzing the effects of different factors on experimental outcomes, allowing for more robust and reliable conclusions. His emphasis on randomization as a fundamental principle ensured that experimental results were unbiased and that statistical analyses were valid. Additionally, his pioneering work on factorial designs and fractional factorial designs allowed for more efficient experimentation, enabling researchers to investigate multiple factors simultaneously while minimizing experimental resources.

The "Kempthorne model" for the ANOVA is widely used in experimental studies and has become a standard reference in the field. This model, developed by Kempthorne, addresses various complexities in experimental design and provides a structured framework for analyzing data. Its application has been instrumental in advancing the understanding of experimental results and ensuring the accuracy of statistical inferences.

Kempthorne's book, *The Design and Analysis of Experiments*, published in 1952, has been a seminal text for generations of students and researchers. The book is renowned for its comprehensive coverage of experimental design principles, its clear exposition of complex concepts, and its practical approach to statistical analysis. It has served as a foundational resource in the field, shaping the education and training of many statisticians and researchers.

Kempthorne played a crucial role in establishing experimental design as a core component of statistical methodology. His work emphasized the importance of rigorous design and analysis in scientific research and industry applications, leading to widespread adoption and integration of experimental design principles. The methodologies he developed continue to be applied across various scientific and industrial domains, reflecting his lasting impact on the field and the continued relevance of his contributions.

Oscar Kempthorne's pioneering contributions to the theory and practice of experimental design have had a lasting impact on the field of statistics and its applications in scientific and engineering research.

George Box and Time Series Analysis

Early Life and Education

George Box's journey into the world of statistics began with his education in mathematics and statistics at the London School of Economics (LSE). Born in 1919, Box's early academic interests were deeply rooted in mathematics, which naturally extended into the field of statistics. His time at LSE provided him with a solid foundation in these disciplines, setting the stage for his future contributions.

Box's academic path was marked by a dedication to understanding and applying statistical methods. His education at LSE was complemented by practical experiences that would later inform his theoretical work. As he progressed through his career, Box's work demonstrated a remarkable ability to bridge the gap between theoretical statistics and practical application, a characteristic that would become a hallmark of his contributions to time series analysis.

Significant Career Spanning Academia and Industry

George Box's career is a testament to his profound influence on both academia and industry. After completing his education, Box embarked on a career that would see him make substantial contributions to the field of statistics, particularly in time series analysis, experimental design, and quality control.

Innovative Theoretical Work: Box's academic career was characterized by his pioneering work in time series analysis. His research led to the development of foundational models and methodologies that are still widely used today. His work on the Box-Jenkins models for time series forecasting remains a cornerstone in the field.

Influential Textbooks: Box co-authored several influential textbooks, including *Time Series Analysis: Forecasting and Control* with Gwilym Jenkins and *Statistical Methods for Research Workers* with William S. Gosset. These texts have been instrumental in shaping the study and application of statistical methods in various fields.

Quality Control and Industrial Applications: Box's work extended beyond academia into practical applications, particularly in the realm of industrial quality control. His contributions to the development of methods for improving manufacturing processes and experimental design had a significant impact on industry practices.

Consulting and Practical Expertise: Box's expertise in statistics was sought after by various industries, and he worked as a consultant to help organizations apply statistical methods to solve real-world problems. His ability to translate complex statistical concepts into practical solutions was highly valued in both academic and industrial settings.

Throughout his career, George Box demonstrated a unique ability to integrate theoretical advancements with practical applications, making significant contributions to the field of time series analysis and beyond. His work continues to influence contemporary statistical practices, and his legacy endures through the models and methods he developed.

Foundations of Time Series Analysis and Forecasting

George Box's foundational contributions to time series analysis and forecasting have had a lasting impact on the field, shaping how data are analyzed and interpreted in various applications.

In the realm of time series analysis, Box is perhaps best known for his work on auto-regressive integrated moving average (ARIMA) models. These models are essential for understanding and forecasting time series data, which often exhibit patterns such as trends and seasonal variations.

ARIMA Models: Box's work with ARIMA models involves defining a class of models that can be used to describe a wide range of time series data. ARIMA models combine autoregressive (AR) components, which express the current value of the series as a function of its previous values, with moving average (MA) components, which account for the relationship between past forecast errors and the current value. The integrated (I) component is used to make the time series stationary by differencing, which helps in stabilizing the mean of the series.

Estimator Constructions: One of the key contributions of Box's work is the development of methods for estimating the parameters of ARIMA models. These estimators are crucial for accurately fitting the model to the data and for making reliable forecasts. Box's approach to parameter estimation emphasizes the use of likelihood-based methods and has been widely adopted in statistical practice.

Seminal 1976 Textbook with Co-Author

In 1976, George Box, along with co-author Gwilym Jenkins, published the seminal textbook *Time Series Analysis: Forecasting and Control.* This book is considered a cornerstone in the field of time series analysis for several reasons:

Comprehensive Coverage: The textbook provides a thorough introduction to time series analysis, including the theoretical underpinnings of ARIMA models, practical applications, and detailed examples. It covers both the theoretical aspects of model construction and the practical techniques for forecasting and control.

Influence on the Field: The publication of this book marked a significant moment in the field of statistics. It provided a unified framework for understanding and applying time series models, and its influence extended beyond academia into various industries that rely on time series forecasting for decision-making.

Practical Applications: The book emphasizes the practical application of time series models to real-world problems, making it a valuable resource for practitioners as well as researchers. It includes numerous case studies and examples that demonstrate the use of ARIMA models in various contexts, from economics to engineering.

Through his work on ARIMA models and his influential textbook, George Box established a solid foundation for the study and application of time series analysis. His contributions have enabled statisticians and data analysts to develop more accurate models and forecasts, and his methodologies continue to be widely used in contemporary statistical practice.

Development of Box-Jenkins Methodology

George Box, along with his collaborator Gwilym Jenkins, developed the Box-Jenkins methodology, which has become a fundamental approach in time series analysis. This methodology provides a structured framework for building, estimating, and diagnosing time series models, making it a widely adopted tool across various fields.

The Box-Jenkins methodology is characterized by its iterative approach to model development, which involves several key stages:

Model Identification: The first step in the Box-Jenkins methodology is to identify a suitable model for the time series data. This involves examining the data to understand its underlying patterns and selecting a model that can adequately represent these patterns. Techniques such as autocorrelation function (ACF) and partial autocorrelation function (PACF) plots are used to determine the appropriate order of the ARIMA components.

Model Estimation: Once a model has been identified, the next step is to estimate its parameters. This process involves fitting the chosen model to the data using methods such as MLE. The goal is to find the parameter values that best describe the observed data and improve the model's accuracy.

Model Diagnosis: After estimating the parameters, it is crucial to assess the model's fit and validity. Model diagnostics involve checking for residuals (the differences between observed and predicted values) to ensure that they are randomly distributed and not correlated. Techniques such as residual plots and statistical tests are used to evaluate the adequacy of the model and to identify any potential issues.

The iterative nature of the Box-Jenkins methodology means that these steps are often revisited multiple times. If the model does not adequately fit the data, adjustments are made based on diagnostic results, and the process is repeated until a satisfactory model is achieved.

Practical Framework Widely Adopted Across Fields

The Box-Jenkins methodology has had a profound impact on time series analysis, with its practical framework being widely adopted across various fields:

Economics and Finance: In economics and finance, the Box-Jenkins methodology is used for forecasting economic indicators, stock prices, and other financial variables. Its ability to model complex patterns and trends makes it a valuable tool for economic analysis and decision-making.

Engineering and Manufacturing: Engineers and manufacturers use the Box-Jenkins approach to monitor and control processes, improve quality, and predict system behavior. The methodology helps in analyzing time series data from production processes, leading to more effective process control and optimization.

Environmental and Social Sciences: Researchers in environmental and social sciences apply the Box-Jenkins methodology to analyze and forecast data related to climate patterns, population trends, and other phenomena. The framework provides a structured approach to understanding and predicting complex time series data.

Through its systematic and iterative approach, the Box-Jenkins methodology has established itself as a powerful tool for time series analysis. Its practical framework continues to be widely used, enabling analysts and researchers to develop accurate models and forecasts across a diverse range of applications.

Contributions to DoEs

George Box's contributions to the DoE have significantly influenced how experiments are planned and analyzed, particularly through his development of RSM and factorial designs. His work has provided valuable tools for optimizing processes and improving the quality of scientific and industrial research.

RSM: Box, in collaboration with his colleagues, developed RSM, a set of statistical techniques used for modeling and analyzing the relationships between a response variable and one or more predictor variables. RSM is particularly useful in optimizing processes and improving quality by exploring the effects of multiple variables and their interactions.

Modeling and Optimization: RSM involves fitting a polynomial model to the response surface, which represents how the response variable changes with the predictor variables. This approach allows for the identification of optimal conditions and the exploration of interactions between variables. It is widely used in experimental settings to understand and optimize complex processes in fields such as manufacturing, engineering, and pharmaceuticals.

Practical Applications: The methodology provides tools for designing experiments that can efficiently explore the effects of multiple factors and their interactions. By using techniques such as central composite designs and Box-

Behnken designs, researchers can create robust experimental plans that lead to improved process understanding and performance.

Factorial Designs: Box's work also includes significant contributions to factorial designs, a class of experimental designs used to study the effects of multiple factors simultaneously. Factorial designs are essential for understanding how different factors and their interactions influence the response variable.

Design Efficiency: Factorial designs involve systematically varying the levels of factors to observe their effects on the response. This approach allows for the estimation of main effects and interactions with fewer experimental runs compared to other design strategies. Box's contributions to factorial designs have helped streamline experimental planning and analysis, making it easier to identify significant factors and optimize processes.

Applications in Science and Industry: Factorial designs are used extensively in scientific research and industrial applications to investigate complex systems and processes. Box's work has helped researchers and practitioners design experiments that provide valuable insights into the relationships between variables and their effects on outcomes.

Data Modeling Philosophy Focusing on Science Applications

George Box's philosophy of data modeling emphasizes the importance of using statistical models to understand and improve scientific and industrial processes. His approach focuses on several key principles:

Model Simplicity and Effectiveness: Box advocated for using the simplest model that adequately represents the data. He believed that complex models are not always necessary and that simpler models can often provide more interpretable and useful results.

Practical Relevance: Box's work emphasizes the importance of applying statistical models to real-world problems. His methodologies are designed to address practical issues in experimental design and data analysis, making them highly relevant for scientific and industrial applications.

Iterative Approach: Similar to his work in time series analysis, Box's approach to experimental design involves an iterative process of model development, testing, and refinement. This iterative approach helps ensure that the models used in experiments are well-suited to the data and provide meaningful insights.

Through his contributions to RSM, factorial designs, and his data modeling philosophy, George Box has greatly enhanced the field of experimental design. His work has provided researchers and practitioners with powerful tools for optimizing processes, understanding complex systems, and improving the quality of scientific and industrial research.

Bayesian and Non-Parametric Approaches

George Box's advocacy for Bayesian and non-parametric methods has had a profound impact on statistical theory and practice, extending far beyond the realm of time series analysis. His work in these areas emphasizes flexibility, robustness, and practical applicability in the face of complex and uncertain data.

Emphasis on Flexibility: Box's support for Bayesian methods highlights their ability to incorporate prior knowledge and update beliefs based on new data. Bayesian statistics offers a flexible framework for modeling and inference, allowing for the integration of prior distributions with observed data to make probabilistic statements about unknown parameters.

Practical Applications: In various fields, including time series analysis, Bayesian methods provide a way to incorporate prior information and update models as new data becomes available. This approach is particularly useful in situations where data are limited or where incorporating expert knowledge can improve model accuracy and decision-making.

Influence on Statistical Practice: Box's work has influenced the adoption of Bayesian methods in areas such as quality control, process optimization, and experimental design. By advocating for Bayesian approaches, he has contributed to a broader acceptance of probabilistic modeling in statistics.

Non-Parametric Methods

Robustness to Assumptions: Non-parametric methods, which do not rely on specific parametric assumptions about the underlying data distribution, have been a key focus of Box's research. These methods are particularly valuable in situations where parametric models may be too restrictive or where the data do not conform to standard distributions.

Applications and Techniques: Box's advocacy for non-parametric approaches includes techniques such as kernel density estimation and empirical distribution functions. These methods provide ways to estimate distributions and make inferences without assuming a particular parametric form, making them useful in a wide range of applications.

Impact on Data Analysis: Non-parametric methods offer greater flexibility and robustness in statistical analysis, allowing for more accurate modeling and inference in complex or non-standard data settings. Box's work in this area has influenced the development and application of these methods in various scientific and industrial contexts.

Influence Beyond Time Series

Cross-Disciplinary Impact: Box's contributions to Bayesian and non-parametric methods have extended beyond time series analysis to influence other areas of statistics and data science. His emphasis on robustness and flexibility has helped shape the development of methods that are applicable to a wide range of problems, including those involving complex or non-traditional data structures.

Integration into Modern Practice: The principles and techniques advocated by Box continue to be integrated into modern statistical practice, influencing fields such as ML, bioinformatics, and econometrics. His work has paved the way for a more nuanced understanding of data and has contributed to the advancement of methods that address real-world complexities.

Through his advocacy for Bayesian and non-parametric approaches, George Box has significantly impacted the field of statistics, providing tools and methodologies that enhance flexibility and robustness in data analysis. His contributions have extended beyond time series analysis to influence a wide range of applications, shaping modern statistical practice and contributing to the development of methods that address complex and uncertain data environments.

Legacy at University of Wisconsin-Madison

George Box's tenure at the University of Wisconsin-Madison was marked by a profound impact on both the institution and the broader field of statistics. His influence extended through his guidance of graduate students, development of research programs, and promotion of practical, discovery-focused statistical work.

Mentorship and Training: At the University of Wisconsin-Madison, Box played a pivotal role in shaping the next generation of statisticians. His mentorship extended to numerous graduate students, many of whom went on to have significant careers in academia, industry, and government. His approach to teaching and advising emphasized critical thinking, practical application, and the importance of robust statistical methods.

Development of Research Skills: Box encouraged his students to engage in innovative research that combined theoretical rigor with practical relevance. This focus on applied research helped to prepare students for careers where they could tackle real-world problems using sophisticated statistical techniques.

Global Influence: The impact of his mentorship was not confined to Wisconsin or even the United States. Many of his students and collaborators have gone on to contribute to statistical science globally, spreading the principles and methodologies championed by Box.

Promoting Practical, Discovery-Focused Statistical Work

Applied Research Emphasis: Box's work at Wisconsin-Madison was characterized by a strong emphasis on applying statistical methods to solve practical problems. He advocated for research that was not only theoretically sound but also relevant to real-world applications, ensuring that statistical techniques could be used effectively in various fields, from engineering to economics.

Innovation and Discovery: Box fostered an environment where statistical innovation was encouraged. His research and teaching often emphasized the importance of discovery and experimentation in statistical practice. This approach helped to advance the field and led to the development of new methods and techniques that have had a lasting impact on both theory and application.

Interdisciplinary Collaboration: Under Box's influence, the University of Wisconsin-Madison became a hub for interdisciplinary collaboration. His work often bridged the gap between statistics and other fields, promoting a collaborative approach that integrated statistical methods with practical problems in diverse areas such as biology, social sciences, and industry.

Enduring Impact

Institutional Legacy: Box's legacy at the University of Wisconsin-Madison is reflected in the continued prominence of its statistics department and its emphasis on practical, applied research. His contributions have helped to establish the university as a leading center for statistical research and education.

Ongoing Influence: The principles and methodologies promoted by Box continue to shape the research conducted at Wisconsin-Madison and beyond. His emphasis on practical application, robust methods, and discovery-focused research has left an enduring mark on the field of statistics and its application to real-world problems.

In summary, George Box's legacy at the University of Wisconsin-Madison is marked by his influential mentorship, commitment to practical and applied statistical research, and the promotion of a discovery-focused approach to statistical science. His impact on the institution and the field of statistics continues to be felt through the achievements of his students, the ongoing research at the university, and the broader application of his methodologies.

Profound and Lasting Impact on Statistics

George Box's contributions to statistics have left an indelible mark on the field, particularly through his work in time series analysis and his broader influence on statistical methodologies. His pioneering efforts have shaped modern statistical practice and earned him recognition as one of the 20th century's most influential statisticians.

ARIMA Models and Methodologies: Box's work on time series analysis, particularly through the development of ARIMA models, has fundamentally transformed how statisticians approach forecasting and data analysis. His seminal textbook, co-authored with Gwilym Jenkins in 1976, provided a comprehensive framework for understanding and applying these models. This work introduced a systematic approach to model identification, estimation, and diagnostic checking, which has become a cornerstone of time series analysis.

Box-Jenkins Methodology: The iterative process of model identification, estimation, and diagnostics, known as the Box-Jenkins methodology, has become a standard practice in the field. This approach has enabled researchers to handle complex time series data more effectively, leading to more accurate forecasts and insights across a range of disciplines.

Influence on Practice: Box's methodologies have been widely adopted in various fields including economics, engineering, and environmental science. The practical impact of his work is evident in the improved accuracy and reliability of time series forecasts and analyses.

Broadening Methodological Horizons

DoEs: Beyond time series analysis, Box made significant contributions to the DoEs. His work in RSM and factorial designs has provided a robust framework for optimizing experimental processes and understanding complex systems.

Innovative Approaches: Box's emphasis on practical applications and robust statistical methods has broadened the methodological horizons of statistics. His work encouraged a focus on real-world problem-solving and the integration of statistical theory with practical applications.

Bayesian and Non-Parametric Methods: Box was also an advocate for Bayesian and non-parametric approaches, which emphasized robust methods that do not rely on strict assumptions. His advocacy helped to expand the toolkit available to statisticians, allowing for more flexible and adaptable approaches to data analysis.

Recognition as a Statistical Pioneer

Influential Textbooks and Research: Box's textbooks and research have been instrumental in shaping modern statistical practice. His influence extends through his seminal works and the methodologies he developed, which continue to be widely used and cited.

Awards and Honors: Box's contributions to the field have been recognized through numerous awards and honors. He is celebrated for his innovative work and lasting impact on both theoretical and applied statistics.

In summary, George Box's profound impact on statistics is evident through his transformative work in time series analysis, his broadening of methodological horizons, and his recognition as a leading figure in the field. His innovative approaches and contributions have shaped modern statistical practice, ensuring his legacy as one of the most influential statisticians of the 20th century.

C. R. Rao and International Contributions

Early Life and Education in India

C. R. Rao's foundational years in India were marked by his academic excellence and early immersion in mathematics and statistics, setting the stage for his future contributions to the field.

Academic Beginnings: C. R. Rao's journey began at the University of Madras, where he pursued undergraduate studies in mathematics.

The University of Madras provided a strong foundation in mathematical principles, nurturing his analytical skills and interest in quantitative methods. This early education in mathematics was instrumental in shaping his future career in statistics.

Focus on Statistics: During his time at the University of Madras, Rao developed a keen interest in statistics, an emerging field with growing importance. His studies in statistics laid the groundwork for his later innovations and research. The combination of rigorous mathematical training and exposure to statistical concepts prepared Rao for his advanced studies and subsequent contributions to the field.

Received PhD from Cambridge University

PhD Studies at Cambridge: C. R. Rao continued his academic journey at Cambridge University, where he pursued a PhD in statistics. Under the guidance of prominent statisticians, Rao conducted research that would later become foundational to the field. His time at Cambridge allowed him to delve deeply into statistical theory and methods, contributing to his development as a leading figure in statistics.

Influential Research: Rao's PhD research at Cambridge was marked by significant contributions to statistical theory. His work included advancements in estimation theory and the development of what is now known as the Rao-Blackwell theorem. This research established him as a leading statistician and set the stage for his future achievements in the field.

In summary, C. R. Rao's early life and education in India, marked by his studies at the University of Madras and his PhD from Cambridge University, provided him with a strong foundation in mathematics and statistics. These formative years were crucial in shaping his future contributions to the field and establishing him as a prominent international statistician.

Career at Indian Statistical Institute (ISI)

C. R. Rao's tenure at the ISI was pivotal in shaping the institute into a premier center for statistical research and education. His work there not only advanced the field of statistics but also fostered a vibrant academic community.

Foundational Role: C. R. Rao joined the ISI in 1956, a period when the institute was still establishing itself as a key player in the field of statistics. His arrival marked a significant turning point for ISI, as he played a crucial role in developing its infrastructure and academic programs. Rao's expertise and vision were instrumental in transforming ISI into a leading institution for statistical research and education.

Research and Development: Under Rao's guidance, ISI expanded its research capabilities and became a hub for statistical innovation. Rao's contributions included developing new statistical methods and theories that advanced the field on an international scale. His work helped to position ISI as a global leader in statistical research, attracting scholars and researchers from around the world.

Developed Influential Faculty and Scholarship Programs

Faculty Development: C. R. Rao was deeply involved in nurturing talent and building a strong faculty at ISI. He attracted and mentored leading statisticians, creating a vibrant academic environment that encouraged research and collaboration. His efforts in faculty development ensured that ISI had a team of skilled researchers and educators who could contribute to and expand the institute's reputation.

Scholarship Programs: Rao also focused on establishing scholarship programs and research initiatives to support emerging statisticians and researchers. These programs were designed to provide financial support and research opportunities for students and scholars, helping to cultivate the next generation of statistical experts. By investing in these programs, Rao helped to sustain ISI's growth and maintain its status as a premier institution.

In summary, C. R. Rao's career at the ISI was marked by his significant contributions to establishing the institute as a leading center for statistical research and education. His efforts in developing influential faculty and scholarship programs were crucial in shaping ISI's reputation and impact on the global statistical community.

Major Methodological Contributions

C. R. Rao's contributions to statistical theory have had a profound impact on the field, particularly through his work on the information matrix inequality, minimum variance bounds, and the Rao-Blackwell theorem. These innovations have become fundamental to statistical inference and estimation.

Information Matrix Inequality: One of Rao's seminal contributions is the development of the information matrix inequality, which provides a lower bound on the variance of an unbiased estimator. This inequality establishes that the variance of an unbiased estimator cannot be smaller than the inverse of the Fisher information matrix. Rao's work in this area formalized the concept of information in statistical estimation and laid the groundwork for understanding the limits of estimator efficiency.

Minimum Variance Bounds: Building on the information matrix inequality, Rao also contributed to the concept of minimum variance bounds. He developed methods to determine the best possible bounds for the variance of unbiased estimators, often referred to as Rao-Cramer bounds or Rao-Blackwell bounds in certain contexts. These bounds are critical for evaluating the efficiency of statistical estimators and ensuring that they are as precise as possible given the available data.

Rao-Blackwell Theorem and Sufficiency Fundamentals

Rao-Blackwell Theorem: Alongside his collaborator David Blackwell, Rao developed the Rao-Blackwell theorem, a fundamental result in statistical estimation. This theorem provides a method for improving an estimator by conditioning it on a sufficient statistic. The Rao-Blackwell theorem states that if you start with an unbiased estimator and improve it by conditioning on a sufficient statistic, the resulting estimator will have a variance that is at least as small as the original estimator. This theorem is central to the concept of sufficiency and has far-reaching implications for constructing efficient estimators.

Sufficiency Fundamentals: Rao's work on the concept of sufficiency has been instrumental in advancing the understanding of statistical inference. The concept of a sufficient statistic refers to a statistic that captures all the information needed about a parameter from the sample data. Rao's contributions to this area have helped establish the foundational principles of sufficiency, including methods for identifying sufficient statistics and understanding their role in statistical inference.

In summary, C. R. Rao's major methodological contributions, including the information matrix inequality, minimum variance bounds, and the Rao-Blackwell theorem, have had a lasting impact on statistical theory. His work has provided critical insights into the efficiency of estimators and the principles of sufficiency, shaping modern statistical practice and theory.

Work on Multivariate Analysis

C. R. Rao's contributions to multivariate analysis have been foundational in shaping the field and providing essential tools for understanding complex data structures. His work laid the groundwork for many techniques and theories that are widely used in multivariate statistics today.

Theoretical Foundations: Rao made significant strides in establishing the theoretical foundations of multivariate statistics. His research addressed the challenges of analyzing data with multiple variables, where traditional univariate methods fall short. He developed methods for estimating and interpreting multivariate distributions, which are crucial for understanding the relationships between several variables simultaneously. Rao's work provided a rigorous mathematical framework for multivariate analysis, making it a vital component of statistical theory.

Estimation Techniques: Rao contributed to the development of estimation techniques specifically tailored for multivariate data. His work included methods for estimating covariance matrices, understanding the distribution of multivariate data, and constructing statistical models that account for multiple interrelated variables. These techniques are fundamental for multivariate data analysis, allowing statisticians to extract meaningful insights from complex datasets.

Textbook A Statistical Paradigm Highly Influential

Publication and Impact: Rao's textbook, A Statistical Paradigm, published in 1987, is a highly influential work in the field of statistics. This comprehensive text provides an in-depth exploration of statistical theories and methods, with a focus on multivariate analysis. It covers a wide range of topics, including estimation, hypothesis testing, and multivariate distributions, presenting them within a coherent framework that integrates theory and application.

Educational Significance: The textbook has been widely adopted in both undergraduate and graduate courses, serving as a key resource for students and researchers alike. Its clear explanations and thorough coverage of multivariate analysis have made it an essential reference for understanding and applying statistical methods. The impact of A Statistical Paradigm extends beyond academia, influencing practitioners and statisticians working in various fields that require multivariate data analysis.

In summary, C. R. Rao's work on multivariate analysis has been instrumental in developing the theoretical and practical aspects of the field. His foundational contributions to multivariate statistics and the influential textbook A Statistical Paradigm have played a crucial role in advancing the understanding and application of multivariate methods in statistical analysis.

International Recognition and Collaboration

C. R. Rao's career was marked by international recognition and extensive collaboration, reflecting his influence and contributions to the field of statistics on a global scale. His work was widely acknowledged, and he played a key role in mentoring and shaping the next generation of statisticians.

Global Academic Positions: Throughout his career, C. R. Rao held prestigious positions at several leading universities around the world. His academic appointments included roles at institutions such as the University of Pittsburgh, Stanford University, and the University of California, Berkeley. These positions not only recognized his expertise and contributions to the field but also allowed him to influence statistical research and education on an international level.

Leadership Roles: In addition to his academic positions, Rao served in leadership roles at various statistical and mathematical societies. His involvement with organizations such as the International Statistical Institute and the IMS further underscored his global impact. These roles enabled him to contribute to the advancement of statistical science through collaboration and international dialogue.

Mentoring Next Generations of Statisticians Globally

Guidance and Influence: C. R. Rao was a dedicated mentor to many statisticians throughout his career. His guidance helped shape the careers of numerous scholars and researchers, who have gone on to make significant contributions to the field. Rao's mentorship extended beyond his direct students, influencing the broader statistical community through his collaborative work and professional relationships.

Educational Contributions: Rao's impact on education was profound. His teaching and mentoring at various institutions influenced countless students and early-career researchers. His emphasis on rigorous statistical methods and innovative research approaches inspired many to pursue careers in statistics and contribute to the field's development. His textbooks and scholarly publications also served as important resources for students and researchers worldwide.

In summary, C. R. Rao's international recognition and collaboration were key aspects of his career, reflecting his significant contributions to statistics and his influence on the global academic community. His appointments at top universities and his dedication to mentoring the next generation of statisticians highlight his enduring impact on the field and his commitment to advancing statistical science worldwide.

Promoting the Field in India and Developing World

C. R. Rao's efforts to promote the field of statistics extended significantly beyond his academic contributions, focusing on addressing broader issues in India and the developing world. His advocacy and initiatives were instrumental in advancing the application and development of statistics in these regions.

Focus on Population and Development: Rao was a strong advocate for using statistical methods to address pressing issues related to population growth and economic development. In India and other developing countries, where resource allocation and policy planning are critical, Rao emphasized the importance of statistical analysis in making informed decisions. His work aimed to apply statistical techniques to solve real-world problems, such as optimizing resource distribution, improving public health, and supporting economic development initiatives.

Influence on Policy and Planning: Rao's advocacy extended to influencing policy and planning efforts. By demonstrating the value of statistical analysis in addressing complex challenges, he helped policymakers and development professionals understand how data-driven insights could lead to better outcomes. His contributions were crucial in promoting evidence-based approaches to policy and planning in developing countries.

Statistical Training Adapted for Varied Contexts

Customized Training Programs: Recognizing the diverse needs and contexts of developing countries, Rao worked to adapt statistical training programs to local conditions. His approach involved tailoring educational programs to address specific challenges faced by these regions. This included designing training materials and courses that were relevant to local data needs and practical applications.

Capacity Building: Rao's efforts in statistical training also focused on building local capacity by training statisticians and researchers in developing countries. This involved not only providing formal education but also fostering collaborations and providing support to local institutions. His initiatives helped establish a network of skilled statisticians who could apply statistical methods effectively in their own countries.

In summary, C. R. Rao's promotion of the field in India and the developing world was marked by his advocacy for using statistics to address population and economic issues and his efforts to adapt statistical training to diverse contexts. His work had a significant impact on improving the application of statistical methods in these regions and advancing development through data-driven insights.

Lasting Global Impact and Recognition

C. R. Rao's contributions to statistics have been recognized globally, highlighting his profound impact on the field and his lasting legacy. His innovative work and dedication have earned him prestigious awards and widespread acclaim.

National Medal of Science: In recognition of his extraordinary contributions to the field of statistics, C. R. Rao was awarded the US National Medal of Science in 2002. This prestigious honor is one of the highest accolades given to individuals who have made significant contributions to science and engineering. The award underscored Rao's exceptional achievements and his influence on the advancement of statistical science.

Other Honors: Rao's contributions have been acknowledged through numerous other awards and honors throughout his career. These include fellowships in major scientific societies and awards from statistical and mathematical organizations. His recognition by these institutions reflects the broad impact of his work and his standing as a leading figure in the global scientific community.

Called "Patriarch of Multivariate Analysis"

Title of Patriarch: C. R. Rao is often referred to as the "patriarch of multivariate analysis," a testament to his pioneering work in the field. This title acknowledges his foundational contributions to the development of multivariate statistical methods and his role in shaping the discipline. His innovations in multivariate analysis have been instrumental in advancing the field and establishing methodologies that are now standard practice in statistical research.

Enduring Legacy: Rao's influence extends beyond his direct contributions to statistical theory and methodology. His work has had a lasting impact on how statisticians approach complex data analysis and has set high standards for statistical research and education. The recognition of Rao as a leading figure in multivariate analysis reflects his enduring legacy and the widespread appreciation of his contributions to the field.

In summary, C. R. Rao's global impact and recognition are highlighted by prestigious awards such as the US National Medal of Science and his esteemed title as the "patriarch of multivariate analysis." His contributions have left an indelible mark on the field of statistics, ensuring that his legacy continues to influence and inspire statisticians and researchers worldwide.

Myron Tribus and Decision Science

Early Life and Education

Myron Tribus's journey into the field of decision science was shaped by his diverse educational background and early experiences. He pursued studies in both engineering and business, which laid the foundation for his later work in applying scientific principles to management and decision-making.

Engineering at MIT: Tribus began his academic career at the Massachusetts Institute of Technology (MIT), where he studied engineering. MIT's rigorous engineering program provided him with a strong analytical and quantitative background, which would later influence his approach to decision science. His time at MIT instilled in him a deep appreciation for systematic thinking and problem-solving, key aspects of engineering that he would carry into his future work.

Business at Harvard: Following his engineering studies, Tribus continued his education at Harvard University, where he focused on business. Harvard's business program equipped him with insights into management and organizational dynamics. This combination of technical and business education allowed Tribus to bridge the gap between engineering principles and practical business applications, a fusion that would become central to his contributions in decision science.

Interest in Applying Science Principles to Management: Tribus's unique blend of engineering and business education fueled his interest in applying scientific principles to management and decision-making. He sought to bring a systematic, quantitative approach to understanding and improving managerial processes, emphasizing the importance of data, statistical analysis, and scientific methodology in making informed decisions.

In summary, Myron Tribus's early education at MIT and Harvard provided him with a solid foundation in both engineering and business. His interest in applying scientific principles to management led him to explore how systematic approaches could enhance decision-making and organizational effectiveness, setting the stage for his influential work in decision science.

Rational Decision Modeling

Myron Tribus made significant contributions to the field of decision science through his work on rational decision modeling. His approach emphasized the application of scientific principles and statistical methods to improve decision-making processes, particularly in real-world scenarios.

Bayesian Framework: Tribus championed the use of Bayesian statistics as a foundation for normative decision rules. Bayesian methods provide a framework for updating probabilities and making decisions based on prior knowledge and new evidence. This approach allows for a systematic and flexible way to incorporate uncertainty and adjust decisions as more information becomes available.

Rational Decision-Making: In the context of rational decision modeling, Tribus advocated for using Bayesian principles to establish normative rules that guide decision-making. These rules are designed to reflect rational behavior, where decisions are made to maximize expected utility based on available information. By applying Bayesian methods, decision-makers can derive optimal strategies and make more informed choices that align with their goals and preferences.

Diagnosing and Improving Real-World Choices

Application to Real-World Problems: Tribus's work extended beyond theoretical modeling to address practical decision-making challenges. He applied rational decision modeling to real-world problems, such as managerial decisions, policy formulation, and resource allocation. By using Bayesian methods and other scientific principles, he sought to diagnose decision-making issues and identify ways to enhance the quality of choices in various domains.

Improvement Strategies: Tribus focused on improving decision-making processes by identifying and addressing common pitfalls and biases. His approach included developing tools and techniques for evaluating and refining decision strategies, ensuring that they are based on sound statistical principles and aligned with rational decision-making criteria. This focus on practical application helped bridge the gap between theory and practice, making rational decision modeling a valuable tool for decision-makers in various fields.

In summary, Myron Tribus's contributions to rational decision modeling involved applying Bayesian statistics to establish normative decision rules and improve real-world decision-making. His work emphasized the importance of systematic, evidence-based approaches to decision-making, helping to enhance the effectiveness and rationality of choices in practical scenarios.

Contributions to Quality Control and Science of Measurement

Myron Tribus's impact on quality control and the science of measurement is notable for its integration of statistical methods and scientific principles to enhance industrial practices and organizational efficiency.

Industrial Quality Control: Tribus applied statistical methods to the field of industrial quality control, focusing on improving the consistency and reliability of manufacturing processes. He emphasized the importance of using statistical techniques to monitor and control production quality, which involves analyzing data to identify variations and ensure that products meet specified standards.

Quality Improvement Methods: His work in quality control included the development and application of methods such as SPC and acceptance sampling. These techniques help businesses detect deviations from quality standards early and implement corrective actions to maintain high levels of product quality. By advocating for a data-driven approach to quality assurance, Tribus contributed to the widespread adoption of statistical tools in industrial settings.

Founding Educational and Organizational Principles

Educational Contributions: Tribus was instrumental in establishing educational frameworks for teaching quality control and measurement science. He developed and promoted educational programs and curricula that incorporated statistical principles and quality management practices. His efforts helped to train a new generation of professionals who could apply these principles in their careers.

Organizational Principles: In addition to educational contributions, Tribus founded and supported organizational principles aimed at improving the effectiveness of quality control systems. His work included promoting the integration of quality management practices into organizational structures and decision-making processes. By emphasizing the importance of a systematic approach to quality control, he helped organizations develop robust frameworks for maintaining and enhancing product quality.

Influence on Standards: Tribus's contributions also extended to influencing industry standards and practices. His work provided a scientific basis for developing standards and guidelines in quality control, helping to shape best practices and ensure that they were grounded in sound statistical principles.

In summary, Myron Tribus's contributions to quality control and the science of measurement were marked by his application of statistical methods to industrial practices and his efforts to establish educational and organizational frameworks. His work significantly advanced the field of quality assurance and helped integrate scientific principles into industrial and organizational settings, leaving a lasting impact on how quality and measurement are approached in practice.

Development of Operations Research

Myron Tribus made significant contributions to the development of operations research, an interdisciplinary field that applies advanced analytical methods to help make better decisions. His work in this area focused on enhancing logistics, optimization, and the integration of diverse perspectives to address complex problems.

Logistics Management: Tribus was a pioneer in applying operations research techniques to logistics and supply chain management. His work involved developing and applying mathematical models to optimize the flow of goods and services, streamline processes, and improve efficiency. By using techniques such as linear programming, queuing theory, and simulation, he helped organizations address logistical challenges and enhance their operational performance.

Optimization Methods: In operations research, optimization is crucial for finding the best solutions to complex problems under constraints. Tribus's contributions included the development and refinement of optimization techniques that could be applied to various domains, from resource allocation to production planning. His work emphasized the importance of using mathematical and statistical methods to identify optimal solutions and make data-driven decisions.

Cross-Fertilization of Perspectives Across Disciplines

Interdisciplinary Approach: Tribus was known for his ability to integrate perspectives from different disciplines to solve complex problems. He encouraged the cross-fertilization of ideas between fields such as engineering, business, mathematics, and economics. This interdisciplinary approach allowed him to develop innovative solutions and methodologies that drew on diverse expertise and insights.

Influence on Management Science: Tribus's work helped bridge the gap between operations research and management science, bringing together theoretical and practical perspectives. His contributions to management science included developing frameworks and techniques for improving organizational decision-making and performance. By combining insights from various disciplines, he advanced the field and provided valuable tools for managers and decision-makers.

Educational and Professional Impact: Tribus also played a role in promoting the integration of operations research into educational programs and professional practice. His efforts included advocating for the inclusion of operations research principles in business and engineering curricula, as well as supporting the development of professional organizations and conferences focused on the field.

In summary, Myron Tribus's development of operations research involved advancing management science techniques for logistics and optimization and fostering interdisciplinary collaboration. His work significantly impacted how complex problems are addressed in various domains, enhancing decision-making processes and operational efficiency through the application of advanced analytical methods.

Establishing Decision Analysis

Myron Tribus played a crucial role in formalizing the field of decision analysis, which focuses on making rational decisions under uncertainty. His contributions laid the groundwork for systematic approaches to decision-making and had a lasting influence on both the theory and practice of the field.

Framework for Decision Analysis: Tribus's work in decision analysis involved creating a structured framework for addressing decisions that involve uncertainty. He applied principles from statistics, probability theory, and operations research to develop methods for evaluating and making choices when outcomes are not deterministic. This formalization provided decision-makers with tools to systematically assess risks, evaluate alternatives, and optimize decisions based on available information.

Quantitative Methods: Tribus advocated for the use of quantitative methods in decision analysis to better understand and manage uncertainty. This approach included the use of decision trees, utility theory, and probabilistic modeling to analyze different decision scenarios and determine the best course of action. By introducing these techniques, he helped establish a rigorous and methodical approach to decision-making that could be applied across various fields, from business to public policy.

Enduring Influence Through Books and Teaching

Influential Publications: Tribus's contributions to decision analysis were widely disseminated through his books and academic papers. His writings provided comprehensive explanations of decision analysis principles and methodologies, making them accessible to both practitioners and scholars. These publications became foundational texts in the field, guiding the development of decision analysis theory and practice.

Teaching and Mentorship: In addition to his written work, Tribus had a significant impact through his teaching and mentorship. He educated and inspired a new generation of decision analysts by sharing his expertise and insights. His courses and lectures helped spread the principles of decision analysis and encouraged students to apply these concepts in their own work.

Legacy in Decision Analysis: Tribus's formalization of decision analysis has had a lasting impact on the field, influencing how decisions are approached and analyzed in various domains. His emphasis on systematic, quantitative methods has shaped the development of decision analysis as a discipline, and his contributions continue to be relevant in contemporary practice.

In summary, Myron Tribus's establishment of decision analysis involved formalizing the process of decision-making under uncertainty through quantitative methods and structured frameworks. His enduring influence is reflected in his influential publications and teaching, which have shaped the field and provided valuable tools for rational decision-making across diverse applications.

Later Career at UCLA

During his later career at the University of California, Los Angeles (UCLA), Myron Tribus continued to make significant contributions by promoting interdisciplinary problem-solving and bridging the gap between theoretical research and practical application. His work at UCLA further solidified his reputation as a leader in decision science and operations research.

Encouraging Collaboration: At UCLA, Tribus was instrumental in fostering interdisciplinary collaboration across various departments and fields. He believed that complex problems often required insights and solutions from multiple disciplines. By encouraging collaboration between researchers in engineering, business, economics, and other areas, he helped create a vibrant environment for addressing challenging problems from diverse perspectives.

Integration of Knowledge: Tribus's approach to interdisciplinary problem-solving involved integrating knowledge and methodologies from different fields. He worked to blend the theoretical insights of mathematics and statistics with practical applications in management, engineering, and public policy. This integration not only enhanced the depth and breadth of research but also facilitated the development of innovative solutions to real-world issues.

Application of Theoretical Research: One of Tribus's key focuses at UCLA was to bridge the gap between theoretical research and practical action. He emphasized the importance of translating theoretical insights into actionable strategies and solutions. By working closely with practitioners and organizations, he ensured that the research conducted at UCLA had practical relevance and could be applied to address real-world problems.

Development of Applied Solutions: Tribus's work involved not only theoretical exploration but also the development of practical tools and methods. He was committed to ensuring that the theoretical advancements in decision science and operations research were accessible and useful to practitioners. This focus on applied solutions helped to enhance the impact of his research and contributed to the broader adoption of his ideas in various industries.

Mentorship and Leadership: As a professor at UCLA, Tribus continued to mentor and guide students and colleagues, sharing his expertise and encouraging them to pursue interdisciplinary approaches to problem-solving. His leadership helped shape the direction of research in decision science and operations research, leaving a lasting legacy at UCLA.

In summary, Myron Tribus's later career at UCLA was marked by his efforts to promote interdisciplinary problem-solving and bridge the gap between theory and practical action. His work fostered collaboration across fields, integrated theoretical research with practical applications, and contributed to the development of effective solutions for complex problems. His leadership and mentorship at UCLA further solidified his influence in the field of decision science and operations research.

Legacy on Data-driven Decision Making

Myron Tribus's contributions to data-driven decision making have had a profound and lasting impact on how organizations approach strategy, management, and problem-solving. His emphasis on integrating scientific principles with decision-making processes laid the foundation for modern business analytics and the application of statistical thinking to complex organizational issues.

Foundation for Analytics: Tribus's work in decision analysis and operations research provided the groundwork for the development of modern business analytics. His emphasis on using quantitative methods to evaluate and make decisions under uncertainty has become a core principle in the field of analytics. Organizations now routinely apply statistical techniques and data analysis to inform strategic decisions, optimize operations, and improve performance.

Data-Informed Strategy: Tribus's legacy extends to the rise of data-informed strategy, where decisions are based on comprehensive data analysis rather than intuition alone. His approach to decision-making emphasized the importance of using empirical evidence and statistical methods to guide organizational strategies. This shift towards data-informed decision making has enabled businesses to make more accurate predictions, identify trends, and develop evidence-based strategies.

Addressing Complexity: Tribus's work highlighted the value of statistical thinking in addressing complex organizational issues. His methods for analyzing uncertainty and optimizing decisions have been applied to a wide range of challenges, from supply chain management to financial planning. By applying statistical principles to these complex problems, organizations can better understand and manage risk, improve efficiency, and achieve their goals.

Enhanced Decision-Making: Tribus's influence on data-driven decision making has led to the widespread adoption of statistical tools and techniques in various organizational contexts. His emphasis on systematic, evidence-based approaches has helped organizations move beyond anecdotal evidence and gut feelings, leading to more informed and rational decision-making processes.

Educational Impact: Tribus's contributions have also had a significant impact on education and training in the field of data science and analytics. His work has inspired the development of curricula and programs that focus on teaching data-driven decision-making skills. This educational impact ensures that future generations of professionals are equipped with the knowledge and tools to apply statistical thinking to real-world problems.

In summary, Myron Tribus's legacy in data-driven decision making is reflected in the modern approach to business analytics and the application of statistical thinking to complex organizational issues. His contributions laid the foundation for data-informed strategy and enhanced decision-making processes, shaping how organizations use data and analytics to achieve their objectives.

David Cox and Foundations of Modern Statistics

Early Life and Education

David Cox's journey into the world of statistics and data science began with a solid foundation in mathematics and a diverse career that would span several influential fields.

Academic Background: David Cox began his academic journey at Cambridge University, where he studied mathematics. His time at Cambridge provided him with a rigorous grounding in mathematical principles and analytical thinking. It was during this period that Cox developed a deep appreciation for the power of mathematical methods in solving real-world problems.

Influence of Cambridge: At Cambridge, Cox was exposed to a broad range of mathematical disciplines, including probability and statistics. The environment at Cambridge, known for its emphasis on both theoretical and practical applications of mathematics, played a significant role in shaping his future contributions to the field of statistics.

Career Spanning Statistics, ML, and More

Early Career in Statistics: After completing his studies, Cox began his career in statistics, where he made significant contributions to the development of statistical theory and methods. His work focused on areas such as survival analysis, statistical modeling, and the development of new methodologies for analyzing complex data.

Influence on Modern Statistics: Over the course of his career, Cox became known for his contributions to the foundations of modern statistics. His development of the Cox proportional hazards model, for example, revolutionized the field of survival analysis and has had a lasting impact on both theoretical and applied statistics.

Interdisciplinary Work: Cox's career also extended into other areas such as ML and applied statistics. His work in these areas demonstrated his ability to bridge the gap between theoretical research and practical application. He explored how statistical methods could be used to address problems in various domains, including medical research, engineering, and social sciences.

Legacy and Impact: Throughout his career, David Cox has been recognized for his contributions to both the theory and practice of statistics. His innovative approaches and methodologies have influenced a wide range of fields and continue to shape the development of statistical science. His ability to apply mathematical principles to diverse problems has established him as a leading figure in the evolution of modern statistics.

In summary, David Cox's early life and education at Cambridge University laid the foundation for his influential career in statistics and beyond. His work has spanned several disciplines, including statistics and ML, making significant contributions to the development of modern statistical theory and practice.

Contributions to Regression and DoEs

David Cox's contributions to the fields of regression analysis and experimental design have been foundational in shaping modern statistics. His work not only advanced theoretical understanding but also established practical methodologies that continue to influence the discipline.

The Regression Analysis of Binary Sequences **(1958):** In this seminal textbook, Cox introduced the Cox proportional hazards model, a revolutionary method for analyzing survival data. This model provided a robust framework for understanding the effects of explanatory variables on the time to an event, such as failure or death. The book was instrumental in defining modern approaches to survival analysis and statistical modeling, significantly influencing both academic research and practical applications in various fields.

Planning of Experiments **(1965):** Another landmark publication by Cox was *Planning of Experiments*, which addressed the DoEs with a focus on optimizing the allocation of resources and improving the efficiency of experimental studies. This book provided comprehensive coverage of experimental design principles, including the use of factorial designs and randomization. Cox's insights into designing experiments to maximize information while controlling for variability have become standard practice in statistical methodology.

Data-modeling Approach Establishing Statistics as a Subject

Advancing Statistical Methodology: Cox's data-modeling approach emphasized the importance of constructing statistical models that accurately represent the underlying data structure. His work highlighted the role of model specification in making valid inferences and drawing reliable conclusions from data. This approach helped establish statistics as a rigorous and systematic field of study, where theoretical development is closely tied to practical application.

Integration of Theory and Practice: By bridging the gap between theoretical statistics and practical implementation, Cox contributed to the establishment of statistics as a discipline that integrates mathematical rigor with real-world problem-solving. His work demonstrated how statistical models could be applied to a wide range of research questions, from clinical trials to industrial experiments, thereby solidifying the role of statistics in scientific inquiry and decision-making.

Impact on Statistical Education: Cox's textbooks and methodologies have had a lasting impact on statistical education, shaping the way statistics is taught and applied. His emphasis on regression analysis and experimental design has influenced curriculum development and provided students with a solid foundation in these critical areas of statistical practice.

In summary, David Cox's contributions to regression analysis and the DoEs have been pivotal in advancing the field of statistics. His influential textbooks from 1958 and 1965 established key methodologies and cemented the foundations of modern statistical practice. His data-modeling approach has played a crucial role in defining statistics as a rigorous and practical subject, influencing both academic research and applied statistics.

Development of RSM

David Cox's work in developing RSM has had a profound impact on the optimization of stochastic processes, with wide-ranging applications in engineering, sciences, and beyond.

Concept and Methodology: RSM is a set of statistical techniques used for optimizing processes by modeling and analyzing the relationship between a response variable and several predictor variables. Cox's development of RSM involved creating a framework for sequentially designing experiments and constructing response surfaces that approximate the relationship between input factors and output responses.

Optimization Process: The essence of RSM lies in its ability to iteratively improve the DoEs based on preliminary results. By using a sequence of designed experiments, researchers can build an empirical model of the response surface and identify the optimal settings for the factors that influence the response. This iterative approach allows for efficient exploration of the design space and helps to find the best conditions for achieving desired outcomes.

Stochastic Processes: In dealing with stochastic processes—where there is inherent variability and uncertainty—RSM provides a systematic approach to understanding and optimizing these processes. By modeling the response surface and analyzing the effects of different factors, researchers can make informed decisions to minimize variability and improve the performance of the process.

Ubiquitous Applications in Engineering and Sciences

Engineering Applications: RSM has become a fundamental tool in engineering for optimizing complex processes and systems. It is widely used in fields such as manufacturing, aerospace, and chemical engineering to improve product quality, enhance efficiency, and reduce costs. By applying RSM, engineers can systematically explore the impact of various factors on performance and identify optimal operating conditions.

Scientific Research: In the sciences, RSM is applied to optimize experimental conditions and analyze the effects of different variables on experimental outcomes. For example, in fields like biology and chemistry, RSM helps researchers design experiments to maximize yield, improve reaction conditions, or study interactions between different factors.

Broad Influence: Beyond engineering and science, RSM has influenced various industries and research areas, including agriculture, pharmaceuticals, and economics. Its ability to provide a structured approach to optimization has made it a versatile and valuable tool in numerous domains.

In summary, David Cox's development of RSM has significantly advanced the field of optimization for stochastic processes. By providing a framework for sequential modeling and analysis, RSM has found widespread applications in engineering, sciences, and beyond, helping to improve processes, optimize conditions, and make informed decisions across various industries.

Proportional Hazards Regression

David Cox's work on proportional hazards regression, particularly through the development of the Cox proportional hazards model, has been seminal in the field of survival analysis and has had a profound impact on various domains, including medicine, epidemiology, and reliability engineering.

Introduction of the Cox Model: In 1972, David Cox introduced the Cox proportional hazards model, which revolutionized survival analysis. The model provides a way to evaluate the effect of explanatory variables on the time to an event (such as death or failure) while accounting for censored data—cases where the event has not occurred by the end of the study period. This model is characterized by its flexibility and ability to handle complex data without assuming a specific baseline hazard function.

Kaplan-Meier Estimator: While Cox's work was pivotal, it builds on earlier methods like the Kaplan-Meier estimator, which Cox and others used to estimate survival functions from lifetime data. The Kaplan-Meier model allows for the estimation of survival probabilities over time, which is crucial for understanding the distribution of event times and the effectiveness of interventions.

Proportional Hazards Assumption: The Cox model assumes that the effect of explanatory variables on the hazard function is multiplicative and constant over time, leading to the concept of proportional hazards. This allows researchers to assess the relative risk of an event based on covariates without needing to specify the underlying hazard function explicitly.

Wide Use in Medicine, Epidemiology, and Reliability

Medical Research: In medicine, the Cox proportional hazards model is extensively used to analyze survival data, such as time to death, recurrence of disease, or time to recovery. It helps in identifying risk factors and evaluating the effectiveness of treatments by modeling how various covariates influence the survival time of patients.

Epidemiology: The model has become a standard tool in epidemiology for studying the impact of exposures and interventions on time-to-event outcomes. It is used to analyze data from cohort studies, clinical trials, and observational studies, providing insights into the relationship between risk factors and disease progression.

Reliability Engineering: In reliability engineering, the Cox model is applied to analyze the time to failure of components and systems. It helps in understanding the impact of various factors on reliability and in predicting the lifespan of products under different conditions.

Broader Applications: Beyond these fields, the Cox proportional hazards model is also used in social sciences and other areas where time-to-event data is of interest. Its adaptability and robustness make it a valuable tool for researchers across diverse disciplines.

In summary, David Cox's development of the proportional hazards regression model has had a transformative impact on survival analysis. The Cox proportional hazards model, along with earlier methods like the Kaplan-Meier estimator, has become a cornerstone in medicine, epidemiology, and reliability engineering, providing crucial insights into the effects of variables on time-to-event outcomes and advancing our understanding of survival and failure processes.

Concept of Sufficiency and Ancillarity

David Cox's contributions to the concepts of sufficiency and ancillarity have provided a rigorous mathematical framework that has shaped modern statistical theory. These concepts are fundamental in statistical inference and have wide-ranging applications in both theoretical and applied statistics.

Sufficiency Concept: The concept of sufficiency is central to statistical inference. A statistic is said to be sufficient if it captures all the information about a parameter contained in the data. Cox formalized this idea, emphasizing that a sufficient statistic effectively summarizes the data without losing any information relevant to the parameter estimation.

Minimal Sufficient Statistics: Cox's work further advanced the notion of minimal sufficiency, which refers to a sufficient statistic that is also minimal in the sense that no other sufficient statistic can be a function of it. This concept is crucial for simplifying statistical analysis and reducing the complexity of inference problems by focusing on the most informative summary of the data.

Mathematical Framework: Cox provided a rigorous mathematical framework for understanding and applying sufficiency. His work includes detailed proofs and theoretical developments that clarify the conditions under which sufficiency holds and how minimal sufficient statistics can be identified. This formalization has become foundational in statistical theory and practice.

Providing Rigorous Mathematical Framework

Ancillarity Concept: Alongside sufficiency, the concept of ancillarity deals with statistics that provide information about the data but are independent of the parameter of interest. Cox's work on ancillarity helps in understanding the role of different statistics in inference and the ways in which they can be used to improve estimation and hypothesis testing.

Implications for Statistical Inference: The rigorous mathematical framework provided by Cox for sufficiency and ancillarity has significant implications for statistical inference. It aids in the development of efficient estimation procedures, hypothesis tests, and confidence intervals by leveraging the properties of sufficient and ancillary statistics.

Application in Statistical Models: The concepts of sufficiency and ancillarity are applied in various statistical models, including linear regression, GLMs, and more complex hierarchical models. Cox's contributions have helped in the development of methods that exploit these properties to improve the precision and reliability of statistical analyses.

In summary, David Cox's formalization of sufficiency and ancillarity has provided a robust mathematical framework that has greatly influenced statistical theory. By defining and elucidating the concepts of minimal sufficient statistics and ancillarity, Cox has advanced our understanding of how to efficiently summarize and analyze data, leading to more effective and rigorous statistical inference.

Later Career and Continued Advances

David Cox's later career was marked by significant contributions as both a researcher and educator, further establishing his influence in the field of statistics and extending his impact into areas such as ML theory.

Imperial College London: After his tenure at Cambridge University, David Cox joined Imperial College London, where he continued to make substantial contributions to the field of statistics. His work at Imperial College solidified his reputation as a leading statistician and a prominent educator. During this period, he was involved in numerous research projects and collaborations that advanced the theory and application of statistical methods.

Research Contributions: At Imperial College, Cox continued to work on a variety of statistical topics, including the development of new methodologies and the refinement of existing techniques. His research during this time further enhanced the understanding and application of statistical models, influencing both theoretical developments and practical applications.

Educational Impact: As a professor, Cox was known for his commitment to teaching and mentoring the next generation of statisticians. His educational efforts included delivering lectures, supervising graduate students, and contributing to the development of educational resources. His influence extended beyond Imperial College, shaping the broader field of statistics through his role as an educator and mentor.

ML Theory: In addition to his work in traditional statistics, David Cox made notable contributions to the field of ML. His research in this area focused on the theoretical foundations of ML, including aspects of algorithm development, model evaluation, and the application of statistical principles to ML problems.

Interdisciplinary Approach: Cox's work in ML reflected his broader interdisciplinary approach to research. By bridging the gap between traditional statistical methods and emerging areas like ML, he helped to integrate statistical thinking into new domains and fostered a deeper understanding of how statistical techniques can be applied to complex data analysis problems.

Enduring Influence: Cox's contributions to ML and related fields have had a lasting impact on the development of modern data science. His work has influenced the development of algorithms, the DoEs, and the application of statistical methods to a wide range of problems, demonstrating the continuing relevance of his ideas in contemporary research.

In summary, David Cox's later career was characterized by a profound influence as both a researcher and educator. His work at Imperial College London and his contributions to ML theory extended his impact on the field of statistics and demonstrated his ability to adapt and lead in evolving areas of research. Cox's legacy includes not only his pioneering work in statistical theory but also his role in shaping the future of data science and ML.

Enduring Impact on Modern Statistics

David Cox's influence on modern statistics is profound and multifaceted, marked by his pioneering methodologies, influential textbooks, and recognition as a leading figure in the field. His work has left an indelible mark on both theoretical and applied statistics, securing his legacy as a "statistical giant" of the 20th century.

Innovative Methodologies: Cox's development of key statistical methods, such as the Cox proportional hazards model and RSM, has fundamentally shaped the field. His contributions to regression analysis, DoEs, and survival analysis have provided statisticians with powerful tools for analyzing complex data and addressing a wide range of research questions. These methodologies have become standard in both academic research and practical applications, influencing how statistical analyses are conducted across various disciplines.

Influential Textbooks: Cox's textbooks, particularly those published in 1958 and 1965, have had a lasting impact on the field of statistics. These texts are not only comprehensive resources on statistical theory and methods but also serve as foundational materials for students and practitioners alike. His clear exposition and rigorous approach to statistical concepts have helped educate generations of statisticians and have contributed to the development of the field.

Educational Contributions: Beyond his textbooks, Cox's role as an educator and mentor has been instrumental in shaping the careers of many statisticians. His teaching at institutions like Cambridge and Imperial College London, along with his involvement in developing educational resources, has fostered a deep understanding of statistical principles and methodologies among his students and colleagues.

Recognition as "Statistical Giant" of the 20th Century

Professional Recognition: David Cox's contributions have been widely recognized within the statistical community and beyond. His groundbreaking work has earned him numerous accolades and honors, affirming his status as one of the leading figures in modern statistics. His achievements are celebrated through awards, fellowships, and positions in prestigious organizations, reflecting the high regard in which he is held by his peers.

Influence on Modern Statistics: The methodologies and theories developed by Cox continue to influence contemporary statistical practice and research. His work has laid the groundwork for advances in statistical modeling, data analysis, and ML, demonstrating the enduring relevance of his ideas in the face of evolving challenges and technologies.

Legacy in Statistical Thought: Cox's legacy as a "statistical giant" is not only due to his individual contributions but also his role in shaping the broader field of statistics. His innovative approaches and commitment to advancing statistical knowledge have set a high standard for research and practice, leaving a lasting impact on how statistical problems are approached and solved.

In summary, David Cox's enduring impact on modern statistics is evident through his pioneering methodologies, influential textbooks, and recognition as a leading figure in the field. His work has fundamentally shaped statistical theory and practice, and his legacy as a "statistical giant" of the 20th century continues to inspire and guide researchers and practitioners in the field of statistics.

John Nelder and GLMs

Early Career in Agriculture and Statistics

John Nelder's early career was marked by a significant intersection of agricultural research and statistical theory, which set the foundation for his later work on GLMs.

Academic

Background: John Nelder's journey in mathematics and statistics began at the University of Cambridge, where he pursued studies in these fields. His time at Cambridge was instrumental in shaping his analytical skills and providing a solid theoretical grounding in mathematics and statistics. The rigorous curriculum and exposure to advanced mathematical concepts equipped Nelder with the intellectual tools needed for his future contributions to statistical science.

Influence on Statistical Thinking: The education Nelder received at Cambridge introduced him to a range of statistical methodologies and mathematical theories. This academic background was crucial in developing his analytical approach and understanding of complex statistical problems, which would later influence his innovative work in GLMs.

Early Career at Rothamsted Agricultural Experiment Station

Position at Rothamsted: After completing his studies, Nelder joined Rothamsted Agricultural Experiment Station, a leading center for agricultural research in the UK. At Rothamsted, Nelder's role involved applying statistical methods to analyze data from agricultural experiments. This experience provided him with practical insights into the challenges of analyzing experimental data, particularly in the context of agricultural research.

Challenges and Innovations: Working with agricultural data exposed Nelder to various complexities, including the need for sophisticated methods to handle diverse experimental designs and data types. These challenges motivated him to seek out and develop more flexible and robust statistical techniques. His experiences at Rothamsted were pivotal in shaping his approach to statistical modeling and analysis.

Foundation for GLMs: The practical difficulties and limitations of traditional statistical methods encountered at Rothamsted led Nelder to explore new methodologies. His work in agricultural statistics laid the groundwork for his later development of GLMs, which addressed many of the challenges he faced in analyzing complex data from agricultural experiments.

In summary, John Nelder's early career was characterized by his studies at Cambridge University and his work at Rothamsted Agricultural Experiment Station. His academic background provided a strong foundation in mathematics and statistics, while his practical experience in agricultural research highlighted the need for advanced statistical techniques. These experiences were instrumental in shaping his development of GLMs, which would become a cornerstone of modern statistical analysis.

Development of GLMs

John Nelder's development of GLMs marked a transformative moment in statistical theory, extending the reach and applicability of linear regression techniques to a broader range of data types and distributions.

Groundbreaking Work: In 1972, John Nelder and his collaborator, Robert Wedderburn, published a seminal paper that introduced GLMs. This publication extended traditional linear regression models to accommodate non-Normal data distributions. The GLM framework allowed for the modeling of various types of dependent variables beyond the assumptions of normality and homoscedasticity that restricted earlier regression models.

Core Innovations: The GLM framework introduced several key innovations:

Link Functions: GLMs use a link function to connect the mean of the response variable to the linear predictors. This allows for the modeling of relationships between variables in cases where the response variable has a distribution that is not normally distributed.

Flexible Distributions: By incorporating exponential family distributions, GLMs accommodate a wide range of data types, including binary outcomes, count data, and continuous measurements with skewed distributions.

Variance Function: The framework includes a variance function that relates the variance of the response variable to its mean, providing flexibility in modeling heteroscedasticity.

Influence and Adoption: The introduction of GLMs revolutionized statistical modeling by providing a unified framework for various types of data and distributions. This flexibility made it possible to apply linear modeling techniques to a wide range of practical problems across different fields, including social sciences, biology, and engineering.

Massively Influential Statistical Framework

Broad Applicability: GLMs have become a fundamental tool in modern statistics, used extensively for analyzing data that do not fit the assumptions of traditional linear regression models. The ability to model various types of response variables and relationships has made GLMs widely applicable in diverse research areas.

Impact on Statistical Analysis: The GLM framework has profoundly influenced statistical analysis by providing a robust and flexible approach to modeling complex data. It has enabled statisticians to handle a variety of data structures and distributions, leading to more accurate and insightful analyses.

Continued Relevance: The principles introduced by Nelder and Wedderburn continue to be integral to statistical practice. GLMs are a standard component of statistical software packages and are taught extensively in statistics courses. Their impact on data analysis and interpretation remains significant, highlighting the enduring legacy of Nelder's contributions.

In summary, John Nelder's development of GLMs in 1972 represented a major advancement in statistical methodology. By extending linear regression techniques to accommodate non-Normal data and providing a flexible framework for modeling a wide range of data types, GLMs have become a cornerstone of modern statistical analysis, with a lasting influence on the field.

Logistic Regression for Binary Response Variables

John Nelder's work on GLMs significantly advanced the field of statistics, particularly through the development of logistic regression for binary response variables. This method has become an essential tool in various research fields, including epidemiology and medicine.

Introduction of the Logit Link Function: Within the framework of GLMs, logistic regression specifically employs the logit link function. The logit link function is a transformation that models the relationship between the binary outcome (e.g., success/failure, presence/absence) and predictor variables. It maps probabilities, which range from 0 to 1, onto the entire real line, making it possible to apply linear modeling techniques to proportions and rates.

Mathematical Foundation: The logit function is defined as the natural logarithm of the odds of the event occurring. This transformation allows the regression model to predict the log-odds of the binary outcome as a linear function of the predictor variables. By doing so, logistic regression handles the bounded nature of probability values and provides a way to estimate the likelihood of a binary event occurring based on various predictors.

Interpretation of Coefficients: In logistic regression, the coefficients of the model represent the change in the log-odds of the outcome for a one-unit change in the predictor variable. This interpretation allows researchers to understand the effect of each predictor on the likelihood of the event and facilitates the estimation of probabilities for different scenarios.

Widespread Applications in Epidemiology, Medicine, and More

Epidemiology and Medicine: Logistic regression has become a cornerstone in epidemiology and medical research. It is widely used to analyze binary outcomes such as the presence or absence of a disease, treatment response, or survival rates. For instance, logistic regression can model the probability of developing a certain condition based on risk factors, helping researchers identify significant predictors and inform public health strategies.

Social Sciences and Marketing: Beyond medical and epidemiological research, logistic regression is also applied in social sciences to study binary outcomes such as voting behavior, employment status, or educational attainment. In marketing, it is used to model consumer choices and the likelihood of purchasing a product based on demographic and behavioral predictors.

ML and Data Science: Logistic regression remains a fundamental technique in ML and data science. It is frequently employed as a classification method to distinguish between two classes in various applications, from credit scoring to spam detection.

In summary, John Nelder's development of logistic regression for binary response variables, facilitated by the logit link function, has had a profound impact on statistical modeling. This method's ability to handle binary outcomes and provide meaningful insights into probabilities has made it indispensable in fields ranging from epidemiology and medicine to social sciences and data science. Its widespread application underscores its significance and lasting influence in statistical analysis.

Nelder-Mead Simplex Algorithm for Optimization

John Nelder, alongside Roger Mead, developed the Nelder-Mead simplex algorithm, a widely used numerical optimization technique designed to handle a variety of optimization problems. This algorithm has had a significant impact on numerical methods and optimization theory.

Numerical Method Handling Non-Differentiable Functions

Overview of the Algorithm: The Nelder-Mead simplex algorithm is a heuristic optimization method that does not require the objective function to be differentiable. This makes it particularly valuable for optimizing functions where derivatives are difficult or impossible to compute.

The algorithm uses a geometric approach to iteratively refine a set of candidate solutions, known as the simplex, to find the optimal value of the objective function.

Simplex Structure: The simplex is a polytope of $n + 1$ vertices in n-dimensional space. The algorithm begins with an initial simplex and iteratively adjusts its shape by performing operations such as reflection, expansion, and contraction. These operations are designed to explore the space of possible solutions and converge towards the optimum.

Key Features: The Nelder-Mead algorithm is known for its simplicity and ease of implementation. It is robust to noisy and discontinuous functions and can be applied to a wide range of optimization problems, including those with constraints and complex landscapes.

Ubiquitous Use for Parameter Estimation

Parameter Estimation: One of the primary applications of the Nelder-Mead simplex algorithm is in parameter estimation. In statistical modeling and ML, the algorithm is used to find the optimal parameters of a model by minimizing a loss function or maximizing a likelihood function. Its ability to handle non-differentiable objective functions makes it suitable for cases where traditional gradient-based methods may fail.

Versatility Across Fields: The Nelder-Mead algorithm has been employed in various fields, including engineering, economics, and operations research. It is used in scenarios where other optimization methods may be impractical or inefficient, such as optimizing complex simulations, calibrating models, or fitting non-linear models to data.

Software and Tools: The Nelder-Mead algorithm is widely implemented in optimization software and libraries, making it accessible for practitioners across different domains. Its integration into tools such as MATLAB, Python's SciPy library, and R's optimization packages demonstrates its broad applicability and enduring relevance.

In summary, the Nelder-Mead simplex algorithm, developed by John Nelder and Roger Mead, is a powerful numerical optimization method that addresses the challenges of non-differentiable functions. Its widespread use in parameter estimation and optimization across various fields underscores its significance and versatility. The algorithm's ability to handle complex and noisy objective functions has established it as a valuable tool in both theoretical and applied optimization problems.

Advances in Statistical Computing

John Nelder's contributions to statistical computing are profound, particularly through his role as a co-developer of the Genstat programming language. His work has greatly influenced the way statistical analyses are conducted and has fostered the integration of computational methods in statistics.

Development of Genstat: Genstat, short for General Statistical, is a comprehensive statistical software package developed in the late 1960s. John Nelder, along with other prominent statisticians, played a crucial role in its creation. The software was designed to provide a flexible and powerful environment for statistical analysis, catering to a wide range of statistical methodologies and applications.

Features and Capabilities: Genstat includes a broad spectrum of statistical techniques, from basic descriptive statistics to advanced multivariate methods and experimental design. One of its key strengths is the ability to handle complex data structures and perform sophisticated analyses, making it a valuable tool for researchers in various fields.

User Friendly Interface: Genstat was designed with both novice and experienced users in mind. Its command-line interface allows for precise control over analyses, while its graphical user interface (GUI) provides an intuitive way for users to interact with the software. This dual approach has made Genstat accessible to a wide audience, from statisticians to applied researchers.

Fostering Computational Applications

Integration of Computing in Statistics: Nelder's work on Genstat exemplifies his commitment to integrating computational methods into statistical practice. By providing a powerful tool for data analysis, he enabled researchers to perform more complex and detailed statistical investigations than was previously possible.

Enhancing Research Productivity: The capabilities of Genstat have significantly enhanced research productivity across various scientific disciplines. Researchers can efficiently analyze large datasets, explore data relationships, and validate their findings using the robust statistical techniques implemented in the software.

Educational Impact: Genstat has also had a significant impact on statistical education. It has been used in teaching statistics at various levels, helping students understand and apply statistical concepts through hands-on experience with real data. The software's comprehensive documentation and user support further facilitate learning and application.

Continued Development and Innovation: Genstat has continued to evolve since its inception, incorporating new statistical methods and computational advancements. This ongoing development ensures that it remains a cutting-edge tool for statistical analysis, reflecting the latest trends and methodologies in the field.

In summary, John Nelder's contributions to statistical computing, particularly through the co-development of Genstat, have had a lasting impact on the field. By fostering the integration of computational applications in statistics, he has enabled more sophisticated and efficient data analysis. Genstat's broad capabilities, user-friendly design, and continued innovation underscore Nelder's influential role in advancing statistical computing.

Later Career at Imperial College London

John Nelder's later career at Imperial College London marked a period of prolific research and influential contributions to the field of statistics. His work during this time spanned a range of topics including designed experiments, GLMs, and optimization. Additionally, his authorship of several key textbooks solidified his reputation as a leading statistician.

Designed Experiments: Nelder continued to advance the theory and application of designed experiments, building on his earlier work at Rothamsted. He focused on the efficient planning and analysis of experiments to maximize information gain while minimizing costs and resources. His insights helped shape modern experimental design practices, making them more robust and widely applicable across various scientific disciplines.

GLMs: Nelder's pioneering work on GLMs continued to evolve at Imperial College. He explored the theoretical underpinnings of GLMs and extended their application to a wider array of data types and distributions. His research contributed to the robustness and flexibility of GLMs, making them an essential tool for statisticians dealing with non-normal data.

Optimization: Nelder's interest in optimization led to further advancements in numerical methods and algorithm development. He focused on practical optimization techniques that could be applied to real-world problems, particularly those involving complex models and large datasets. His contributions to optimization theory and practice have had a lasting impact on the field, influencing both academic research and applied statistics.

Authorship of Influential Textbooks

Textbooks and Publications: Throughout his career, Nelder authored and co-authored several influential textbooks and research papers that have become foundational in the field of statistics. These publications have been widely used in academic settings and have significantly contributed to the education and training of new generations of statisticians.

Educational Influence: Nelder's textbooks are known for their clarity, rigor, and practical orientation. They cover a broad range of topics, from the basics of statistical theory to advanced methods in experimental design, GLMs, and optimization. His ability to convey complex concepts in an accessible manner has made his books invaluable resources for students, educators, and practitioners alike.

Legacy of Thought Leadership: Nelder's writings have not only provided comprehensive coverage of statistical methods but also offered new perspectives and innovative approaches. His emphasis on practical applications and real-world relevance has ensured that his work remains pertinent and widely respected in the statistical community.

In summary, John Nelder's later career at Imperial College London was marked by significant research contributions in designed experiments, GLMs, and optimization. His authorship of influential textbooks further cemented his status as a thought leader in statistics, shaping the education and practice of future statisticians. His legacy continues to influence the field, underscoring the enduring impact of his work.

Profound and Lasting Impact on Statistics

John Nelder's contributions to the field of statistics have left an indelible mark, particularly through his development of GLMs. His work has enabled the analysis of a wide variety of data types, making sophisticated statistical techniques accessible to researchers across numerous disciplines.

Versatility of GLMs: Nelder's introduction of GLMs in 1972 transformed statistical analysis by extending linear regression to handle non-normal data distributions. This innovation allowed statisticians to model relationships between variables in a more flexible manner, accommodating different types of response variables such as counts, proportions, and binary outcomes.

Broad Applications: The versatility of GLMs has led to their widespread adoption in diverse fields, including epidemiology, medicine, social sciences, and engineering. Researchers can now apply GLMs to study phenomena where traditional linear models fall short, thus broadening the scope and applicability of statistical analysis.

Logistic Regression: One of the most notable applications of GLMs is logistic regression, which is used for modeling binary response variables. This technique has become essential in fields such as epidemiology, where it is used to analyze the relationship between risk factors and disease outcomes, and in social sciences for studying dichotomous events.

Influential Textbooks: Nelder's textbooks and publications have educated countless statisticians and researchers, providing a comprehensive understanding of complex statistical methods. His clear and practical approach to explaining statistical concepts has made his works enduring resources in both academic and professional settings.

Awards and Honors: Nelder's contributions have been widely recognized by the statistical community. He has received numerous awards and honors, reflecting his status as a leading figure in the field. These accolades underscore the significance of his work and the high regard in which he is held by his peers.

Legacy of Innovation: Nelder's innovative approach to statistical modeling and analysis has influenced subsequent generations of statisticians. His development of GLMs and other statistical methods continues to inspire new research and applications, ensuring that his legacy endures in the ongoing evolution of the field.

In conclusion, John Nelder's profound and lasting impact on statistics is evident through his development of GLMs, which have enabled the analysis of a wide range of data types. His work has transformed statistical practices, earning him recognition as one of the most influential statisticians of the 20th century. His legacy continues to shape the field, guiding future advancements and applications in statistical science.

Gerard Salton and Information Retrieval

Early Life and Education

Gerard Salton's formative years and education were pivotal in shaping his future contributions to the field of information retrieval. His academic background in engineering and mathematics laid the groundwork for his pioneering work in computer science and information retrieval.

Undergraduate Studies: Gerard Salton began his academic journey at the University of Chicago, where he pursued studies in Electrical Engineering and Mathematics. The University of Chicago, known for its rigorous academic environment, provided Salton with a strong foundation in both theoretical and applied aspects of engineering and mathematics. His exposure to these disciplines fostered his analytical skills and problem-solving abilities, which would later become crucial in his work in information retrieval.

Influences and Interests: During his time at Chicago, Salton developed an interest in applying mathematical and engineering principles to solve complex problems. This interest was instrumental in shaping his future research directions, particularly in the development of algorithms and methods for managing and retrieving information. His education at Chicago was marked by a strong emphasis on analytical thinking and technical proficiency, setting the stage for his groundbreaking contributions to the field.

Advanced Degrees in Computer Science from Harvard

Graduate Studies: After completing his undergraduate education, Salton continued his academic journey at Harvard University, where he pursued advanced degrees in Computer Science. At Harvard, he engaged with cutting-edge research in computer science and information systems, which provided him with the tools and knowledge to tackle emerging challenges in the field of information retrieval.

Research Focus: Salton's time at Harvard was marked by a deep dive into the emerging field of computer science, with a focus on information systems and retrieval. His research during this period laid the foundation for his later work in developing information retrieval models and algorithms. The advanced education and research opportunities at Harvard enabled him to build on his earlier studies and contribute significantly to the development of information retrieval technology.

In summary, Gerard Salton's early life and education at the University of Chicago and Harvard University were characterized by a strong foundation in engineering, mathematics, and computer science. His academic experiences provided him with the skills and knowledge necessary to make pioneering contributions to the field of information retrieval.

Foundations of the Vector Space Model (VSM) for Information Retrieval

Gerard Salton's work on the VSM has been fundamental in shaping modern information retrieval systems. The VSM introduced a systematic way to represent and compare documents and queries, significantly advancing the field of information retrieval.

Vector Representation: In the VSM, both documents and queries are represented as vectors in a high-dimensional space. Each dimension of this space corresponds to a unique term (word) from the corpus. The weight assigned to each term in the vector is typically based on its frequency in the document or query, adjusted by its importance across the entire corpus. This weight, often referred to as term frequency-inverse document frequency (TF-IDF), reflects the relevance of the term to the document or query.

Term Weights: By representing documents and queries as weighted term vectors, the VSM allows for a quantitative comparison of textual content. The weight of each term captures how often it appears in a document or query relative to its frequency in the whole collection. This representation helps in distinguishing between important and less important terms, making it easier to identify relevant documents based on the content of a query.

Calculating Similarity as Cosine of the Angle Between Vectors

Cosine Similarity: One of the key innovations of the VSM is the use of cosine similarity to measure the relevance between documents and queries. Cosine similarity calculates the cosine of the angle between two vectors (representing a document and a query) in the vector space. This measure quantifies how closely related the two vectors are, regardless of their magnitude. A smaller angle (or a higher cosine value) indicates a higher similarity between the document and the query.

Normalization: The cosine similarity is particularly useful because it normalizes the vectors, focusing on the orientation rather than the length of the vectors. This normalization helps in comparing documents of different lengths and ensures that the similarity measure is not biased by the length of the text. The cosine similarity score ranges from 0 (no similarity) to 1 (perfect similarity), making it a straightforward and effective measure for retrieving relevant documents based on a given query.

In summary, Gerard Salton's introduction of the VSM revolutionized information retrieval by providing a robust framework for representing and comparing documents and queries. By using weighted term vectors and cosine similarity, the VSM enabled more effective and efficient retrieval of relevant information, laying the foundation for many modern IR systems.

SMART Retrieval System

The SMART Retrieval System, developed by Gerard Salton and his colleagues, represents a significant advancement in information retrieval technology. This system was a large-scale implementation of the VSM and played a crucial role in demonstrating and refining the principles of modern information retrieval.

System Development: The System for the Mechanical Analysis and Retrieval of Text (SMART) was developed in the 1960s and 1970s at Cornell University. It was one of the first large-scale implementations of the VSM, incorporating the theoretical foundations of Salton's work into a practical and operational system. The SMART system was designed to handle large collections of documents and queries, providing a robust platform for testing and applying information retrieval techniques.

Technical Features: The SMART system utilized the VSM to represent documents and queries as vectors in a high-dimensional space. It employed various techniques for term weighting, document indexing, and query processing. The system's implementation allowed for efficient retrieval of relevant documents based on the similarity between document and query vectors, showcasing the effectiveness of the VSM in practical applications.

Evaluation Experiments and Groundbreaking Demonstration

Evaluation and Testing: One of the key contributions of the SMART system was its rigorous approach to evaluation. Salton and his team conducted extensive experiments to test and refine the system's performance. They used a variety of evaluation metrics to assess the accuracy and effectiveness of the retrieval algorithms. These experiments provided valuable insights into the strengths and limitations of the VSM and contributed to the development of best practices in information retrieval.

Demonstration of Effectiveness: The SMART system demonstrated the practical benefits of the VSM in large-scale information retrieval. Its ability to efficiently process and retrieve relevant documents based on a user's query was groundbreaking at the time. The success of the SMART system helped establish the VSM as a foundational approach in the field of information retrieval, influencing subsequent developments and innovations.

In summary, the SMART Retrieval System was a pioneering project that showcased the practical application of the VSM in information retrieval. Its large-scale implementation, combined with rigorous evaluation experiments, provided a groundbreaking demonstration of the effectiveness of Salton's approach and set a benchmark for future advancements in the field.

Development of TF-IDF Weighting Scheme

The TF-IDF weighting scheme, developed by Gerard Salton and his colleagues, represents a cornerstone in the field of information retrieval. This method provides a statistical measure of the importance of a word within a document, and its development has had a profound and lasting impact on IR techniques.

TF: The TF component of the TF-IDF weighting scheme measures how frequently a term appears within a specific document. The underlying idea is that the more frequently a term occurs in a document, the more significant it is likely to be for that document. This is a straightforward measure that captures the prominence of a term within the document's content.

IDF: The IDF component addresses the commonness of a term across a collection of documents. It decreases the weight of terms that appear in many documents, emphasizing those that are unique or rare. The IDF is calculated as the logarithm of the inverse proportion of documents containing the term. This component helps to balance the TF measure by accounting for the term's overall relevance within the broader corpus.

Combining TF and IDF: The TF-IDF weighting scheme combines these two components to provide a balanced measure of a term's importance. By multiplying the TF by the IDF, the TF-IDF score reflects both the term's significance within a particular document and its rarity across the document collection. This approach ensures that terms that are both frequent and specific to a document are given higher importance.

Remains a Fundamental IR Weighting Technique

Enduring Relevance: Since its development, TF-IDF has become a fundamental technique in information retrieval. It is widely used in search engines, document indexing, and text mining to evaluate and rank the relevance of documents in response to a query. The simplicity and effectiveness of TF-IDF have made it a standard tool in various IR systems.

Influence on Modern Methods: Although newer techniques such as word embeddings and deep learning models have emerged, TF-IDF remains influential. It continues to be used in combination with more advanced methods and serves as a baseline for comparing the performance of newer algorithms. The principles behind TF-IDF have also informed the development of other weighting and ranking techniques.

In summary, the development of the TF-IDF weighting scheme by Gerard Salton represents a significant advancement in information retrieval. By providing a statistical measure of word importance, TF-IDF has become a fundamental technique in the field, influencing both traditional and modern IR approaches. Its enduring relevance underscores its importance in the effective retrieval and ranking of documents based on textual content.

Improvements to Boolean Retrieval Systems

Gerard Salton's contributions extended beyond the development of the VSM and TF-IDF; he also made significant advancements in improving Boolean retrieval systems. These improvements enhanced the functionality and effectiveness of search systems, leading to broader adoption in the information retrieval industry.

Proximity Search: Traditional Boolean retrieval systems often struggled with the context and relationships between terms. Salton's enhancements included proximity search, which allowed users to specify the relative positions of terms within documents. By introducing proximity-based querying, users could retrieve documents where the search terms appeared within a certain distance of each other, improving the relevance of the results and capturing more nuanced contextual information.

Phrase Search: Phrase search capabilities were another improvement. This feature enabled users to search for exact sequences of words, such as specific phrases or expressions. By enhancing Boolean retrieval systems with phrase search, Salton's work addressed the need for more precise matching of word sequences, which is particularly useful for finding documents containing specific phrases or idiomatic expressions.

Semantic Search: Salton's improvements also included advancements towards semantic search, where the focus shifted from exact word matching to understanding the meaning and context of queries. Although fully semantic search systems were not yet realized during his time, the groundwork laid by Salton's enhancements paved the way for later developments in semantic retrieval, where the goal is to understand and retrieve content based on the underlying meaning rather than just keyword presence.

Growing Adoption by IR Industry Players

Impact on IR Industry: Salton's enhancements to Boolean retrieval systems were adopted by industry players as they sought to improve search functionalities and user satisfaction. These advancements addressed some of the limitations of traditional Boolean systems, such as rigid matching criteria and lack of contextual understanding. As a result, search engines and information retrieval systems began incorporating these features to provide more relevant and accurate results.

Influence on Search Technologies: The improvements made to Boolean retrieval systems influenced the development of more sophisticated search technologies and algorithms. By incorporating proximity, phrase, and early semantic search capabilities, Salton's work contributed to the evolution of search systems that better understood user intent and context. This influence can be seen in the advancements of modern search engines and information retrieval systems that continue to build upon these foundational enhancements.

In summary, Gerard Salton's improvements to Boolean retrieval systems significantly advanced the field of information retrieval. By introducing features such as proximity search, phrase search, and early semantic search capabilities, he addressed key limitations of traditional systems and facilitated their broader adoption in the industry. These enhancements played a crucial role in the evolution of search technologies, contributing to more effective and relevant retrieval of information.

Contributions Beyond Information Retrieval

Gerard Salton's work extended well beyond the core area of information retrieval, influencing a wide range of fields including text analysis, classification, clustering, and statistical natural language processing (NLP). His methodologies and ideas have had a lasting impact on various aspects of text-related research and applications.

Text Analysis: Salton's innovations, particularly the VSM and TF-IDF weighting, laid the groundwork for advanced text analysis techniques. These methods are widely used in analyzing textual data to extract meaningful patterns and insights. For example, TF-IDF is instrumental in identifying significant terms within documents, which can be used to summarize content, detect themes, and understand document structure.

Text Classification: In the realm of text classification, Salton's techniques provided a foundation for developing algorithms that automatically categorize documents into predefined classes or categories. The VSM and TF-IDF are commonly used in text classification tasks such as spam detection, sentiment analysis, and topic categorization. By representing documents as vectors, these methods enable effective feature extraction and classification based on term relevance.

Clustering: Salton's contributions also influenced text clustering methods, where documents are grouped based on their similarity. The VSM facilitates clustering by quantifying the similarity between documents, enabling algorithms to cluster similar documents together. This is useful in various applications, including organizing large document collections, identifying related research papers, and segmenting text data for further analysis.

Statistical NLP Influence

Statistical Methods in NLP: Salton's work contributed to the development of statistical approaches in NLP. By employing statistical measures such as TF-IDF and VSM, he demonstrated the value of quantitative methods in understanding and processing natural language. This statistical approach became a cornerstone of modern NLP, influencing the development of algorithms for parsing, machine translation, and text generation.

Foundations for Modern NLP: The methodologies pioneered by Salton have laid the groundwork for many contemporary NLP techniques. Statistical NLP models that rely on TF and document frequency concepts trace their origins to Salton's work. These models have evolved into more sophisticated techniques, including probabilistic language models and deep learning approaches, but the principles established by Salton remain integral to the field.

In summary, Gerard Salton's contributions have had a profound impact beyond information retrieval, influencing text analysis, classification, clustering, and statistical NLP. His innovative methods provided a strong foundation for various text-related applications and have shaped the development of modern NLP techniques, underscoring his lasting legacy in the field of computational text analysis.

Legacy on Modern Search and Data Discovery

Gerard Salton's contributions have had a profound and enduring impact on the field of search and data discovery. His pioneering work laid the groundwork for many of the advanced capabilities seen in modern search engines and data retrieval systems.

Foundational Theories and Models: Salton's introduction of the VSM and TF-IDF weighting has become foundational in information retrieval. These concepts enabled the development of more sophisticated search techniques that can handle vast amounts of data and provide users with highly relevant search results. The principles of VSM and term weighting continue to underpin modern IR systems, influencing how documents are indexed, queried, and retrieved.

Advanced IR Capabilities: By addressing limitations of earlier retrieval systems, Salton's work enabled advancements such as improved ranking algorithms, relevance feedback mechanisms, and more effective handling of diverse query types. Features like proximity search and phrase matching, which Salton helped develop, are now standard in modern search engines, enhancing the ability to retrieve precise and contextually relevant information.

Enduring Influence on Behavior of Search Engines

Search Engine Design: The principles introduced by Salton have shaped the design and functionality of contemporary search engines. Modern search engines incorporate advanced algorithms that build on the VSM, using TF-IDF and similar techniques to rank and retrieve documents. Salton's work has influenced how search engines process and interpret queries, leading to improvements in search accuracy and user satisfaction.

Impact on Data Discovery: Beyond search engines, Salton's methodologies have influenced various aspects of data discovery. The techniques developed for IR are now applied in other domains such as document management, content recommendation systems, and data mining.

Salton's innovations have facilitated the development of tools that help users discover relevant information in large and complex datasets, supporting a wide range of applications from academic research to business intelligence.

In summary, Gerard Salton's legacy in search and data discovery is profound and far-reaching. His foundational contributions have shaped the field of information retrieval, enabling advanced capabilities that drive modern search engines and data discovery systems. The principles he developed continue to influence the design and functionality of these systems, underscoring his lasting impact on how we access and interact with information in the digital age.

Grace Wahba and Splines in Statistics

Early Life and Education

Grace Wahba's journey into the world of statistics and mathematics began with a solid foundation in mathematical sciences. Born into an environment ripe with intellectual curiosity, she pursued her undergraduate studies at the University of Colorado. There, she delved into the intricacies of mathematics, laying the groundwork for her future contributions to the field. Her time at Colorado was marked

by a growing fascination with the potential applications of mathematics to real-world problems.

Wahba's academic path took a significant turn when she moved to the University of California, Berkeley, for her graduate studies. At Berkeley, she encountered a stimulating environment where rigorous mathematical theory intersected with practical application. The vibrant academic atmosphere at Berkeley was instrumental in shaping her approach to statistical problems, fostering an interest in the applications of mathematics beyond pure theory.

Her doctoral research was a testament to her pioneering spirit. Wahba's work during this period began to bridge the gap between abstract mathematical concepts and their practical applications. This early research laid the foundation for her future work, which would significantly influence the field of statistics. Her innovative approach to mathematical modeling and problem-solving set the stage for her subsequent contributions to splines and smoothing techniques in statistics.

Wahba's academic journey was not just a personal pursuit but also a reflection of the broader trends in mathematics and statistics during the latter half of the 20th century. Her education at two prestigious institutions provided her with a unique perspective, combining a strong theoretical background with an appreciation for practical applications. This blend of theory and practice would become a hallmark of her career, influencing her work in developing statistical methods that address complex real-world problems.

Overall, Grace Wahba's early life and education were marked by a deep commitment to mathematics and statistics. Her academic experiences at the University of Colorado and Berkeley equipped her with the skills and insights that would later define her pioneering work in statistical modeling and splines. Her journey from these early academic endeavors to her influential contributions in the field exemplifies a career driven by curiosity, innovation, and a dedication to advancing statistical science.

Foundations of Smoothing Splines

Grace Wahba's seminal work on smoothing splines revolutionized the field of non-parametric regression by introducing a powerful method for analyzing and modeling data without relying on stringent parametric assumptions. Her research provided a new way to approach data smoothing, enabling statisticians and data scientists to address complex relationships between variables more flexibly and effectively.

Smoothing splines emerged from Wahba's quest to find a robust method for data fitting that could adapt to various types of datasets while avoiding the limitations of traditional parametric models. The core idea behind smoothing splines is to balance the trade-off between fitting the data closely and maintaining a smooth, interpretable model. This balance is achieved by minimizing a roughness penalty functional, a concept central to Wahba's approach.

In her work, Wahba proposed a method for non-parametric regression that involves fitting a smooth curve to data points while penalizing excessive fluctuations in the curve's second derivative. The roughness penalty is a crucial component, as it ensures that the fitted curve does not become too wiggly or overly complex, which could lead to overfitting. By introducing this penalty, Wahba's method allows for a smooth representation of the underlying relationship in the data, while still capturing important trends and patterns.

The smoothing spline approach can be understood through the lens of functional analysis and optimization. Wahba's methodology involves solving an optimization problem where the objective is to find a spline function that minimizes both the sum of squared residuals (representing the fit to the data) and the roughness of the spline. This dual objective ensures that the final model is both accurate and smooth, avoiding the pitfalls of overfitting and underfitting.

Wahba's introduction of smoothing splines marked a significant advancement in statistical modeling. It provided researchers with a versatile tool for non-parametric regression that could be applied to a wide range of data types and research questions. Her work not only advanced theoretical understanding but also had practical implications, influencing various fields where flexible modeling of complex data is essential.

Overall, Grace Wahba's foundational contributions to smoothing splines established a new paradigm in statistical modeling. By developing a method that effectively balances fit and smoothness, Wahba provided a valuable framework for analyzing data that continues to be widely used and appreciated in both theoretical and applied statistics. Her innovative approach to non-parametric regression remains a cornerstone of modern statistical methodology.

Leave-One-Out Cross-Validation (LOOCV) for Model Selection

Grace Wahba's development of LOOCV represented a significant advancement in model selection and evaluation within the realm of non-parametric estimation. This technique, inspired by the Jackknife method, provided a robust approach to choosing smoothing parameters and assessing model performance, addressing a crucial need in statistical modeling.

LOOCV involves systematically evaluating a model's performance by iteratively leaving out one observation from the dataset, fitting the model to the remaining data, and then assessing the model's prediction accuracy on the omitted observation. This process is repeated for each data point, and the overall model performance is averaged across all iterations. The approach provides a thorough assessment of how well the model generalizes to new, unseen data, making it a powerful tool for model validation.

Wahba's innovation with LOOCV was particularly impactful in the context of smoothing splines and non-parametric regression. Choosing the optimal smoothing parameter is a critical step in non-parametric modeling, as it affects the trade-off between fitting the data closely and ensuring a smooth, interpretable model. LOOCV offered an automatic and data-driven method for selecting this parameter, helping to avoid the pitfalls of overfitting and underfitting that can arise with arbitrary parameter choices.

The Jackknife-inspired approach of LOOCV involves computing the model's performance metrics by leaving out one observation at a time and assessing the prediction error. By averaging these errors, LOOCV provides an estimate of how well the model will perform on new data, thus aiding in the selection of the smoothing parameter that minimizes prediction error. This method's robustness and simplicity make it widely applicable across various non-parametric estimation problems.

Wahba's introduction of LOOCV significantly influenced statistical practice by offering a systematic, empirical approach to model evaluation and parameter selection. The technique has become a standard tool in the field, particularly for non-parametric and ML models where flexibility and adaptability are crucial. Its ability to provide unbiased estimates of model performance and its applicability to a wide range of estimation problems have cemented its place as an essential method in statistical analysis.

In summary, Grace Wahba's work on LOOCV exemplifies her contributions to improving model selection and validation techniques. By introducing an automatic, data-driven method for choosing smoothing parameters, Wahba advanced the field of non-parametric statistics and provided researchers with a valuable tool for enhancing model accuracy and reliability. Her innovative approach to cross-validation continues to be widely used and highly regarded in the statistical community.

Applications Across Science and Engineering

Grace Wahba's work on splines has had far-reaching impacts across a diverse array of scientific and engineering disciplines, revolutionizing the way complex data is analyzed and interpreted. Her pioneering contributions in smoothing splines and non-parametric regression have found applications in fields such as time series forecasting, medical imaging, and meteorology, showcasing the interdisciplinary influence of her work.

Time Series Forecasting: In the realm of time series analysis, splines have become instrumental in modeling and forecasting trends and patterns. Wahba's techniques allow for flexible modeling of temporal data, accommodating the non-linearities and complexities inherent in time series.

This flexibility is crucial for accurate forecasting and understanding of time-dependent phenomena. For example, in financial markets, smoothing splines help in modeling price trends and volatility, providing more reliable forecasts and insights for investors and analysts.

Medical Imaging: Wahba's splines have also made significant contributions to medical imaging, where precise data modeling is essential. In areas such as magnetic resonance imaging (MRI) and computed tomography (CT), splines are used to enhance image reconstruction and improve the quality of diagnostic images. By applying smoothing splines to imaging data, researchers and clinicians can achieve more accurate representations of anatomical structures, leading to better diagnosis and treatment planning.

Meteorology: In meteorology, splines are utilized to model and predict weather patterns and climate variables. The ability to fit smooth curves to complex meteorological data enables more accurate climate modeling and weather forecasting. Wahba's methods facilitate the analysis of large-scale atmospheric data, helping meteorologists to understand and predict weather phenomena with greater precision.

Interdisciplinary Influence and Collaboration: Wahba's work has fostered interdisciplinary collaboration, as the techniques she developed are applicable to a wide range of scientific and engineering problems. Her influence extends beyond traditional statistics, intersecting with fields such as engineering, biology, and environmental science. Researchers from various disciplines have adapted and applied her spline methods to address complex problems, illustrating the broad utility and impact of her contributions.

In summary, Grace Wahba's development of splines has had a profound impact on numerous fields, enhancing the ability to analyze and interpret complex data across science and engineering. Her methods have improved forecasting, diagnostic imaging, and weather prediction, and have facilitated interdisciplinary research and collaboration. Wahba's legacy is reflected in the widespread adoption and adaptation of her techniques, demonstrating their enduring relevance and influence.

Later Techniques for Functional Data

Grace Wahba's contributions to the field of functional data analysis have advanced the way researchers handle and interpret data that varies over a continuum, such as time or space. Her later techniques, particularly in basis function methods and statistical shape analysis, have further extended the utility of her spline-based approaches, addressing complex data challenges across various domains.

Basis Function Methods for Curves and Functions: Building on her foundational work with splines, Wahba developed and refined techniques for analyzing functional data using basis function methods. These methods involve representing curves and functions as linear combinations of basis functions, such as splines or wavelets. By choosing appropriate basis functions, researchers can efficiently model and smooth data that are inherently functional in nature, such as growth curves, temperature variations, or other phenomena observed over continuous domains. This approach allows for flexible and accurate fitting of complex patterns in the data while maintaining interpretability and reducing overfitting.

Statistical Shape Analysis of Anatomical Structures: In the field of medical imaging and anatomical studies, Wahba's later work contributed to statistical shape analysis. This area focuses on understanding the variability and structure of shapes, such as anatomical structures or biological forms, using statistical techniques. Wahba's methods enable the analysis of shapes by representing them as smooth curves or surfaces, allowing researchers to study shape variations and their associations with different factors, such as diseases or developmental stages. For example, in studies of brain morphology, statistical shape analysis helps in understanding structural changes associated with neurological conditions.

Applications in Various Disciplines: The application of these techniques spans several disciplines. In biomedical research, functional data analysis and statistical shape analysis provide insights into developmental changes, disease progression, and individual variability. In environmental science, these methods assist in modeling and interpreting spatial and temporal data related to climate change, pollution patterns, and ecological processes. Furthermore, in engineering, functional data techniques support the analysis of data from sensor networks, structural health monitoring, and quality control processes.

Advancement of Statistical Theory and Practice: Wahba's later techniques represent a significant advancement in statistical theory and practice, enhancing the ability to handle complex functional data and providing tools for more nuanced and detailed analysis. Her contributions have led to the development of more sophisticated models and methods that address the challenges posed by functional data, improving the accuracy and applicability of statistical analyses in diverse fields.

Leadership in the Statistics Community

Grace Wahba's influence extends beyond her pioneering research to her significant leadership roles within the statistics community. Her contributions to the field have been complemented by her active involvement in shaping the future of statistical science through editorial positions, organizational roles, and mentorship.

Editor Roles with Major Journals and Professional Organizations: Wahba has played a crucial role in the editorial landscape of statistics. As an editor for prominent journals, she has contributed to the advancement of the field by overseeing the review and publication of cutting-edge research. Her work with journals such as The Annals of Statistics and Biometrika has ensured the dissemination of high-quality research, fostering the growth and evolution of statistical methodologies. Her editorial leadership has helped shape the direction of statistical research, promoting rigorous standards and innovative approaches.

In addition to her editorial roles, Wahba has been actively involved with professional organizations in statistics. Her participation in organizations such as the ASA and the IMS has allowed her to influence the broader statistical community. Through committee work and leadership positions, she has contributed to the development of policies and initiatives that support the advancement of statistical science and the professional growth of statisticians.

Mentorship of Next-Generation Researchers: Wahba's commitment to mentorship has been a cornerstone of her career. She has guided numerous graduate students and early-career researchers, offering them valuable insights and support as they navigate their careers. Her mentorship has extended beyond technical guidance to include professional development and advice on navigating the complexities of academia and research. Many of her former students and mentees have gone on to make significant contributions to the field, reflecting the impact of her guidance and support.

Through her leadership in the statistics community, Grace Wahba has not only advanced the field through her research but has also played a vital role in nurturing the next generation of statisticians. Her work as an editor, involvement with professional organizations, and dedication to mentorship have collectively shaped the direction of statistical science and ensured its continued growth and relevance.

Lasting Impact on Non-Parametric Methods

Grace Wahba's contributions to non-parametric statistics, particularly through the development and popularization of smoothing splines, have left an indelible mark on the field.

Her innovative work has established splines as a fundamental tool in statistical analysis and has significantly influenced the way data-driven learning techniques are approached.

Established Splines as a Fundamental Statistical Tool: Wahba's seminal work in introducing and formalizing the use of smoothing splines revolutionized the way statisticians handle non-parametric regression. By developing a methodology that balances the fit of the data with the smoothness of the function through a roughness penalty, she provided a robust framework for tackling complex data structures without imposing rigid parametric assumptions. This approach has become a cornerstone of modern non-parametric statistics, enabling more flexible and accurate modeling of diverse data sets. The technique's widespread adoption across various fields underscores its foundational role in statistical practice.

Recognition as a Pioneer of Data-driven Learning Techniques: Beyond splines, Wahba's influence extends to the broader domain of data-driven learning. Her work laid the groundwork for a range of techniques that rely on data-driven methods to model complex relationships and make predictions. By advocating for and advancing methods that prioritize data flexibility and adaptability, Wahba has helped to shape the landscape of statistical learning and prediction. Her contributions have paved the way for the development of sophisticated algorithms and models that are now integral to data analysis and ML.

Wahba's impact is evident in the continued use and evolution of splines and related techniques in both theoretical and applied statistics. Her pioneering work has not only enriched the methodological toolkit available to statisticians but has also influenced the development of new techniques and applications in data science. Through her research and advocacy, Grace Wahba has established herself as a leading figure in the advancement of non-parametric methods, leaving a lasting legacy that continues to shape the field.

Bradley Efron and Resampling Methods

Early Life and Education

Bradley Efron's journey into the world of statistics and resampling methods began with a solid foundation in mathematics and a keen interest in the evolving field of statistics.

Caltech Undergraduate Studies: Efron's academic journey began at the California Institute of Technology (Caltech), where he pursued undergraduate studies in mathematics. Caltech's rigorous mathematical environment provided Efron with a strong analytical background and introduced him to various advanced mathematical concepts. This early exposure to  mathematics laid the groundwork for his later contributions to statistics and statistical theory.

Graduate Studies at Berkeley: After completing his undergraduate degree, Efron continued his education at the University of California, Berkeley. At Berkeley, he expanded his focus to include both mathematics and statistics, allowing him to bridge the gap between theoretical mathematics and practical statistical applications. His time at Berkeley was crucial in shaping his understanding of statistical methods and their applications, and it set the stage for his groundbreaking work in resampling methods.

Influence of Faculty and Peers: During his studies, Efron was influenced by prominent statisticians and mathematicians, which helped to refine his interests and approach to statistics. His education at Berkeley exposed him to innovative statistical techniques and theories, fostering his development as a leading figure in the field of statistics.

In summary, Bradley Efron's early life and education, marked by his studies in mathematics at Caltech and his advanced work in mathematics and statistics at Berkeley, provided him with a strong foundation for his future contributions to resampling methods and statistical theory.

Foundations of the Bootstrap Method

Bradley Efron's 1979 paper, "Bootstrap Methods: Another Look at the Jackknife," marked a significant milestone in statistical methodology by introducing the bootstrap method. This innovative technique transformed how statisticians approach the estimation of sampling distributions and uncertainty.

Introduction of the Bootstrap Method: Efron's bootstrap method emerged from his work on resampling techniques as an alternative to traditional statistical inference methods. The bootstrap approach involves repeatedly sampling from the observed data with replacement to approximate the distribution of a statistic. This method provided a powerful tool for estimating the variability and confidence intervals of statistical estimates, addressing challenges associated with small sample sizes and complex data structures.

Influence and Reception: The publication of this paper was well-received in the statistical community, as it offered a practical and intuitive method for dealing with sampling distributions. The bootstrap method quickly gained attention for its simplicity and effectiveness, leading to widespread adoption in various fields of research and application.

Intuitive Approach for Estimating Sampling Distributions

The bootstrap method's intuitive approach allowed statisticians to estimate sampling distributions and uncertainty in a straightforward and accessible manner.

Resampling with Replacement: The core idea of the bootstrap method is to generate multiple resamples from the original dataset by sampling with replacement. This process creates numerous bootstrap samples that mimic the variability of the data, allowing for the estimation of sampling distributions for different statistics. By calculating the statistic of interest on each bootstrap sample, researchers can approximate the distribution of the statistic and derive confidence intervals or standard errors.

Practical Applications: The simplicity of the bootstrap method made it a valuable tool for practical applications in statistics. It provided a flexible approach for assessing the reliability of statistical estimates, particularly in cases where traditional methods were difficult to apply. The method proved useful in various contexts, including hypothesis testing, model evaluation, and parameter estimation.

Impact on Statistical Inference: Efron's bootstrap method significantly impacted statistical inference by offering an alternative to parametric approaches. It allowed researchers to make robust inferences based on empirical data rather than relying solely on theoretical distributions. The method's intuitive nature and broad applicability contributed to its widespread adoption and continued relevance in modern statistics.

In summary, Bradley Efron's 1979 paper introduced the bootstrap method, a groundbreaking resampling technique that revolutionized the estimation of sampling distributions and uncertainty. The method's intuitive approach, involving resampling with replacement, provided a practical and effective tool for statistical inference, leading to its widespread use and influence in the field.

Other Resampling Method Contributions of Efron

Bradley Efron's contributions extend beyond the bootstrap method, encompassing several other resampling techniques and innovative statistical methods. His work in these areas has had a significant impact on statistical theory and practice.

Jackknife Method: Prior to the bootstrap, Efron contributed to the development and popularization of the jackknife method. The jackknife is a resampling technique used to estimate the bias and variance of a statistical estimator. It involves systematically leaving out one observation at a time from the dataset and recalculating the estimate. This approach provides insights into the stability and reliability of the estimator, helping to assess its robustness.

Cross-Validation: Efron also made important contributions to cross-validation, a technique used to evaluate the performance of statistical models. Cross-validation involves partitioning the data into subsets, training the model on some subsets, and validating it on the remaining ones. Efron's work helped to formalize and refine cross-validation techniques, enhancing their application in model selection and performance evaluation.

Permutation Tests: Efron contributed to the development of permutation tests, a non-parametric approach for hypothesis testing. Permutation tests involve rearranging the data to create a distribution of the test statistic under the null hypothesis. This method allows for the assessment of significance without relying on specific distributional assumptions, providing a flexible alternative to traditional hypothesis tests.

Stacked and Empirical Bayes Methods

Stacked Methods: Efron explored stacked methods, which involve combining multiple models or estimators to improve predictive performance. Stacking, or stacked generalization, integrates predictions from different models to create a final ensemble prediction. Efron's contributions in this area helped to advance the understanding of how to effectively combine different statistical techniques to achieve better results.

Empirical Bayes Methods: Efron's work also includes contributions to empirical Bayes methods, which combine Bayesian principles with empirical data to estimate prior distributions. Empirical Bayes methods use data to estimate the prior distribution, making Bayesian techniques more practical and accessible. Efron's innovations in this area helped to bridge the gap between theoretical Bayesian methods and practical applications.

In summary, Bradley Efron's contributions to resampling methods include the development of the jackknife, cross-validation, and permutation tests, as well as innovations in stacked and empirical Bayes methods. These contributions have broadened the scope of statistical techniques and enhanced the tools available for data analysis, solidifying Efron's role as a leading figure in modern statistics.

Local Bootstrap Methods of Efron

Bradley Efron's advancements in resampling techniques include the development of local bootstrap methods, designed to address challenges associated with dependent or clustered data. These methods extend the classic bootstrap approach to handle more complex data structures.

Local Bootstrap Approach: Traditional bootstrap methods are often applied to independent and identically distributed data. However, when dealing with data that exhibit dependence or clustering, such as time series or spatial data, the standard bootstrap can be less effective. Efron introduced local bootstrap methods to address these issues by adapting the resampling procedure to account for the local structure of the data.

Smoothing Techniques: Local bootstrap methods involve smoothing techniques that preserve the local dependencies or clustering present in the data. For instance, in time series analysis, where observations are correlated over time, the local bootstrap might involve resampling blocks of data to maintain temporal dependencies. Similarly, in spatial data, the method can resample data in a way that respects spatial correlations. These adaptations help to provide more accurate and reliable estimates for statistics derived from complex data structures.

Addressing Problems with Standard Bootstrap

Challenges with Standard Bootstrap: Standard bootstrap methods assume that data points are independent and identically distributed. When this assumption is violated, as in cases of dependence or clustering, the traditional bootstrap can yield biased or misleading results. For example, in time series data, resampling individual observations without considering their temporal order can distort the inherent structure of the data.

Improvements with Local Bootstrap: Efron's local bootstrap methods address these problems by modifying the resampling process to account for dependencies. By resampling within local regions or blocks that reflect the data's inherent structure, these methods provide more accurate estimates of statistical properties. They improve the reliability of inference by maintaining the dependencies or clustering patterns present in the original data, leading to better performance in real-world applications.

In summary, Bradley Efron's local bootstrap methods represent an important extension of the classic bootstrap approach, designed to handle dependent or clustered data. By incorporating smoothing techniques and addressing the limitations of standard bootstrap methods, these innovations enhance the accuracy and reliability of statistical inference in complex data environments.

Later Career at Stanford University

Bradley Efron's tenure at Stanford University marked a period of significant contributions to various fields within statistics, expanding his research directions and applications.

Monte Carlo Techniques: During his time at Stanford, Efron delved into Monte Carlo methods, a class of computational algorithms that rely on random sampling to obtain numerical results. His research in this area aimed to refine and enhance these techniques, which are widely used for simulating and analyzing complex systems where analytical solutions are challenging to obtain.

Applications and Innovations: Efron's work in Monte Carlo methods contributed to their application in various statistical problems and improved the efficiency and accuracy of simulations. His contributions helped advance the theoretical understanding and practical implementation of Monte Carlo techniques, making them a valuable tool for statistical inference and computational experiments.

Work in Disease Clustering, Genomics, and Ecology

Disease Clustering: Efron applied his statistical expertise to the study of disease clustering, focusing on understanding spatial and temporal patterns of disease occurrence. His research aimed to identify clusters of diseases and investigate factors contributing to their spatial distribution. This work has implications for epidemiology and public health, aiding in the design of targeted interventions and policies.

Genomics: In genomics, Efron contributed to the development of statistical methods for analyzing high-dimensional data from genomic studies. His work in this area included developing techniques for analyzing gene expression data and understanding genetic variations. Efron's contributions have supported advancements in personalized medicine and our understanding of genetic influences on health and disease.

Ecology: Efron's research extended to ecological studies, where he applied statistical methods to analyze environmental data and ecological patterns. His work in ecology involved studying species distribution, biodiversity, and the impacts of environmental changes. By applying statistical techniques to ecological data, Efron contributed to a better understanding of ecological processes and conservation efforts.

In summary, Bradley Efron's later career at Stanford University was marked by significant contributions to Monte Carlo methods and a broad range of applications in disease clustering, genomics, and ecology. His research advanced computational techniques and provided valuable insights across various scientific domains, reinforcing his impact on modern statistics and its applications.

Legacy as Founder of Modern Resampling Field

Bradley Efron's legacy in the field of statistics is most prominently marked by his pioneering work in resampling methods, which has had a profound and lasting impact on statistical practice.

Resampling Methods Revolution: Efron's introduction of the bootstrap method in 1979 represented a groundbreaking shift towards computer-intensive statistical techniques. Prior to this, many statistical methods relied heavily on theoretical distributions and assumptions. Efron's bootstrap method, along with other resampling techniques he developed or advanced, allowed for empirical estimation of statistical properties through computational resampling. This approach marked a significant departure from traditional methods and laid the groundwork for modern statistical practice.

Innovation in Computation: The resampling methods pioneered by Efron ushered in a new era of statistical analysis that leverages computational power to solve complex problems. By using resampling techniques like the bootstrap, jackknife, and permutation tests, statisticians could perform robust analyses without relying solely on parametric assumptions. Efron's work demonstrated how computational methods could be harnessed to address real-world data challenges and provide more accurate and practical statistical inferences.

Enduring Influence on Statistical Practice

Broad Adoption: Efron's contributions have had a lasting influence on statistical practice across a wide range of fields. The resampling methods he developed are now standard tools in statistical analysis, widely used in areas such as epidemiology, finance, and ML. His methods have become integral to modern data analysis, providing researchers with versatile techniques for estimating uncertainty, testing hypotheses, and validating models.

Educational Impact: Efron's work has also had a significant impact on statistical education. His methods and ideas are featured prominently in statistical textbooks and courses, shaping how resampling techniques are taught and applied. His emphasis on computer-intensive methods has influenced the curriculum and training of statisticians, ensuring that new generations of researchers are well-versed in these powerful techniques.

Ongoing Research and Application: The foundational concepts introduced by Efron continue to inspire ongoing research and innovation in statistical methods. New developments in computational statistics, including advances in ML and data science, build upon the principles established by Efron. His work remains relevant as statisticians and researchers continue to explore and refine resampling techniques and their applications.

In summary, Bradley Efron's legacy as the founder of modern resampling methods is characterized by his pioneering contributions to computer-intensive statistical techniques and their enduring influence on statistical practice. His innovations have transformed how data analysis is conducted and have left a lasting impact on both the theoretical and practical aspects of statistics.

Looking to the Future of Statistics

What We Expect from the Future Statisticians

As we look to the future of statistics, the field stands on the precipice of exciting transformations driven by advancements in technology, evolving data landscapes, and interdisciplinary integration. The role of statistics in contemporary research and decision-making is more critical than ever, and its future promises to be shaped by several key trends and developments.

Integration with Emerging Technologies: One of the most significant trends shaping the future of statistics is its integration with emerging technologies such as AI and ML. These technologies rely heavily on statistical principles for building models, making predictions, and deriving insights from vast amounts of data. As AI and ML techniques become more sophisticated, statisticians will play a crucial role in developing and refining these methods, ensuring they are robust, interpretable, and aligned with real-world applications.

Big Data and Advanced Analytics: The explosion of data from various sources, including social media, IoT devices, and digital transactions, presents both opportunities and challenges for statisticians. The ability to process and analyze large-scale datasets, often referred to as "big data," will drive innovations in statistical methodologies and tools. Advanced analytics, including real-time data processing and predictive modeling, will become increasingly important, requiring statisticians to develop new techniques for managing and interpreting complex data structures.

Ethical Considerations and Data Privacy: As the use of statistical methods in areas such as predictive policing, healthcare, and financial markets grows, so do concerns about data privacy and ethics. Statisticians will need to address these challenges by developing frameworks for ethical data use, ensuring transparency in statistical models, and safeguarding individuals' privacy. The future of statistics will involve a greater emphasis on ethical considerations, including the responsible handling of sensitive data and the mitigation of biases in statistical analyses.

Interdisciplinary Collaboration: The future of statistics will also be marked by increased interdisciplinary collaboration. Statisticians will work closely with professionals from diverse fields such as biology, economics, engineering, and social sciences to tackle complex problems that require a blend of domain expertise and statistical rigor. This interdisciplinary approach will lead to the development of novel methodologies and applications, enhancing the impact of statistics on solving real-world challenges.

Education and Training: As the field evolves, so too will the education and training of future statisticians. The curriculum will need to adapt to include new statistical techniques, computational tools, and ethical considerations. Emphasizing practical experience and interdisciplinary learning will prepare statisticians to meet the demands of a rapidly changing landscape. Additionally, fostering collaborations between academia and industry will ensure that educational programs remain relevant and aligned with current needs.

Innovative Statistical Methodologies: The development of new statistical methodologies will continue to drive the field forward. Innovations in areas such as Bayesian statistics, causal inference, and statistical learning will enhance our ability to model complex phenomena and make informed decisions. Statisticians will need to remain at the forefront of methodological advancements, continually refining techniques and exploring new approaches to address emerging challenges.

Conclusion: The future of statistics is bright and full of potential. As the field continues to evolve, statisticians will be at the heart of transforming data into actionable insights, guiding decision-making across various domains, and addressing the pressing issues of our time. By embracing technological advancements, fostering interdisciplinary collaboration, and prioritizing ethical considerations, the statistical community will shape a future where data-driven insights lead to meaningful progress and positive change. The journey ahead promises to be as dynamic and impactful as the rich history of the statisticians who have paved the way.

As the field of statistics continues to evolve, these trends and areas of focus will shape the future direction of the discipline, ensuring that statistical methods and tools remain relevant, impactful, and responsive to the complex challenges of the 21st century. Happy learning!

List of Abbreviations

1. ML - Machine Learning
2. EDA - Exploratory Data Analysis
3. AI - Artificial Intelligence
4. GLM - Generalized Linear Model
5. CLT - Central Limit Theorem
6. MLE - Maximum Likelihood Estimation
7. UCL - University College London
8. ANOVA - Analysis of Variance
9. RCBD - Randomized Complete Block Design
10. ANCOVA - Analysis of Covariance
11. SPC - Statistical Process Control
12. JUSE - Japanese Scientists and Engineers
13. PDCA - Plan-Do-Check-Act
14. TQM - Total Quality Management
15. DMAIC - Define, Measure, Analyze, Improve, Control
16. IMU - International Mathematical Union
17. NBG - von Neumann-Bernays-Gödel
18. IAS - Institute for Advanced Study
19. CPU - Central Processing Unit
20. MANOVA - Multivariate Analysis of Variance
21. ASA - American Statistical Association
22. FFT - Fast Fourier Transform
23. DFT - Discrete Fourier Transform
24. IMS - Institute of Mathematical Statistics
25. MCMC - Markov Chain Monte Carlo

26. RSM - Response Surface Methodology
27. LSE - London School of Economics
28. ARIMA - Auto-Regressive Integrated Moving Average
29. ACF - Autocorrelation Function
30. PACF - Partial Autocorrelation Function
31. DoE - Design of Experiments
32. ISI - Indian Statistical Institute
33. MIT - Massachusetts Institute of Technology
34. UCLA - University of California, Los Angeles
35. GUI - Graphical User Interface
36. VSM - Vector Space Model
37. TF-IDF - Term Frequency-Inverse Document Frequency
38. TF - Term Frequency
39. IDF - Inverse Document Frequency
40. SMART - System for the Mechanical Analysis and Retrieval of Text
41. NLP - Natural Language Processing
42. LOOCV - Leave-One-Out Cross-Validation
43. MRI - Magnetic Resonance Imaging
44. CT - Computed Tomography

References

1. Euler, L. (1741). Introductio in Analysin Infinitorum. Marcum-Michaelem Bousquet, Lausanne.

2. Dunham, W. (1999). Euler: The Master of Us All. The Mathematical Association of America.

3. Gauss, C. F. (1809). Theoria Motus Corporum Coelestium in Sectionibus Conicis Solem Ambientium. Perthes et Besser, Hamburg.

4. Dunnington, G. W. (1955). Carl Friedrich Gauss: Titan of Science. The Mathematical Association of America.

5. Pearson, K. (1901). On Lines and Planes of Closest Fit to Systems of Points in Space. Philosophical Magazine.

6. Porter, T. M. (2004). Karl Pearson: The Scientific Life in a Statistical Age. Princeton University Press.

7. Gosset, W. S. (1908). The Probable Error of a Mean. Biometrika.

8. Ziliak, S. T., & McCloskey, D. N. (2008). The Cult of Statistical Significance. University of Michigan Press.

9. Fisher, R. A. (1925). Statistical Methods for Research Workers. Oliver & Boyd, Edinburgh.

10. Box, J. F. (1978). R. A. Fisher: The Life of a Scientist. Wiley.

11. Jeffreys, H. (1939). Theory of Probability. Oxford University Press.

12. Howie, D. (2002). Interpreting Probability: Controversies and Developments in the Early Twentieth Century. Cambridge University Press.

13. Neyman, J., & Pearson, E. S. (1933). On the Problem of the Most Efficient Tests of Statistical Hypotheses. Philosophical Transactions of the Royal Society of London.

14. Reid, C. (1982). Neyman: From Life. Springer-Verlag.

15. Deming, W. E. (1986). Out of the Crisis. MIT Press.

16. Gabor, A. (1990). The Man Who Discovered Quality: How W. Edwards Deming Brought the Quality Revolution to America. Penguin Books.

17. Wald, A. (1950). Statistical Decision Functions. Wiley.

18. Mangel, M., & Samaniego, F. J. (Eds.). (2004). Abraham Wald's Contributions to Statistical Decision Theory. Springer.

19. Kolmogorov, A. N. (1933). Foundations of the Theory of Probability. Chelsea Publishing Company.

20. Shiryaev, A. N. (2003). Kolmogorov: Life and Creative Activities. Annals of Probability.

21. von Neumann, J. (1951). Various Techniques Used in Connection with Random Digits. National Bureau of Standards Applied Mathematics Series.

22. Macrae, N. (1992). John von Neumann: The Scientific Genius Who Pioneered the Modern Computer, Game Theory, Nuclear Deterrence, and Much More. Pantheon Books.

23. Wilks, S. S. (1948). Order Statistics. Wiley.

24. Olkin, I., & Tate, R. F. (1964). Samuel S. Wilks (1906-1964). Annals of Mathematical Statistics.

25. Wolfowitz, J. (1957). Coding Theorems of Information Theory. Springer.

26. Slepian, D. (1971). Jacob Wolfowitz 1910–1981. Biographical Memoirs of the National Academy of Sciences.

27. Tukey, J. W. (1977). Exploratory Data Analysis. Addison-Wesley.

28. Brillinger, D. R. (2002). John W. Tukey: His Life and Professional Contributions. Annals of Statistics.

29. Kendall, D. G. (1953). Stochastic Processes Occurring in the Theory of Queues and their Analysis by the Method of the Imbedded Markov Chain. Annals of Mathematical Statistics.

30. Johnson, N. L., & Kotz, S. (1993). Leading Personalities in Statistical Sciences: From the Seventeenth Century to the Present. Wiley.

31. Savage, L. J. (1954). The Foundations of Statistics. Wiley.

32. O'Hagan, A. (1994). Kendall's Advanced Theory of Statistics. Wiley.

33. Kempthorne, O. (1952). The Design and Analysis of Experiments. Wiley.

34. Speed, T. P. (2001). Oscar Kempthorne: A Memorial Tribute. Statistical Science.

35. Box, G. E. P., & Jenkins, G. M. (1976). Time Series Analysis: Forecasting and Control. Holden-Day.

36. Hunter, J. S. (2001). George Box's Contributions to Quality and Statistics. Quality and Reliability Engineering International.

37. Rao, C. R. (1945). Information and the Accuracy Attainable in the Estimation of Statistical Parameters. Bulletin of the Calcutta Mathematical Society.

38. Sen, P. K., & Singer, J. M. (1997). Rao's Centenary Tribute: Selected Contributions of C. R. Rao to Statistics. Springer.

39. Tribus, M. (1969). Rational Descriptions, Decisions, and Designs. Pergamon Press.

40. Tribus, M. (1979). Thermostatics and Thermodynamics: An Introduction to Energy, Information and States of Matter, with Engineering Applications. Van Nostrand Reinhold.

41. Cox, D. R. (1958). Planning of Experiments. Wiley.

42. Reid, N. (1994). David Roxbee Cox: An Appreciation. International Statistical Review.

43. Nelder, J. A., & Wedderburn, R. W. M. (1972). Generalized Linear Models. Journal of the Royal Statistical Society.

44. McCullagh, P., & Nelder, J. A. (1989). Generalized Linear Models. Chapman & Hall.

45. Salton, G. (1971). The SMART Retrieval System: Experiments in Automatic Document Processing. Prentice-Hall.

46. Buckley, C., & Salton, G. (1995). Improving Retrieval Performance by Relevance Feedback. Journal of the American Society for Information Science.

47. Wahba, G. (1990). Spline Models for Observational Data. SIAM.

48. Gu, C. (2002). Smoothing Spline ANOVA Models. Springer.

49. Efron, B. (1979). Bootstrap Methods: Another Look at the Jackknife. Annals of Statistics.

50. Efron, B., & Tibshirani, R. J. (1993). An Introduction to the Bootstrap. Chapman & Hall.

51. https://mathshistory.st-andrews.ac.uk/Biographies/

52. https://www.britannica.com/Biographies

53. https://en.wikipedia.org/